Creggan
more than a history

MICHAEL McGUINNESS &
GARBHÁN DOWNEY

First published in November 2000
Typeset and designed by
GUILDHALL PRESS
Unit 4, Community Service Units
Bligh's Lane, Derry BT48 0LZ
T: (028) 7136 4413
F: (028) 7137 2949
info@ghpress.com
www.ghpress.com

ISBN 0 946451 59 1
Cover photographs courtesy Mickey Kivelehan, *Derry Journal*, Larry Doherty and Eamonn Melaugh

PREFACE

There is a story, very possibly apocryphal, about a young boy playing ball in the fledgling Creggan estate when it was only a couple of dozen houses standing on a green mountain top. The lad is bouncing the ball against a gable wall to the rhythm: *The Protestants have all the houses, the Protestants have all the houses.* With that, a priest comes up and, an early exponent of political correctness, tells the youngster: 'That's not true, son, sure wasn't our Lord himself born in a stable?' Duly chastened, the wee lad recommences his bouncing to the time of: *Our Lord was born in a stable, because the Protestants have all the houses . . .*

That Creggan was built as an estate for Catholics is in little doubt, nor is the fact that it was a vital development for Derry, where people were dying because of appalling housing conditions. That the estate was built where it was, in the old South electoral ward, to keep Nationalists in the one electoral area and so ensure Unionist control of the Corporation, is also widely accepted. But what few could have imagined is that the community created would thrive, excel and contribute so much to both its host city and beyond.

Fifty years on, and tens of thousands of people have passed through the 3,000 or so houses which constitute Creggan. There has been much to mourn, but equally there has been much to celebrate. The recent Creggan 50th Festival provided residents and 'ex-patriots' the opportunity to welcome what everyone hopes will be a peaceful and prosperous new dawn. And it also allowed them to revisit an often troubled, but always fascinating, past.

Importantly for the editors, the festival sowed the seeds for this book. A series of articles was commissioned by the *Derry Journal* charting Creggan's story, through the eyes of local inhabitants, historians and political pundits. These pieces were collated and, with the newspaper's very kind permission, were used to form the skeleton of what we hope will serve as a 'people's history' of Creggan.

The story, as told here, is by no means complete. We have heard tales we would love to have included for colour, craic or completeness, but, as with any work, there are sensitivities to be observed. (More particularly, perhaps, there are lawyers to be satisfied!) However, we hope we do manage to convey the essence of what makes Creggan a place apart.

Dozens of people have aided this production and to them all we extend a heartfelt thanks: to all those interviewed, for their time; to the writers, for their reminiscences; to the historians, for their records; to the politicians, economists and industrialists, for their visions and analyses; to Larry Doherty, Eamonn Melaugh, Dan O'Donnell and all who donated photographs; to Mary Crumley and Eamon Baker for their persistent support; to Guildhall Press, our publishers, in particular Paul Hippsley, Joe Mc Allister and Declan Carlin, for having the patience to wait the extra two years; to our most generous funders, without whom this book would never have seen the light of day; and to our wives and families for being great.

Go raibh maith agaibh uilig.

Foreword
by Councillor Cathal Crumley
Mayor of Derry

Stand at the top of Southway, the winding stretch of road that steeply ascends from the Lone Moor Road, past the Carmelite Fathers' Retreat House, Termonbacca, to reach its summit at St Peter's High School, and witness one of the most spectacular views of the River Foyle and city of Derry. Down river, the double-deck Craigavon Bridge acts as a sort of gateway behind which lie the spires of cathedrals, the clock tower of the Guildhall, and the crumbling chimneys of old factories poking up as markers of familiar streets. These markers guide the eye on towards the quayside, the site of the old docks and the departure point for thousands of emigrants over the past three centuries. Further on, the eye catches sight of Lough Foyle and the suggestion of the Atlantic Ocean beyond. More often than not, this view is obscured by mist and cloud, but on a crystal clear day, it reveals a Derry that is picturesque, unique and startling.

Now turn around and contemplate this rocky ground you stand upon: Creggan, a place apart, a housing estate whose geography dictates that it is an integral part of this city. Seen from Prehen, across the river, Creggan is indeed 'a green hill far away', as immortalised by Dame Alexander. And on the surface, there is nothing particularly special about Creggan today – physically it is identical to hundreds of other housing estates of similar age, size and population throughout Ireland. It could have been built anywhere. Certainly those of us who grew up in Creggan were not aware of anything special or remarkable about it other than the fact it was home, where we went to school and where we played. So why is the name Creggan recognisable throughout the world?

What makes Creggan remarkable is a combination of its inception, geography and the pivotal role it played in the history of Derry and Ireland in the 20th century. Creggan was built as a Catholic, Nationalist enclave within a partitioned state. Through gerrymandering, planners intended to ensure a Unionist majority in the old Corporation and hence secure Unionist domination in the foreseeable future. Creggan is an excellent example of the jaundice that governs supremacist and sectarian views, for in their pursuit of political expediency, the individuals who conceived of Creggan failed to appreciate that they were 'giving away' possibly the most valuable property in the city to a population they scorned. Irony indeed.

In the early years, people in Creggan were happy to have homes of their own, leaving behind the crowded conditions of multi-family dwellings in Fahan Street and the Bogside. But it was not long before they and their children began to demand their rightful role in the city. And herein lies more irony. For a people who were supposed to live on the periphery of the city, be excluded and be denied their rights, they had an inherent instinct to be full participants in the affairs of Derry. This was a community very much at the forefront of community and political development. But the more Creggan people tried to participate fully in the development and growth of the city, the more the political masters of the time resisted. This collective experience induced a cauldron of discontent that saw Creggan at the forefront of political conflict in the past 30 years.

The most graphic demonstration of the Nationalist pursuit of equality and the resistance it received at the hands of the state was the 1972 Civil Rights march, now known as Bloody Sunday, that began in Creggan and ended in Rossville Street with 14 innocent people shot dead But a quick read through the local print media of the time or a few hours spent in conversation with residents will reveal how the political conflict of the past 30 years affected the entire estate. Virtually every family in Creggan was touched and traumatised by the conflict. Nearly everyone was connected to someone who was incarcerated for his or her beliefs and aspirations. A substantial number of Republican volunteers were from Creggan and many lost their lives. Most street corners and back lanes were the settings for acts of resistance. The collective experience of Creggan will be studied by students of contemporary Irish history for generations.

During decades of economic hardship, social exclusion and political upheaval, Creggan people led productive lives and raised large families. They took an active but compassionate interest in their neighbours, sharing their moments of happiness and sorrow. They participated in sport and the arts. Despite the adversities, they tried to live their lives as fully as possible and they succeeded.

The Creggan diaspora gives testimony to their intelligence and ability. Thousands of people who originated in Creggan left to take up eminent positions in the fields of government, the media, politics, medicine, education, the arts, sport and entertainment; others left simply to build new lives abroad. All possess that unique quality that distinguishes a Creggan man or woman from anyone else in the world – a quality that is immediately recognisable to another Creggan person, no matter where they meet.

Creggan people rose above the restrictions intended for them back in 1947 when work began on the first houses. Their experiences fuelled a desire within many of them to play a full role in the city and to excel in their chosen fields. They were, and still are, a unique and special people And these special people are what make Creggan a place apart.

And yet Creggan is Derry and Creggan people are Derry people.

Creggan: More Than a History is a volume that is long overdue. In it, editors Garbhán Downey and Michael McGuinness bravely undertake a challenging piece of work, for it is not easy trying to encapsulate something as mercurial as Creggan Man or Creggan Woman. It is a credit to them and their skill that they gained the trust of those who recount their stories. This collection of memories and stories is essential reading for anyone who would like to understand what Creggan is and who Creggan people are. This volume will give the reader a glimpse into the psyche and collective experience of the thousands of individuals and characters who hail from Creggan, built on the rocky ground overlooking the Foyle.

Yes, they were kind souls – compassionate, sensitive, strong, intelligent, the salt of the earth. They possessed humour and humility and they were proud of who they were. They were a brave people. They were truly giants in the face of adversity.

Muintir an Chreagáin: na daoine is fearr ar an domhan.

About the Editors

Michael McGuinness is co-ordinator of the Derry Community History and Heritage Project. A former senior footballer, he worked for ten years in the BSR factory in Creggan and more recently was chairperson of the History Committee which oversaw the exhibitions for the Creggan 50th Festival.

Garbhán Downey was responsible for writing and compiling features on Creggan for the *Derry Journal* during the Creggan 50th Festival. He currently works for the BBC.

Acknowledgements

We greatly appreciate the support received for this publication from Derry City Council, NI Voluntary Trust, NI Community Relations Council and Creggan Enterprises Ltd. Our thanks also to Michael O'Hanlon, Marie O'Doherty and Michael McCarron.

This book has received support from the Cultural Diversity Programme of the Community Relations Council, which aims to encourage acceptance and understanding of cultural diversity. The views expressed do not necessarily reflect those of the NI Community Relations Council.

GP Media/Guildhall Press receives financial support from the District Partnership for the Derry City Council Area under the European Special Support Programme for Peace and Reconciliation and from the Londonderry Development Office under the Londonderry Regeneration Initiative. We would also like to thank Derry City Council's Recreation and Leisure Department for generous Community Services Grant Aid.

Contents

All articles by the editors unless otherwise attributed. The views expressed do not necessarily reflect the views of the editors or publishers.

Chapter 1

Rocky Ground, Rocky Beginnings . . .

Creggan Estate, as you would perhaps expect, given the singular nature of the place, isn't built on Creggan at all. When developers began the build in the '40s, they selected three ancient townlands – including Creggan, which translates from the Irish as 'Rocky Ground' – as the site. But as Mickey McGuinness will explain in this chapter, all the work took place on the other two patches, with Creggan ignored in all but name. Nonetheless, 'Creggan' it was christened, and it's as 'Creggan' that it will go down in history.

But to imagine that Creggan only became a place of prominence in the latter half of the 20th century would be completely wrong. There is evidence of a Bronze Age settlement at Creevagh; there was of course the medieval Rath where the 'Cropie' roundabout currently lies; and, in the 17th century, King James used the area to pitch camp while he besieged the Williamites (working out, like many after him, that the sloping hills give great height advantage in battle). In the 19th century, Foyle Hill was home to one of Derry's wealthiest families, the Scotts, whose tragic legacy sparked a host of ghost stories, one of which is recounted here. Later, the Scotts' Manse was to become the Old Foyle Hill Hospital, another important pre-war Creggan landmark. In the earlier part of the 20th century, the Creggan back road to the border was a famous walk for both pleasure seekers and smugglers alike, and was used by no less a personage than Éamon de Valera, who was banned from entering the North by more conventional routes.

Throw in the fact that Creggan can also claim to be the inspiration for one of the most famous hymns ever written, and you begin to get some idea of the timeless substance of Derry's 'Rocky Ground'. No, Creggan was a place apart long before it was an estate apart.

In the Beginning . . .
Ancient Graves and Townland Names

From about 7000 BC, Mesolithic people began settling in Ireland. Settlement would have occurred by sea and along rivers in an age when dense forests covered Ireland and survival depended on hunting and gathering. A very significant and important site for the study of this period is Mount Sandel, near Coleraine. Local finds of artefacts belonging to this period show that these Mesolithic people moved inland along the River Foyle. Later incursions brought Neolithic settlers with farming skills.

The discovery of a Bronze Age 'Cist' grave on Foster's farm in Creevagh (reported in the *Derry Journal* on 24 April 1956) confirms the continued presence of human habitation in the area encompassing and surrounding the Creggan housing estate over thousands of years. Another grave discovered recently in Shantallow was reconstructed and put on display in the Tower Museum, Derry. It contains human skeletal remains and an urn similar to those found in the Creevagh grave.

A requirement for the study of the early historic period is an examination of one of the country's ancient divisions, namely the townlands. Of these it has been said:

> Many townland and parish names possess an ancientness far greater than the present shape of the names would suggest and have behind them the hoary antiquity of several centuries.

Researchers, who wish to determine where Creggan Estate is, with respect to the ancient townland divisions, will be surprised to discover that it lies in the townlands of Edenballymore and Ballymagowan – not in Creggan. In the absence of any firm evidence on the decision to name the estate at that stage, one may attempt an explanation.

In 1944, land was vested for housing in the adjoining townlands of Edenballymore, Ballymagowan and Creggan, and obviously a name was required for this new development. In the absence of long-term projections, and given the fact that Creggan townland had seen no urban growth, unlike Edenballymore and Ballymagowan, the naming of the new estate as 'Creggan' is understandable. The inclusion of the Creggan Reservoir within the newly vested area must also have been a factor in arriving at the choice of name. As it turned out, however, the Creggan housing estate was built on the townlands of Edenballymore and Ballymagowan. Information on all three townlands and other related areas is required to complete the scant evidence of the early historic period. Little reference to this townland is made in historical sources consulted other than to give the translation which is 'Rocky Ground'.

Edenballymore can be translated as 'the large townland on the brow (or face) of the hill'. The Ordnance Survey Memoir of 1837 elaborates:

> The Irish word Eudan . . . generally signifies the human forehead, but when used topographically it signifies the brow of the hill – generally, but

> not always, the southern or sunny side, and the opposite of cul, the back, or northern side, of a hill. It appears from the Down Survey, which was finished in 1657, that 224 acres of townland were then held under lease by Captain Alexander Staples, and 12 acres of the south-eastern corner of it a controversy [sic]. It seems to have been included in the Bishop's land, called the quarter of Craggin and Drumniurny, and the half-quarter of Courneglogh, which lay on the northern side of the bog, near the island of Derry. The quarter of Craggin and Drumniurny, and the half-quarter of Courneglogh – both of which seem to be included in the present townlands of Creggan and Edenballymore – belonged to the Bishop, and the townland of Ballynagalliagh, as its name imports, was part of the property of the nunnery (from Inquisition taken at Derry in 1609).

This reference to the Bishop's lands helps explain the sector of land in Edenballymore, marked Bishop's Demesne on 19th-century maps, and it indicates the origins of the name Demesne Avenue. Much of the present Creggan estate is laid out on this land formerly owned by the Church of Ireland Bishop. This would also indicate that the origins of the Bishop's Field are much earlier than is suggested by the transaction to purchase land for St Mary's Catholic Church and schools in the 1950s.

Ballymagowan is derived from Ballynagananagh – the townland of the Canons. This townland is listed with others belonging to the abbey of St Columbcille. The others include Ballougry, Ballynagard, Ballynashallog, Creevagh, Killea, Mullenan and Termonderry. That church lands were not always havens of peace and tranquillity is evident from the incident recorded in *The Annals of the Four Masters* for 1537, which records that:

> The son of O'Doherty was slain in a nocturnal assault by Rury, son of Felim O'Doherty, at Baile-na-gcananach (Ballymagowan) in the Termon of Derry.

Ballymagowan was also included in The Quarterlands, or Fifteen Hundred Acres. These lands were the source of centuries of extensive litigation when ownership claims and counterclaims were made by the Protestant Bishop, The Irish Society and the Corporation.

Termonderry, the Ordnance Survey says:

> . . . considered as a townland, the City, or more correctly the island of Derry, appears to have anciently borne the name of Termonderry, or the sanctuary of Derry. An Inquisition of 1603 found that the southern half of the island of Derry then belonged to St Columb's Monastery, and the northern half to the Nunnery.

Bligh's Lane is interesting for a number of reasons. Early estate maps show it as leading to Hugh Blee's farm in Sheriff's Mountain. The derivation of its modern name is obvious. The lane also delineated the border between Edenballymore (to the north) and Ballymagowan (to the south) townlands. In ancient times, natural features were often used as territorial markers, and it would seem that the stream, alongside which Bligh's Lane eventually developed, performed this function. Before the opening of St Mary's Church, there was, apparently, a quasi-parochial divide by which Creggan Catholics to the north of Bligh's Lane were encouraged to use St Eugene's Cathedral and those to south, the Long Tower Chapel. Thus, 20th-century informal Church administrative divisions reflected centuries-old divisions which, in the early historic period, included Church lands. The site of Creggan housing estate was, therefore, far from being an empty wasteland. It has been inhabited for thousands of years and disputed for some of that time. It was also to play a part in one of the crucial events of Irish history, namely the Siege of Derry in 1689.

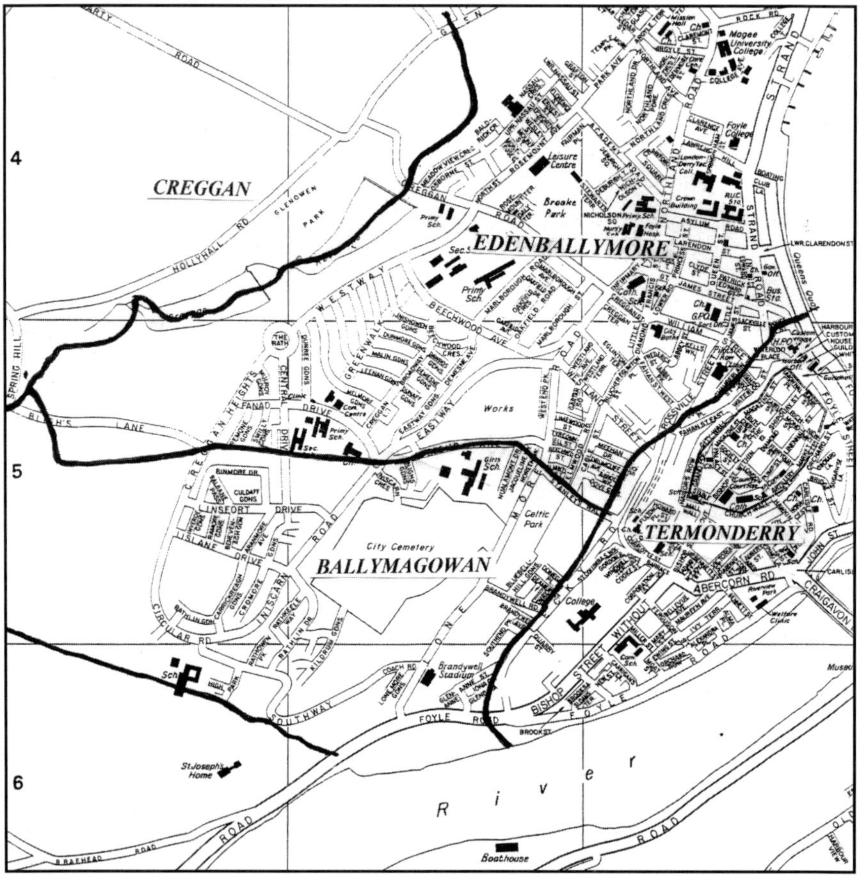

Detail from Creggan map showing Townland Divisions. (Ordnance Survey NI)

THE CREGGAN RATH
THE FORT ON A MOUNTAIN TOP

The so-called Creggan Rath is an apparently circular, earthen platform almost 80 metres in diameter and covering an area of just one acre. It is situated on sloping ground on the east side of a hill at an altitude of 300 feet in the former townland of Edenballymore. There are marvellous views from the site, over Derry and the Foyle Valley, but obviously these would have been more extensive before the present suburbs of the city, which surround the site, were built. The site currently serves as a roundabout at the junction of Westway and Central Drive and may have been disturbed at the time the roads were being constructed. On the south and west (higher) side, the platform rises no more than 0.5 metres (1 foot 6 inches). The platform is relatively level and no other features are visible now. Previous reports, preserved in Northern Ireland Sites and Monuments' records, suggest that, until comparatively recently, an enclosing bank and fosse were to be seen. Until the mid-1950s, the rath was covered with mature trees. A local informant reported that after the trees had been removed the site was artificially heightened and levelled with material brought from the demolition of Watt's Distillery in William Street.

There are two slightly contradictory descriptions of the site dating from the mid-1940s. In 1944, A McL May from Coleraine (who is responsible for most of the entries for County Londonderry in the Preliminary Survey of Ancient Monuments in Northern Ireland) described the rath as an earthen ring 66 yards in diameter surrounded by an earthen rampart 6-feet high and 6-feet broad in places. A 6-feet-wide fosse lay inside the rampart and at the time of his visit a spring issued into the fosse, although May did not think this had been used to keep the fosse flooded. He suggested that a break on the rampart on the east side was evidently the small entrance. The interior had a level surface except for a few stones which protruded from the grass, but these did not suggest the ruin of some structure. He interpreted the site as a cattle enclosure for use during summer pasture. The only evidence he gives for this view is firstly that the site did not look to him as if it had been built for strong defence, and secondly, the presence of the spring. Neither reason seems persuasive.

DA Chart, the former Deputy Keeper of the Public Records Office of Northern Ireland, visited the site fairly close to the time of Mr May's inspection. However, his description of the 'single ringed fort', as he calls it, differs in a number of places. He says that the 'single ringed fort' was from 1 foot 6 inches to 3 feet in height and confirms that it had disappeared from one quadrant of the circle. Presumably this was the east side as indicated by May. The internal 'trench' dropped about 2 feet below the surface of the interior and was around 6½-feet wide. He adds that from one point on the circumference, a kind of radial hollow leads to the centre. According to Chart, there was possibly an entrance on the west or south west where the internal trench rises to the field (internal) level. He adds that the city surveyor at the time, Mr Andrew, and an S Hamilton who accompanied him on his visit to the site, reckoned that the fort is geometrically an accurate circle.

It seems possible to reconcile these two descriptions. A circular space was enclosed, except to the west to south west side, by a fosse 2-feet deep and around 6½-feet wide. Outside of this, a low earthen rampart, at no point more that 3 feet in height internally, elsewhere considerably less, and, in places, (especially on the east side) totally absent, defined the edge of the site. This rampart was up to 6-feet wide at its base, and dropped 6 feet and more to the external ground level. It is possible that an entrance existed on the west to south west side where the interior was close to the outside ground level, and where there was no fosse. It is not clear whether the difference in level internally and externally on the north east side was due to natural or artificial causes.

Although often referred to as the 'Creggan Rath', the site is known locally as the 'Cropie' or the 'Cropie Camp' (the word is often pronounced as if written crow-pay). No satisfactory explanation exists for the name. A French word, 'croupe', occasionally used in English, signifies the rounded top of a hill. Although not strictly on the summit, the views from the site give the impression of a great altitude. If the site was in existence at the time of the Siege of Derry in 1689, then a possible explanation for the name might be that it derives from French troops, allies of King James II, who were encamped in the vicinity of Creggan.

Without excavation, it is impossible to be certain as to the nature or date of this monument. However, a number of possibilities suggest themselves. In chronological order, the original features and traditions of the monument might suggest that it could be: (a) a henge-type monument of the early Bronze Age; (b) a hill-fort type monument of the late Bronze or Iron Age; (c) a ringfort (rath) of the early historic (Christian) period; (d) an emplacement of some kind built during the Siege of Derry and (e) an ornamental tree-ring of the 18th or 19th centuries.

(a) Henges are embanked circular enclosures usually of great diameter and associated with the so-called Beaker People of the early Bronze Age. Little is known about them, but they were probably places of ritual (they take their names from Stonehenge). The main argument against the interpretation in this case is the slight nature of the surrounding banks. It should be pointed out, however, that there is plenty of evidence for the presence of early Bronze Age construction in these hills and the surrounding area.

(b) The large diameter and location of this univallate earthen enclosure might suggest that the site is a hill-fort. The presence of the internal fosse would suggest a comparison with similar (probably ritual) features at several 'Royal' sites. However, the accurate circularity of the site would seem to preclude the possibility of it being a hill-fort.

(c) A number of ringfort type monuments are known to have existed on these hills overlooking the monastic settlement at Derry. However, the great size, circularity, slight banks and internal fosse of the Creggan Rath (at least in its recent and present form) would seem to preclude this identification. A story in Manus O'Donnell's *Life of Colmcille* refers to a number of raths between Derry and the Grianan of Aileach. One of these seems to have been known in O'Donnell's time as 'Rath na Fledh' (the rath of the banquet), but there appears to be no way in which the location of this can be determined.

(d) Neville's map of the Siege of Derry shows a large circular enclosure on the hills overlooking the city and certainly not far from the location of the Creggan Rath, although correlation with modern Ordnance Survey maps is difficult. The legend accompanying the map says that this is the 'Fort built by them (the besieging soldiers) soon after their approach to the town'. This fortification is unusually shaped, as the other specially built defences are linear or angular. It is possible that this 'Fort' reused an older monument. Neville, however, shows two circular 'Danish Forts' reused by the besiegers, one in the vicinity of the present Southway, and the other possibly in the vicinity of Bluebell Hill. It is difficult to understand why he would not similarly describe the large enclosure if it likewise were a secondary usage.

The 'Danish Forts' are shown by two closely spaced concentric circles, the inner circle having a thinner line. In the case of the large enclosure, the circles are further apart and the thin line is on the outside. It is not clear, however, what these differences in convention are supposed to represent on the ground. The name used locally for the rath nowadays, as well as the reported finding of cannon balls in its vicinity, would support the identification with the enclosure shown on Neville's map, whatever about an older ancestry.

(e) Ornamental circular tree plantations either on, or in imitation of, raths, became popular from the late 17th century. The imitative forms are known as tree-rings and among the features which allow them to be distinguished from earlier raths are true circularity, slight proportions of the banks and standardisation of diameters on the same estate. These features appear to be present at the Creggan Rath, although the large diameter would seem unusual.

The site was located in the former demesne lands of the Church of Ireland Bishop of Derry. A number of maps show that tree planting in circular groups (or in some variation such as a quadrant or a semi-circle), was being practised on the estate from the late 18th century during the incumbency of Frederick Augustus Hervey, the Earl Bishop who was noted for the grandeur of his estates. The diameters of these plantations are all quite large and, although they vary, a number conform to a relative standard size. The Creggan Rath, shown on the 19th-century Ordnance Survey maps to have had a diameter then of 220 feet, would be an average.

A small oval-shaped tree-ring with diameters 60 feet (length) and 40 feet (width) was shown 140 feet NNE of our monument. A second tree-ring of 120 feet in diameter was located 120 yards to the NE, but was partially truncated by a field boundary on its SE, 820 yards almost due East of the Creggan Rath, in the area now known as Oakfield. Another large slightly oval tree-ring 210 feet in diameter was shown on a number of maps. This seems to have survived, at least partially, in outline until the area was engulfed by housing in the late 19th century. The actual site was not built on until quite recently.

Another large plantation, in the form of two quadrants with radii ranging from 130 to 150 feet, was located at either side of the entrance to the demesne in the area where today Eastway joins Lone Moor Road. There were also other quadrant or triangular-shaped plantations scattered about the demesne. These would all have been visible (although it is unlikely that they were as yet mature) from Hervey's palace on the site of the present Masonic Hall in Bishop Street Within and his casino in the grounds of the present Lumen Christi College in Bishop Street Without.

It is quite clear that the Creggan Rath functioned as a tree-ring from at least the time of the first edition of the Ordnance Survey map (surveyed in 1830) although, strangely, it is not shown on another official map of 1831. There seems to be strong, but not conclusive, evidence to identify the site with a large enclosure marked on Neville's map of c.1690. If this is the case, although Neville says that it was newly built, it seems more likely that it compares with the other 'Danish Forts' shown by him within a radius of about a mile. The term 'Danish Fort', by an unhistorical association with the Vikings, was commonly used in the 17th and 18th centuries to describe ringforts (raths) of the early Christian period, but it is also clear that a wide range of ancient enclosures and mounds were similarly referred to. It therefore seems that the Creggan Rath might turn out to be a monument of ancient times which has been repeatedly reused down to its present 'vocation' as a road roundabout, but it is unlikely that there will ever be certainty about the matter until the site is archaeologically excavated.

This archaeological account of the Creggan Rath was contributed by Brian Lacy, former Head of Derry City Council's Museum Services and Michael McGuinness, Co-ordinator, Derry Community History and Heritage Project. Originally published in Templemore, Journal of the North West Archaeological and Historical Society (Vol 1, 1984/5).

Creggan Rath in the '50s; note house-building in progress.

The Jacobites Arrive

The French Pitch Camp for the Siege of Derry

Since the 6th century, an ecclesiastical settlement had flourished on the island of 'The Derrie'. In 1566, the first English settlement, a military one, was attempted there, but sickness and an explosion in the magazine put paid to this attempt within two years. A more permanent settlement was ensured with the arrival of Elizabethan soldier Colonel Henry Docwra leading an invasion force of 4,000 foot and 200 horse in 1600. The Elizabethan Nine Years War ended with a defeat for the Irish cause when O'Neill surrendered in 1603, which allowed Docwra, who remained as Governor, to proceed with commercial development.

On 11 July 1604, Docwra was presented with a charter for the incorporation of the city, which identified its suitability as a colony, declaring:

> The town or borough of Derry is, by means of natural seat and situation thereof, a place very convenient and fit to be made both a town of war and a town of merchandise, and so might in many ways prove serviceable for the Crown, and profitable for the subject.

On 4 September 1607, the departure from Rathmullan of the defeated Ulster chieftains O'Neill and O'Donnell, known as the 'Flight of the Earls', was the beginning of the end for Gaelic rule in Ireland. The O'Doherty Rebellion, which began in April 1608, was regarded as the final act of treason and the lands previously held by them and other Gaelic leaders in Ulster were confiscated.

A new era in the history of Derry was dawning. A systematic plan for colonisation, the 'Plantations in Ulster', was devised. Loyal British Protestant colonists were to supplant the defeated Gaelic population. Plans for Derry departed from the rules applied elsewhere. The ancient London Livery Trades Guilds were persuaded to become involved in this new colonial venture. From their membership a new body was formed which we now know as 'The Honourable The Irish Society'. Part of its responsibility was to build a new walled city on the old site of Derry.

A new charter was presented in March 1613 which changed the name of the city from Derry to Londonderry. The walls were completed in 1618 and seemed to fulfil the aspirations expressed in the 1604 charter, which thought it 'a place very convenient and fit to be made both a town of war and a town of merchandise.'

Reservations over how defensible the city might prove in the event of war arose in the report of the Royal Commission of 1628, which observed that the city was:

> . . . so ill-situated that the walls, houses and streets lie open to the command of any shipping that shall come into the harbour, and also to divers hills about the town, and to many other inconveniences.

It concluded that it was 'not a place of defence nor tenable if any foreign enemy should come before it'. The real test, however, was still some years ahead.

The new city was to meet its first military test, successfully surviving the siege of 1649, when it was defended by Sir Charles Coote for the English Parliament. The second challenge was made during the Great Siege of 1689. Creggan was not to escape involvement in the historic series of events which were crucial formative influences in Derry's and Ireland's history. Indeed, much of our present failure to reach political accommodation locally has its origins in the events of over 300 years ago.

When James II succeeded to the throne of England in February 1685, he proceeded to replace Protestants in his administration and army with Catholics. A predictable consequence was the heightening of fears in the Protestant colony of Derry. Consternation increased with the arrival in the Waterside of the Earl of Antrim's Catholic troops who were expecting to garrison the city. While their officers were negotiating terms with the City Fathers, some of the Earl's soldiers began to arrive on the West Bank. Perceiving danger, 13 apprentice boys closed Ferryquay Gate in an act of defiance which was a crucial event leading to the siege. Hoping for a voluntary end to this defiance, James appeared in person at Bishop's Gate on 15 April 1689. Not only did the citizens refuse to capitulate, but they also fired shots at James's party, hitting some of his retinue. The Siege of Derry had begun; it was to cause much suffering and loss of life and was to become a pivotal point in Irish history.

The Neville map (see page 27), drawn immediately after the event by Captain Francis Neville, provides fascinating evidence of Creggan's part in the Siege of Derry. It depicts the situation in the latter half of the action when the town had become more closely besieged. Previously, heavy mortar had come from Stronge's Orchard (in the vicinity of Ebrington Barracks) in the Waterside. By mid-June, mortar fire was directed from the cityside in the vicinity of Creggan. Siege historian JG Simms describes Jacobite [a follower of King James] commander Richard Hamilton's difficulties and the limitations of the Jacobite armoury:

> His chief lack was artillery. A limited number of guns did arrive, but few were more than field guns. Nothing less than 24-pounders would be effective against the walls, and Hamilton had only one of these; his next largest gun was a solitary 18-pounder. For most of the time, these two were kept down at the boom a couple of miles away. There were some mortars, one of which was very large and threw a bomb of 270lbs, but the high trajectory of mortar bombs made them suitable for destroying houses, not fortifications. No big guns were brought from France and, if they had been, their transport over the Irish roads would have been extremely difficult.

The feature marked **4** on Neville's map is described by him as:

> A platform for three mortars, which played [was aimed] at the Church [St Columb's Cathedral] and Bishop's House. And of the great number of

> bombs which were discharged and fell thick about both, on the first there fell but three, one of which fell on the steeple amongst the bells and did no harm. Another fell on the battlement on the south side, tumbled easie on the leads and broak there with little harme, the people being there in the church. The third fell on the north. It broak a little hole in the lead and, by a strange providence, rebounded, came over the battlement of four-foot high and broak in the Church yard.

Twenty bombs in all were fired that day, killing one man and wounding another. The garrison did not always get off so lightly. One account estimates that 337 bombs were launched between 21 June and 21 July. This is the period when the mortars were moved to the West Bank (ie the mortar battery identified by JG Simms as being located above the present Eastway Road). On 27 June, a diarist of the siege, Captain Thomas Ash, recorded:

> Ten bombs flew into the city. One fell on Joseph Gallagher's house in Bishop Street, where two barrels of powder were lodged. There were 14 killed by it, viz six grenadiers belonging to our regiment, four horsemen and four women.

One famous mortar bomb must have been launched from the Eastway site, namely that which landed in the city on 10 July. Instead of powder it contained terms for surrender and read:

> To the soldiers and inhabitants of Derry. The conditions offered by Lieut Gen Hamilton are sincere. The power he hath of the King is real; be no long imposed upon by such as tell you contrary; you cannot be ignorant of the King's clemency towards his subjects. Such of you as chuse to serve the King, shall be entertained without distinction in point of Religion. If any chuse to leave the Kingdom, they shall have passes. You shall be restored to your estates and livings, and have free liberty of Religion whatsoever it be. If you doubt the powers given to Gen Hamilton by the King, twenty of you may come and see it with freedom, under the King's hand and seal. Be not obstinate against your natural Prince; expose yourselves no longer to the miseries which you undergo, which will grow worse and worse if you continue to be opinionate, for it will be too late to accept of the offer now made you when your condition is so low that you cannot resist the King's forces longer. *July 10th, 1689.*

Not for the first time the reply was to be 'No Surrender', a phrase which has echoed down to the present. This mortar shell is now on display in St Columb's Cathedral. The feature marked **1** on Neville's map is identified as '. . . an old Danish fort repaired by the enemy, in which they kept a strong guard at all tymes'. The site has been identified as the ground above Southway. Indeed, this vantage point overlooking town and river would have been hard to ignore.

The Rath roundabout at the top of Westway, pictured (page 19) in the 1950s, is the feature in Creggan which has the strongest claim to antiquity. Brian Lacy has suggested putative prehistoric origins with the possibility that it was re-used over the centuries and developed as a fort during the siege (see Creggan Rath article on page 15). An encounter which probably took place there is described by historian CD Milligan:

> An engagement at Creggan, which occurred on 18 May and lasted until night, parted the combatants, and was marked by the murder of Captain John Cunningham. A party of the garrison numbering a hundred were led out to the open fields by Captain Cunningham, Captain Noble, Captain Archibald Sanderson and others. They sieged a fort the enemy had made on a hill. Then a force from Galmoy's horse, coming between the garrison soldiers and the town, attempted to cut them off. Fifteen or sixteen of the garrison were killed and many wounded, some dying a few days later. Captain Noble and others managed to get away, except Captain Cunningham, who was taken prisoner. Although quarter had been given, he was basely murdered.

The site of the present Rath roundabout suggests that it would have been a natural choice for strategic reasons. Important skirmishes were fought at Pennyburn Mill, and the Rath commanded the safe route along the Creggan Burn (The Glen) to Pennyburn Mill, sheltered from the city's guns. It also commanded the road to Burt. Fleet commander Kirk's landings at Inch posed the threat of a Williamite invasion from there. The most accessible, quickest, and therefore most dangerous route for the Williamite forces, was the Burt Road.

Although the Jacobite encampment on the West Bank stretched from Balloughry Hill to Culmore, by far the greatest concentration on the West Bank was above the town. This campsite has been identified by historian JG Simms, who has deduced that it ran along the contour of Creggan Heights. This location would have given the Jacobites protection from the city's guns. Francis Neville described the sod huts built at Derry in the absence of tents.

> The ground on which they quartered shews, as much for having but few tents, they were forced to make Hutts, the walls of which being made of sods. My drawing . . . shews each camp very plaine, especially those within half a myle of the City whose huts . . . were sunk about four or five feet underground least the random shott of the great Artillery from the Citty should doe them any harme.

French officials and officers also sent highly critical reports back to France which further illuminate conditions 'at the camp before Derry' in the wet summer of 1689.

Former University of Ulster History Lecturer Frank D'Arcy has summarised their contents and given some examples below. The letters give a picture of the state of the army camped around the city and of the conditions endured by the troops. They complain about the lack of material to conduct a siege – the lack of suitable cannon, the lack of tools for making trenches, the lack of wood for making ladders, the lack of armourers to repair weapons. The troops had to live for a long period without cover. The rain was constant and the heights were cold. There was a lack of money to pay the troops. They were deserting in droves. So went the reports back to France. The letters are very critical of the Irish officers and the army generally. At one point, they claim there were only 3,000 men out of 15 battalions and 300 cavalry capable of bearing arms. There was a fever sweeping through the camp. There were only nine surgeons for several hundred sick or wounded. Medical supplies were short and a hospital was set up in Strabane. One letter ends bleakly:

> Finally Sir, it's an army of wanderers and mutineers, and there is also a good number of ill-disposed people.

What The French Generals Wrote

The following excerpts of correspondence from the French generals leading the siege give an indication of the difficulties suffered by the Jacobite troops.

30 June 1689

> The troops here are extremely tired and many fall sick. They have been on a campaign for four months – without tents and in a countryside where there is no cover and where it is always raining and where the nights are very cold . . . I can assure your Majesty that the troops and most of the officers are extremely discouraged for several reason – they are badly clothed, badly paid and too exposed to the weather. If things drag on, and I am sure they will, there is a danger that the troops will disappear altogether. Already a quarter of them are in the mountains with their officers.

8 July 1689

> The cavalry regiments of Tirconnel and Galmois, which are here, are very fine. They have, however, shrunk in numbers because of the course of action which the King has made them follow since his visit here and also because a number of their horses have been stolen while grazing, since there is no hay here for them to be kept tethered at picket. These sort of thefts are very common, for all the troops pilfer from each other.

> Whatever there are of new regiments of cavalry and dragoons are established only by taking horses from wherever they can find them. It often happens that they dismount each other and when one wants to talk about his, the gentleman who has taken the horses wants to go away and all the regiment want to follow him.

13 July 1689

> The army ebbs away day by day, some through illness and others because they are not paid and because they are disheartened by the fire from the besieged and by the work. Besides that, there is a good deal of negligence on the part of officers of all categories – for which they are mostly not fitted. I do what I can to instruct them but I do not succeed.

1 August 1689

> The Siege of Dery is still in the same state as I had the honour to tell you in my letter of 16 July. The King's amnesty-general took place on the 19th. The besieged had asked for this before entering into a settlement. After a whole day of conferences which the aforesaid commissioners spent in drinking well, most of them being tipsy, they broke up without deciding anything. During this conference, the people from the town and our soldiers were allowed to talk together and walk through the trenches. A fever is raging in the camp, and it spreads like a kind of plague, but the country is not hot enough for it to be able to develop entirely. Everyone has been attacked and several are dead: Monsieur Rose had had a violent bout, and Monsieur De Lery as well, but they have not gone away yet.

What emerges from the correspondence is a picture of troops who are demoralised, poorly housed, poorly armed and not equipped for breaching the walls of Derry. Inhospitable weather and sickness added to their difficulties. Derry's defensive weaknesses had been alluded to by the Royal Commission of 1628 which remarked on the city's vulnerability to attack from the river.

Threats from shipping, however, did not materialise during the siege as the Williamite fleet commanded Loughs Foyle and Swilly. It was left to the besiegers to exploit the 'divers hills about the town'. The importance of securing the high ground around Windmill Hill (in what is now Lumen Christi College in Bishop Street) was recognised by both sides. Occupation, for the besiegers, would have given them a shorter range from which they could hope to breach the walls on the Bishop's Gate side. It was, consequently, fiercely fought over, the besiegers eventually losing out.

The high ground at Creggan was to become more important as the siege wore on. The higher region, out of range of cannon fire from the walls, provided for the bulk of the Jacobite encampment. Here reserves could be safely accommodated. Reinforcements

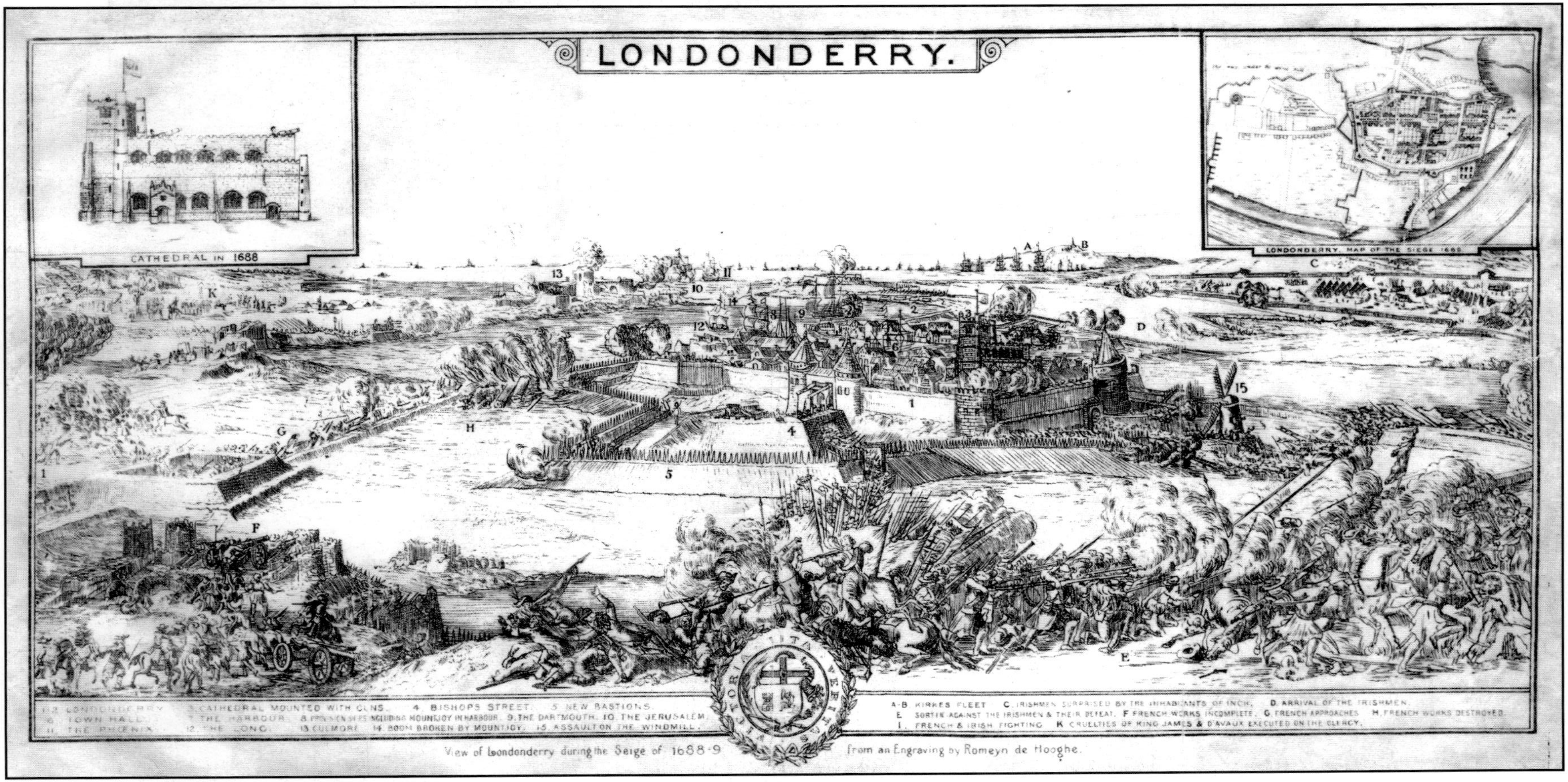

Contemporary illustration of the Siege of Derry 1689 from the vicinity of Creggan.

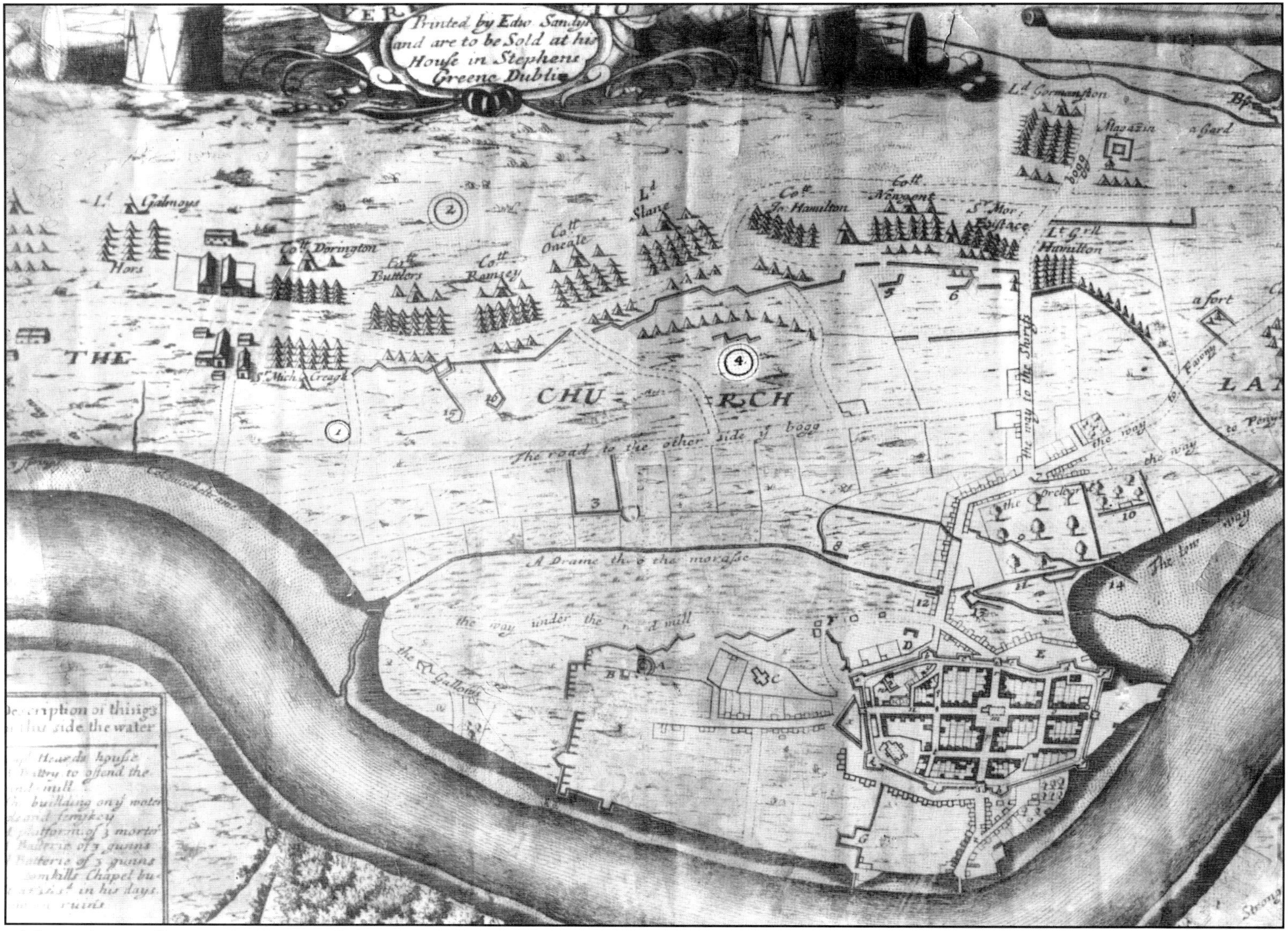

Detail from the Neville map drawn just after the siege. A portion of the Jacobite encampment is clearly on the ground now occupied by Creggan Estate.

could, and did, issue from the camp to engage with raiding parties, as they did at the daylong battle at the Rath. From here also would have come relays of foot soldiers to man earthworks and trenches around the Bogside and adjoining areas.

The manned forts at Southway and the Rath helped, along with trenches, earthworks and other forts, to complete the blockade that increasingly became the besiegers' tactic. A successful blockade would, eventually, have starved out the defenders. The other element of Jacobite activity, namely that of causing as much damage, injury and loss of life as possible, was not to be abandoned. The decision to move the mortar battery from Stronge's Orchard in the Waterside to the West Bank on 21 June, ensured that mortar fire would come from the Eastway site. From the diary of Thomas Ash, it has been calculated that as many as 337 bombs were fired from here between 21 June and 21 July. The highest figure for one day was 30 on 3 July. In the end, the combination of bombardment and blockade was to fail. The fortitude and courage of the defenders and the breaking of the boom on 28 July 1689 brought an end to the Siege of Derry.

Many historic siege events were enacted over the area now occupied by Creggan Estate. Continental forces fought here and reverberations were felt in Europe. Long-term consequences were most keenly experienced in Ireland and particularly in Derry, where the legacy is still disturbingly relevant. In an ironic twist of history, another Siege of Derry, involving Creggan and the Bogside was ended by Operation Motorman on 31 July 1972, only in the second case, the Jacobites (or at least the inheritors of the Jacobite tradition) were the besieged.

A Green Hill Far Away

How Creggan Moved Dame Cecil Alexander to Song

The famous hymn writer, Cecil Frances Alexander, daughter of Major John Humphrey, was born in Dublin in 1818. When she was seven, the family went to live in Wicklow where her father became agent to the incumbent Earl. Another move in 1833 took them to Milltown House, Strabane, where the Major was appointed agent to the Marquis of Abercorn. While living in Strabane Cecil Frances published, in 1848, her *Hymns for Little Children.* Written to explain the Apostles' Creed to children, their appeal to a wider audience is evident in the contemporary remark that 'these children's hymns are not childish'. Three of the most famous are: *Once in Royal David's City; All Things Bright and Beautiful*; and *There is a Green Hill Far Away.*

Various claims have been made for the location of the 'Green Hill' which inspired the latter hymn. Her biographer, EW Lovell, has looked at several possibilities and concludes:

> We cannot overlook the probability, however, that if any scene inspired Fanny (Cecil Frances) to write her well-known lines, it was the view of some grassy slope outside the walls of Derry.

The lines *There is a green hill far away, without a city wall* would seem to support the argument for the walled city of Derry. Although she did not move to Derry until after the hymn was published, she was close enough to receive her inspiration from the city. As a religious woman, deeply influenced by several noted churchmen, Cecil Frances would have been familiar with the development of Derry and its place in the history of the Church of Ireland.

The proximity of Strabane would have allowed frequent visits to Derry where she would have looked out from the Bishop's Palace and the walls around Walker's Pillar and St Augustine's Church. The green hill viewed from these vantage points is where the Creggan estate now stands. The hill also had a tract of land owned by the Bishop and known as the Bishop's Demesne. Such knowledge would have enhanced the religious dimension for the poetic observer.

In 1850, Cecil Frances married a young clergyman named William Alexander, son of the Rev Robert Alexander, a rector in the Derry diocese. Prior to his wedding, William Alexander had, in 1847, been ordained to the curacy of St Columb's Cathedral. At the height of the great famine he had ministered to the hungry and diseased until he himself contracted fever.

After his recovery and their marriage, the couple moved to the parish of Termonamongan. Here, as a rector's wife, Cecil Frances Alexander performed many exemplary charitable works. EW Lovell reveals:

> The parish clerk remembered her carrying food to the sick and poor in the most remote parts of the parish, and in the most inclement weather,

Detail of Cecil Frances Alexander window in St Columb's Cathedral which contains the opening lines of the famous hymn. (Lorcan Doherty)

> and often he saw her returning from errands wet through. It was also remembered that for six weeks she attended one woman (a Roman Catholic), suffering from cancer, and daily dressed the sore. From her slender resources, she paid for the education of a young man whom she enabled to become a National School teacher. Finding an elderly paralysed woman in a cottage who had insufficient blankets for her bed, Fanny removed her own shawl and wrapped it round the invalid. It was typical of her that she would allow neither distance nor weather, nor the personal inconvenience involved, to interfere with her visits to those she could help.

William was appointed to the parish of Upper Fahan in 1855, where they spent the next five years, after which, in 1860, they were moved to the parish of Camus-Juxta-Mourne in Strabane. In 1867, William Higgins, Bishop of Derry and Raphoe, died and William Alexander was offered the vacant bishopric. As wife to the Bishop, Cecil Frances Alexander remained in Derry for 28 years until her death in 1895.

She continued her good works ministering to the poor. Her fame had grown as her hymns became more popular and spread over the English-speaking world. A particular tribute to the words of the hymn *There is a Green Hill Far Away* was paid by French composer Charles Gounod who said:

> They set themselves to music.

On her death, she was mourned by the whole community and it was said:

> She was revered not only as a gifted hymn writer, but more intimately as the gentle and constant friend of the poor and the sick and the needy.

Cecil Frances Alexander found a final resting-place on a green hill outside the city walls. In October 1895, she was buried in the City Cemetery, part of the green hill which houses the present Creggan housing estate. A simple white cross marks her grave and the inscription reads:

> Your sons and daughters shall prophesy,
> Your old men shall dream dreams,
> Your young men shall see visions.
> (Joel 3:1)

Modern view of 'The Green Hill' from the Walls of Derry, near the Bishop's Palace. (Lorcan Doherty)

The Headless Horseman

Nineteenth-century Creggan was to spawn its own Victorian ghost story and quite a sinister one at that. The tale centres on Scott's House, a 'gentleman's seat' about a mile outside Derry, which stood on Foyle Hill until the latter half of the 20th century. The mansion, older generations may remember, was used by the Corporation as a fever hospital in the early part of the 20th century. Then, in the late 1940s, a number of dwellings collapsed at Nailor's Row in the city centre, and the old Scott's House was converted into flats for homeless families before they were eventually given houses in Creggan Estate. But it is to the 1860s that we return now for the tale of the Headless Horseman, related here by James Campbell, the late editor of the 1960s Creggan magazine, The Latest.

The long winding road up the steep slope into Foyle Hill affords a panoramic view of the River Foyle. The eye can take in the sweep of the river into the heart of Donegal and on a clear day ships can be seen sailing majestically towards the mouth of the Lough, and beyond to the Atlantic Ocean. Such a view without the industrial trappings of modernity must have presented itself to the inhabitants of the city in the 19th century. The same inhabitants could well have been acquainted with the horseman, whose ghost, it is alleged, still thunders down the modern Southway driving his black coach and sleek horses where he once thundered down the old tree-lined, bleak and forbidding Coach Road. Who he was or why he was there, few could ever say. But he was headless, they swear, and he cursed (if a headless man can curse) the horses and whipped them into a frenzy as if pursued relentlessly by some unknown follower. But who would want to chase a headless ghost?

Derry people for many generations past have seen him. Fortunate were those who only heard him, but even these will speak excitedly of the cold, icy air that swept through them as the dreaded sound passed by. One of these folk who has heard him, but never seen the apparition, tells me that the very trees bent, rustled and creaked on a very calm night. But for those who are sceptical, the origin of the story must be traced.

In the middle of the 19th century, the land on which Foyle Hill Estate now stands was the property of a retired Army Officer, Captain William Scott. The 'Big House', as his residence was known, was on the site of the Old Foyle Hill Hospital. The land of Termonbacca, and stretching further beyond, belonged to the captain, an authoritarian but respected figure in the neighbourhood. He wasn't above taking a whip to any young lad found trespassing on his lands, but he was judged to be fair in his dealings with the native peasantry, his tenants. Perhaps on those occasions when he did beat some local unmercifully, he was only venting his spite against the world for the misfortune that an erring son daily inflicted on him. They didn't come any wilder than his son, John 'Terror' Scott, the principal in the story of the headless horseman.

Handsome to a fault, with a thick mop of brown curly hair, fine, proud features and a sensuous mouth that betrayed his weakness; he was irresistible to women. Indeed, women and drink were his downfall. At 18, he was shipped off to a military establishment in England, but soon found himself in disgrace for some civil transgression. He was dishonourably discharged and returned home to face an irate father. It might be that the offence was his first and it may have been minor, but for an honourably retired and respected captain, a son who brought the family name into disgrace was unfit to be his heir. The young Scott was informed that he no longer had an inheritance to claim. It was only out of a self-righteous feeling of charity that he was allowed to remain in the family home. His father's treatment of him could not have been kind, but he might eventually have been forgiven. John Scott didn't petition for forgiveness. The drinking dens and places of ill repute became his haunts.

Nightly he summoned his father's groom and ordered him to get the coach and horses ready, the only liberty his father allowed him to take.

Come saddle my horses,
Bold James McAfee,
The night's for carousing
Throughout the country,
And if you'll drive me
Into the town,
We'll drink and we'll sing
Till daylight comes round.

But the groom was too respectable for that and he didn't fancy his young master's habit of taking over the reins and whipping the horses wildly down the Coach Road.

Begging your pardon,
My young Master John,
But my Captain don't like
Your wild goin's on.
Now when ye've danced
And drunk your fill
Take the horses right aisy,
Ye'd die in a spill.

The groom's advice was unheeded. With a wild laugh, young Scott would leap up on the coach and the horses would feel the sting of the whip all the way into town. The groom would be left shaking his head sadly, murmuring softly to himself 'he'll come to a bad end'. Little did James McAfee know that he himself would figure prominently when the end would come.

Captain Scott was wealthy and John was his only son. For this reason, he was quite prepared to tolerate his son's drinking habits and degenerate behaviour, provided the son was discreet enough not to add further disgrace to the family. The gambling debts came in and were duly paid. It was a small price to pay to keep his wayward son happy. But John Scott developed what in his father's eyes and the groom's eyes was an unforgivable habit. He left the sweating and excited horses unattended for most of the night and often he was to be found staggering home by the side of the ditch with the horses nowhere in sight. Frequently, James McAfee had to go into Derry to fetch them and found coach and horses outside an inn, or worse, outside a house of ill repute. Captain Scott didn't like the son's sins to be the talking point of the town.

An opportunity arose to be quit of him in the form of an offer from a friend who had a plantation in Ceylon. Young Scott was prevailed upon to accept the offer as manager of the plantation. The boredom of provincial life weighed heavily on him and he was anxious for romance and adventure. In 1865, at 23 years of age, he set sail for Ceylon. For three years the coach wheels turned at a more leisurely pace. But like many a rogue, the people missed him and always they asked for news of him at the 'Big House'. Nevertheless, the captain was glad to be rid of him and refused to even mention his name. It was left to James McAfee to pass on scraps of news that filtered through the house. John Scott was not the boy to keep them waiting.

In 1868, three years after he left Ireland, he was on his way home again having killed a young English officer in a duel. It is said they quarreled over a woman and, even though Scott was of English planter descent, being called 'Irish scum'. Scott challenged him to a duel and shot him between the eyes. His retreat from the East was a matter of diplomacy.

Come, fight me a duel
My bold Grenadier
And be ready to die
When the morrow draws near.
Calmly Scott sneered
At the gallant's fine clothes
And sent the ball home
Through the bridge of his nose.

The news of the deed had gone before him and it was with much misgiving that his father received him back into the fold. But where he had nothing but contempt for him previously, he was now inclined to boast that his son had acquitted himself bravely and honourably. After all, he had faced death in a duel and won. Military pride was uppermost in generations of Scotts. John Scott was re-instated as heir. The prodigal son had returned. But he was still prodigal. His recklessness and degeneracy increased. Fine black horses were run into the ground. Gambling debts increased. He was seldom sober. Men were challenged to duels every night. None accepted. His reputation as a dead shot grew as time passed and his insults had to be accepted.

I'll fight any man
In this fair town
With pistol and shot
I'll shoot him down.
I'll fight any man
With pistol and shot
And I'll shoot him down
Or my name's not Scott.

For two years he drove coach and horses recklessly throughout the countryside. People scattered when they heard the sound of the wheels and, rising from the ditch after he had passed by, muttered angrily, 'There goes "Terror" Scott', for so he had been named.

The coaches were driven
At a mad pace
And the horses were lathered
With the sweat of the race.

Captain Scott again cut him off, giving him nothing but food and lodging, forbidding him to drive the coach and horses.

The 'Terror' was not to be kept down. Regularly at midnight he would steal into the stables, hitch the horses to the coach and drive into Derry. His father's anger increased when he discovered that the coach and horses were missing one morning. He was to find out later that day that they had been sold in Letterkenny just about the time the stable doors were found lying wide to the wall.

No money for horses
No money for sin,
Scott sold the horses
For a barrel of gin.

About 1870, the descent into tragedy began. James McAfee's daughter Molly fell in love with the wild young man. Clandestine meetings took place between the pair on the lonely Coach Road. James McAfee had solemnly warned his 16-year-old daughter never to see the young master, but his warning fell on deaf ears. Before two months of this clandestine association had passed, Molly was pregnant. It was inevitable and Scott's behaviour on learning the dismal news was also inevitable. He found it convenient to ignore her.

In the fourth month of her pregnancy, Captain Scott died. John was lying drunk in the stables when they informed him. He entered the house to find five ministers of his faith grouped solemnly around the blazing hearth fire. One of the ministers, a relative of the Scotts, upbraided him for not being at his father's deathbed. 'Terror' Scott, far from mourning, smiled grimly.

Stand close to the fire,
Feel the heat on your back.
I'm the master now,
The devil is back.

Indeed he became the master of the estate, successfully contesting the will that had not provided for him. Molly McAfee was by this stage too far advanced to hide the truth from her father. It was a grim and outraged groom who confronted the new

Front elevation of Foyle Hill House, circa 1896. (courtesy Derry City Council Heritage and Museum Service)

owner and demanded that Scott should marry her. Scott in a drunken stupor not only refused but also dismissed the groom from his employment. McAfee privately swore revenge. His reasons for revenge were dramatically heightened the following evening when his heartbroken daughter, finally accepting that Scott would never marry her, drowned herself in a pool of water that lay not 50 yards from the 'Big House'. Scott heard the cries of one of his workers and rushed to the pool. He saw her billowing dress. When he brought her out, she was dead.

For three weeks Scott never left the house, nor did he touch a drop of drink. It was the only tragic event that had ever shook him. James McAfee never approached the house. His revenge appeared to consist of nothing more than a silent condemnation of Scott. Messengers were sent daily to McAfee with money and food, but they were coldly refused.

It would have been better for Scott if he had decided to give up drink and his mad, midnight race. But weakness got the better of him and he gave the order to hitch up the coach.

It was a clear moonlit night in October when Scott set off from Foyle Hill down the Coach Road. Out of character, he started out at a leisurely pace. The moon stealing across the sky and the thought of the dead girl may have prompted him to lash the horses, spurring them on faster and faster. Suddenly disaster struck. A wheel came off with a splintering of wood. The coach overturned and the horses screamed. Scott's terrible scream rent the calm of the night. He was flung onto the roadway like a broken doll. The shattered coach careered into the ditch and the horses, free of their burden, galloped into the night.

Scott was probably dead, but a figure armed with an axe emerged from the trees. It was the man who had tampered with the wheel of the coach, James McAfee.

Bending over Scott, never looking to see if he was dead or alive, he severed the head from the body with one violent blow of the axe. With a macabre touch, 'Terror' Scott's head rolled several yards down the road. So the legend of the 'Headless Horseman' had begun.

Rural Creggan

The land over which Creggan Estate now extends was not just sterile property awaiting urban development. It once housed small farms, a brickworks, a reservoir for a local industry and, for a short time, a greyhound-racing track. As a green area adjacent to a densely populated town, it also provided a place of recreation where town dwellers could escape into the countryside.

Tommy McCallion is a long-term resident, having lived in Leenan Gardens for over 50 years. His family connections, however, go back much further. The McCallion family was installed in a small farm in Bligh's Lane as early as the 1880s. Tommy's grandfather was landsteward and assistant coachman to the Watt family, who owned the distillery of the same name, and the McCallion family were to have other transactions with the Watts. The McCallions specialised in chicken farming and did good business with the distilling family, who regularly placed large orders to grace the tables at their many functions.

Another responsibility which came with the position of landsteward was that of caring for the reservoir, now the site of Oakland Park. This was also owned by the Watts and fed, by way of a stone culvert, into Watt's other reservoir nearer the distillery which was known as The Bull (now Bull Park). As a young man, Tommy remembers being allocated the task of opening an outlet valve there when the water level got too high in the reservoir.

He has fond childhood memories of innocent rambles and blackberry-picking forays all over Creggan. A favourite walk was out past Sarah and Jimmy Mitchell's shop, which was near the site of Piggery Ridge and where the brandy balls they stocked made the journey worthwhile. He remembers other landmarks. There was the Dane's Field, now the site of St Cecilia's College, and King James's Well, which was situated where lower Bligh's Lane comes to a stop at Eastway. This would seem to indicate the persistence in folk memory of sites identified with the Jacobite encampment during the Siege of Derry. The information on a map, drawn immediately after the siege, which identifies a feature as a Danish Fort, and the unearthing of a sword (since disappeared) in the area some time ago, would lend credence to this oral tradition.

The brickworks, later the site for the BSR factory and the Brickfield Cottages, speaks of an activity long gone from the area. Apart from this small industry and the existence of Watt's reservoir, economic activity seems to have been primarily farming.

Hugh Hamilton was raised on the family farm situated close to what became the British Army camp at Piggery Ridge during the *Troubles*. In fact, the by then derelict farmhouse was thought to have been blown up by the Army to secure its base. It had also been used as a billet for gunners who manned anti-aircraft guns during the Second World War. He fondly remembers a childhood dominated by farming activities, where he was expected to do his share of the work after school hours, and where evenings were regularly given over to storytelling, a gift Hugh has inherited.

His memories of previous occupants of the area are vivid. He rhymes off a list of former residents, starting at the bottom of Bligh's Lane. There were the Kildeas, who lived opposite the BSR gate; just above that, the McCallions; and above that again was the 'nine-acre field', owned by William McCafferty, who operated a greyhound-racing track there. On the right side of Bligh's Lane, just below the present Ráth Mór complex, were the Moores and below that again, the Brickfield Cottages, where the Stewart, Ross and Hamilton families lived. There was the Anderson farm, near where the lane intersects Creggan Heights, and the McFeeters and Doherty farms on Foyle Hill. Just above Creggan Heights near the Watery Lane was the home of Jack Deeney, whose unusual carvings are now housed in the Harbour Museum. A walk out along Bligh's Lane to Springhill Road would have taken you to the B-Specials' Drill Hall, known as the Black Hut, where locals of all persuasions attended dances.

Familiar to Tommy McCallion was the Morgan (formerly the McGuinness) house and farm at the top of Beechwood Avenue, which had originally been Watt's property; the house was to serve as a temporary parochial house for the priests of Creggan and later as premises for the Society of St Vincent de Paul. The Boys' Club used the outbuildings for a while until all, including the Tierney house alongside, were demolished to make way for new development. The last house in Beechwood Avenue before this modern development was Harry Scott's. Cost Cutters now stands on the site of the house, and the buildings from there to the taxi stand are built on ground that was formerly Scott's garden.

Reports of occurrences in the area in the first half of the 20th century have resonances for the history of that period. One is reflected in the existence of a field known as the Volunteers' Field. This is reputed to be where local Irish Volunteers trained prior to the outbreak of the First World War.

The other report is of de Valera being smuggled into Derry through Creggan to appear illegally at a meeting in the city. Hugh Hamilton has some detail, as told to him by his father. Apparently de Valera, accompanied by an O'Donnell from Donegal and another man, took the route from Carstruse, then up over the hill to the Bonnemaine Road, over the Holywell Hill, down the Peat Cadger's Lane and then on to Bligh's Lane. The account ends at Mary B's Bar. His transfer to the meeting is another story. Apart from these activities, rural Creggan seems to have experienced nothing to disturb its rural equilibrium in the years leading up to the birth of the new housing estate.

A sentimental piece, expressing regrets over the changes ushered in by urban developments, was published in the *Derry Journal* in 1953:

Bligh's Lane

To my old friend in America
By William Sharkey, Derry

Old friend, I wish you were here again
To see the change in our Bligh's Lane.
McCallions are gone and everything new,
There is nothing left but the basin brew.

A new road made up the old Demesne
And new houses along to Watery Lane.

A cottage built where we cut the corn,
You would almost get lost where you were born.

Our picnics my memory oft recalls
To Gracy Mitchell's for brandy balls,
And on past Sam's to roam at will
To a heather bed on Holywell Hill.

Sometimes with glasses I look down
On the peaceful scenes around our ancient town,
The well-kept farms and beautiful soil,
With a heavenly breeze from the silvery Foyle.

Perhaps you may return again,
And visit the place we called Bligh's Lane.
Gone are your friends and their innocent joys.
Where is your Bligh's Lane and where are the boys?

Many have left our old Glassagh home
Like you, dear friend, it was their fate to roam.
But if you come back, don't leave in despair
Just ask around and you'll find McCallions still there.

One story which links this rural hinterland to the present is the 'Story of the Medals' which is best told in their own words by the authors, Tommy and Pat McCallion of Glassagh and Creggan:

> At the end of the 19th century, our grandfather was landsteward for Watt's Distillery. The Watt family had a large holding of land in what we now know as Creggan, but in those days was known as Glassagh in the townland of Ballymagowan. The farmhouse was located about 100 yards from where St Mary's Church now stands.
>
> Times were hard and people depended on their neighbours for friendship and support in times of need. Regular visitors to the people of the area were the nuns from Termonbacca, who were warmly welcomed into all homes. On one such visit, two American nuns, visiting our grandparents, Tom and Elizabeth McCallion, for the last time before their return home, gave our grandfather four Miraculous Medals with instructions to bury them at the four corners of the farm so that all who lived there would always be in the care of Our Blessed Lady.
>
> The four medals were duly buried as instructed and the 'Story of the Medals' and their locations was passed down from our grandfather to our father and then on to our families and us. The farm was quite big by the standards of those days, but the exact location of each medal was known

to all of us. Eventually the farm was sold and the new Creggan Estate appeared on the fields where we used to play and work. One field, however, the 'Field of the Black Gates', was left untouched and it was in this field that the fourth medal was buried. When it was decided that Creggan should have its own chapel, the 'Field of the Black Gates' was the obvious site, and the layout of the new St Mary's placed the sanctuary exactly on the site of the buried Miraculous Medal.

Often in the re-telling of the 'Story of the Medals' to our families, I think back to the promise of the American nuns to our grandfather that Our Blessed Lady would always look after us and feel it was no accident that our church was built where it now proudly stands, dedicated to none other than Our Blessed Lady.

St Mary's was to have its expected quota of sad and happy occasions, as families experienced the normal trials and joys of life, but as the *Troubles* developed, it was to witness events which could never have been foreseen when it was built as a haven of peace and comfort.

Hugh Hamilton (front) with sister Kathleen on his right and brother Willie on his left. The adult is their uncle Johnny. Taken over 60 years ago in front of Ballymagowan House which was about 200 yards from Piggery Ridge. It was later used by anti-aircraft personnel during the Second World War. (Hugh Hamilton)

Tommy McCallion, 2000. (Larry Doherty)

THE CREGGAN PARK RACING TRACK

One sport which flourished for a short while in Creggan, but did not survive the urban development of the housing estate, was greyhound racing. Jimmy Breen, entrepreneur, turf accountant, philosopher and storyteller, remembers the early days. Jimmy's interest was stirred when his uncle, Willie Lynch, took him to a race meeting in Omagh when he was only eight years of age. Years later, when the Creggan dog track opened in 1941, Jimmy, then a young man, was a very interested spectator. Up to then, Celtic Park had been the Mecca for followers of the sport, but the Catholic Bishop's disapproval was enough to have racing terminated there. Apparently he had reached the conclusion that the lure of 'the dogs' was proving too great an attraction for weaker church members who, when faced with a choice between religion and the track, chose the excitement of the track.

The search for a new venue for the dog-racing fraternity began. Applications to organise racing in the Brandywell Grounds were rejected by Derry Corporation, and Creggan was one of a number of alternatives sought. A field, owned by William McCafferty and situated near the present Rinmore Drive, was duly prepared as a 325-yard sprint track and for a few years hosted the noble sport. Two meetings were held every Sunday and one every Friday. Serious competition was encountered from another venue. Meetings clashed with those in Boundary Park, well named, as it was situated at Springtown within sight of the city boundary post. A compromise was reached, however, as evidenced in a notice in the *Derry Journal* of 18 June 1945. This advised punters of an arrangement between the Creggan management and its competitor, Boundary Park, to have meetings on alternate nights commencing the following Friday.

Jimmy Breen, who was to become a bookmaker of note himself, fondly remembers earlier members of his calling who operated in Creggan, among whom were Hugh O'Neill, 'Poet' McLaughlin, 'Boodyim' Doherty, Peter and 'Buff' Meenan and Jim McCaul. Operating with Jim was a very talented clerk, Dinky Anderson – father of current Derry City Councillor Peter Anderson. Also prominent were Tully Deehan, 'a small man with a voice bigger than himself' and 'Liza' Doherty, who, although he could neither read nor write, was, according to Jimmy, the best boardman and the fastest calculator he ever knew. Prince among punters was 'Porky' Green.

'Porky' Green, Prince of Punters, late '40s. (courtesy Gerry Downey)

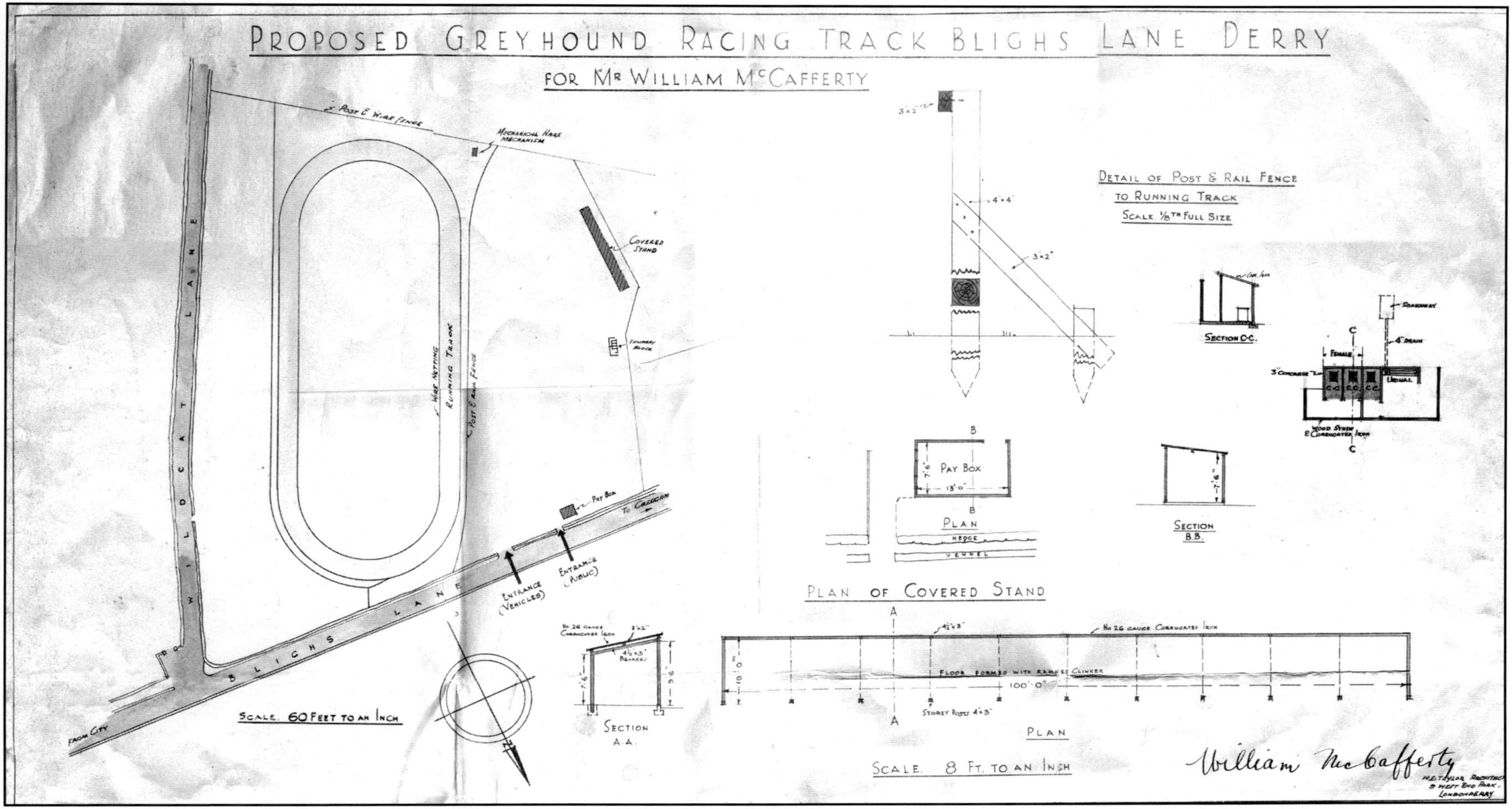

William McCafferty's plans for proposed Greyhound Racing Track, August 1944. (courtesy Derry City Council)

The Christmas Programme for 1944 was advertised in the *Derry Journal*. A look at the cards should stir memories of another generation:

CREGGAN PARK GREYHOUND RACING TRACK

Great Xmas Programme
Sunday, at 2.30 p.m.
8 Well-graded Races. Sweepstake Heats And Trials

Christmas Day, 2.30 p.m.
Special Attraction:
Great Challenge Sprint – £25 a-side
Mr William Doherty's BOND STREET
V
Mr Michael Barr's GOLDEN CLOUD
Also Sweepstake Final and a well-graded Card
Usual admission. ALL MUST PAY

NEXT SUNDAY'S CARD
Sweepstake (375 yards), 1st, 2nd and 3rd to run in final on Christmas Day.
Heat 1 – Killarney Girl, Short Speed, Joe's Luck, Cream Queen, Bulldozer, Hazelbank.
Heat 2 – Messines Boy, Too Late, Miss Lagoon, Lancer, The Hood, Sammy Blair.
525 – Swanee Rebel, Froggy, Red Glory, Dead Stop, That's That, Star Turn.
375 – All Alone, Coal King, Hot Pepper, Phoenix Boy, Jackie, Miss Darkie. Sub. – Rebel Girl.
525 – John L., Red Cap, White Row, Ham Bone, Find the Lady, Lizzie's Fancy. Subs. – Voltaire. Golden Nib.
375 – Lady Luck, Lady Lagoon, Monty, Red Don, Full Moon, Mill Boy. Sub. – Lucky Stroke.
525 – Brilliant Patch, On The Road, Flip, Ask Archie, Fawn Cloud. Sub. – Carrick Boy.
525 – Hopeful Sign, Mr M. Cosey Corner, Off You Pop, Can't Run, Steelstown.

XMAS DAY CARD
375 – Fair Head, Souped Again, Happy Lady, Glendarragh Boy, Rambler, Hazeltree.
525 – Bogside Lass, Miss Miniver, Hopeless, Know Nothing, Short Service, Flash Parade. Sub. – Foyle Bank.
Final of 375-yard Sweepstake.
Challenge Sprint (£25 each side bet)
Mr Wm. Doherty's BOND STREET.
Mr M. Barr's GOLDEN CLOUD.
375 – True Form, Honest Penny, Black Flash, Fair Jack, Dark Cloud, Dodger.
375 – Red Robin, Larry's Gift, Fairway Caught Again, Packets, Red Sail. Sub. – Wise Guy.
375 – Chelsea Lad, Clydeside, May Queen, Pin-up Girl, Old King Sol, Newmarket.
375 – Silver Sixpence.. Jamie's Pal, Dark Print, Slemish Lass, Golden Girl, Hi Cisco.

The special attraction for Christmas Day, a challenge between William Doherty's *Bond Street* and Michael Barr's *Golden Cloud*, with side bets of £25, is interesting, because of the size of the bets and the personalities involved. Twenty-five pounds in 1944 was a sum not to be sniffed at. Jimmy Breen identifies Mickey Barr from Buncrana and William Doherty from Derry as two of the great characters of greyhound racing in Derry. The challenge sprint was not won by the favourite. Jimmy would not be drawn on any interpretation of the outcome other than to say it was unexpected.

Derry's contribution to winning the Battle of the Atlantic during the Second World War meant that many nationalities would pass through the port. It was to be expected that many would have welcomed opportunities for a gamble, especially at a spectator sport. Although local punters would generally have outnumbered others, many nationalities did attend. Among Jimmy's many jobs was that of chauffeur to officers at the American Naval base. Commodore Perry Johnston of the US Navy was a regular patron. On race nights, Jimmy picked him up at the Clooney base and delivered him to Creggan. The noble Commodore's investments would have been all the more successful for the advice offered by his knowledgeable and astute chauffeur.

The demise of the Creggan Park Racing Track had nothing to do with any decline in business; all the evidence points to consolidation and expansion. William McCafferty certainly had expansion in mind when, on 10 August 1944, he submitted plans to the Corporation for an improved and restructured facility; the plans were approved on 31 October. However, within three weeks the death knell was sounded.

The *Derry Journal* of 20 November published details of the order informing the public of the Government's intention to vest land for the new housing estate of Creggan. This was to include McCafferty's land, on which stood the Creggan Park Racing Track. Thus, while racing continued for some time after, the fate of greyhound racing in Creggan had, in a few short weeks, swung from that of a healthy enterprise to one facing extinction.

William McCafferty's son Lewis remembers listening to a conversation between his parents that hinted at the success of the track; the conversation probably took place in late 1944. As the young Lewis lay in bed, he overheard his father expressing satisfaction to his mother at their good fortune, adding that it was almost too good to be true. Part of this good fortune, he revealed, was that a profit of £20 was made on minerals (soft drinks in modern parlance) alone at each race meeting. William's conversations were punctuated by puffs on his favourite pipe, and as he savoured thoughts of his good fortune, he spat on the hearth and his spittle landed on a spider. A superstitious man, William regarded any injury caused to a spider to have earned misfortune for the perpetrator. He pondered for a while, considered his recent expressions of his good fortune and added: 'But maybe not for much longer.' Within weeks, the order vesting his land had been published. William, however, was able to accept that there was a positive outcome for the wider community, when, after hearing of the vesting order, he observed that at least a lot of children would benefit from this new development. Whether fate intervened, the story of the Creggan Park Greyhound Racing Track is one of unrealised potential, or at least the story of what might have been.

Chapter 2

Moving In

The history of the modern Creggan housing estate may be said to have begun with the approval, at a meeting of the Derry Corporation with City Surveyor Andy Hamilton in January 1944, of plans for the erection of from 500 to 1,000 houses at Creggan. The estate would incorporate a shopping centre and all modern facilities, including recreational spaces.

On 20 November 1944, the vesting notice for lands required for this new housing development was published in the *Derry Journal.* A major step had been taken in converting plan to reality. However, it was August 1946, following much procrastination, before houses started to appear, but only after desperate families had taken the extreme measure of squatting in vacant military encampments all around the city. Ironically, the first movement of squatters was to Bligh's Lane, led by Adam Smith, a man whose Christian name must have seemed appropriate in the circumstances.

The extreme deprivation suffered by many, and the urgent need for substantial housing, are demonstrated by the experiences of two families. Adam Smith delivered this opinion:

> We have endured squalor too long. For eight years, my wife and myself and five children – four boys and a girl of ages from seven to 18 years – have had to live in one room at 37 Limewood Street. Can you imagine what it was like, all eating and sleeping in one small room? Desperation drove me to this; I couldn't have stood it any longer.

Meanwhile, in an article entitled *Twenty-three in Three-roomed House*, the *Derry Journal* reported:

> Easily the worst case was that of Mr Joe Doherty, who, with his wife and nine children, shared one small room in a three-roomed house in which altogether there were 23 people, the tenant, Mr George Doherty, having eight of a family. The Doherty family included twins born six weeks ago. One of them died and, in the words of the mother: 'Was it any wonder? Some of us had to sleep in the scullery, and every night we had to lift the cradle up on the table to leave room for the others to lie down.'

Although the development of the Creggan estate was to contribute to the easing of this desperate housing problem, the choice of site, which was to become overwhelmingly Catholic, was interpreted as being influenced by its position to the South ward electoral division. Increased numbers of Catholic voters would do little to alter Unionist domination at local government level.

Given the origins of the recent *Troubles*, which were in large measure a response to injustices caused by gerrymandered boundaries and the measures taken to retain minority control, the observations of one man over 60 years ago were to prove prophetic. Archie Halliday, a Unionist, attended the 1936 inquiry into the redrawing of the city wards. When asked for his opinion on the proposals, his reply revealed his misgivings:

> You know perfectly well that if you put justice underground, if you take a course that is unjust, disguise it as you may, it will come out and arise sometime – maybe not immediately, but sometime or other – and will wreak havoc which you probably did not see and should have foreseen when you planted that injustice.

This turned out to be an unexpected insight from a Unionist politician which in its way predicted the emergence of opposition, led by the residents of Creggan and the Bogside, to the agencies which had initiated and maintained political inequality in Derry for decades.

Adam Smith, first squatter in Bligh's Lane, August 1946. (*Derry Journal*)

Built to Suit Unionists

Despite a strong Catholic majority in Derry, careful manipulation of electoral boundaries would allow Unionists to retain control of the city's Corporation. And it was in an attempt to maintain this gerrymander that Creggan was sited where it is, as former Derry Journal *editor Frank Curran explains here.*

Derry's Creggan is the estate which was built many years before it should have been, but long after it was desperately needed. That statement seems to be a contradiction in terms. Let me explain. From 1840 – when the British Parliament passed the Municipal Corporation (Ireland) Act which provided a local government vote for every person whose dwelling had a yearly valuation of not less than £10 – until 1896, the Unionists had total control of Derry Corporation. The population of the city had grown to 33,000. Catholics numbered 18,322 and all others 14,561. Yet on the Municipal Voting Register there were only 182 Catholics and 600 all others. That, of course, reflected the fact that the Catholics were so much worse off economically that few of them had homes meeting the £10 valuation voting imperative.

The much wider parliamentary franchise, which gave a vote to all who paid rates and lodgers who paid £10 or more a year, suited the Catholics much better. In 1892, the Unionist Member of Parliament, Mr John Ross, had beaten a Nationalist by only 20 votes. When another election was announced in 1895, the Unionists knew they faced a very difficult contest. The Nationalist Party selected a young Protestant solicitor, Vesey Knox, as its candidate. The Unionist candidate, again Mr Ross, expressed Unionist fears when he declared that the boundary of the city constituency should be expanded to include the Upper and Lower Liberties (which included places like Culmore, Ballyarnett, Shantallow, Coshquin and Sheriff's Mountain, then all predominantly Protestant demographically). Then, he declared, there would be no need for a contest at all. However, the worst fears of the Unionists were realised when Mr Knox won the seat by 2,033 votes to 1,994, a Nationalist majority of 39. The Unionists knew that with the Catholic majority increasing year by year, they would never win the seat again.

While the loss of the parliamentary seat was a dreadful shock to a Unionist community accustomed to unquestioned ascendancy in Derry, there was an even worse spectre looming. The Westminster Parliament was planning to extend the parliamentary franchise to municipal elections. The Unionist majority in Derry Corporation was in deadly danger. So, out of dire Unionist political necessity was born the first of several gerrymanders of the city's electoral wards, which in the 20th century earned Derry the damning title 'Ireland's Fascist city'.

Derry had three electoral wards – East, North and South. On a £4 valuation qualification, the respective electoral strengths were calculated as: East ward, Catholics 342, all others 658; North, Catholics 467, all others 540; South, Catholics 854, all others 700. Thus the Nationalists would win the South, the Unionists the East, and probably the North. But Catholic voting numbers were increasing and a Catholic

Derry Journal

Established 1772

FRIDAY MORNING, AUGUST 11, 1950

GERRYMANDER AND DERRYMANDER

Reproduction of cover illustration of the latest pamphlet of the Mansion House Anti-Partition Conference

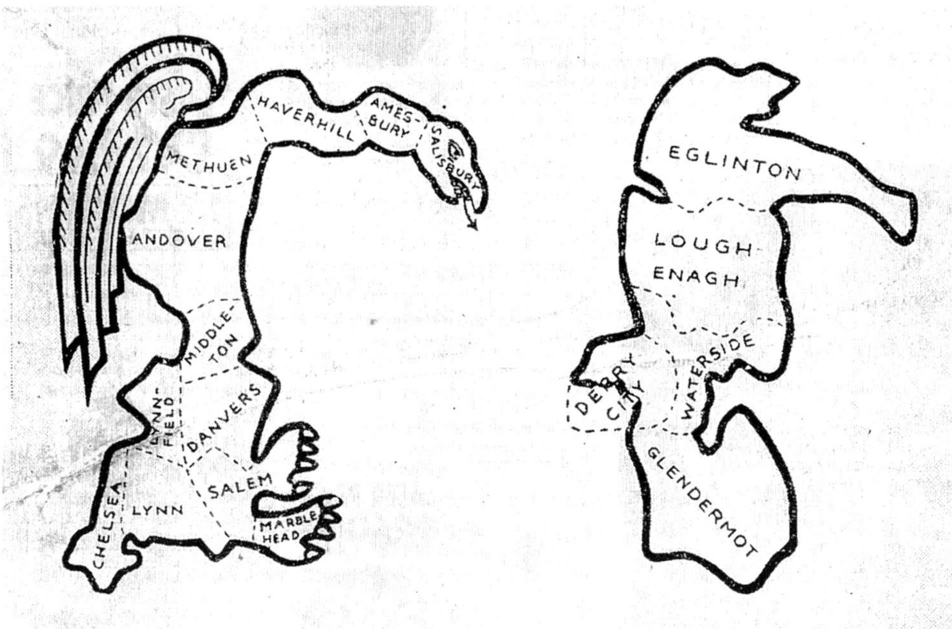

ONE MONSTER –

– AND ANOTHER

The classic example of boundary manipulation for which the name Gerrymander was coined. The electoral areas in Essex County, Massachusetts, U.S.A., were rearranged when Governor Elbridge Gerry was in office giving an outline to which the artist, Gilbert Stuart, finding it in the office of Benjamin Russel, the Boston editor, added wings, beak and claws, and said it was like a salamander "Better say a Gerrymander," growled Russel; and a new word entered the world's dictionaries.

A modern example of boundary manipulation in the partitioned area of North-East Ireland. In order to gerrymander the Nationalist majority in Derry out of representing that city in Parliament, a new City Division was designed by the Belfast Government. Part of the city is omitted altogether, and rural areas up to eight miles away have been brought in to outvote the Nationalists in the city proper.

The Unionist gerrymander was a bone of contention in Derry for decades – as the graphic above taken from the *Journal* in 1950 shows.

majority in the North, and therefore a Catholic majority of seats in the Corporation, was inevitable within a few years.

The Unionists proposed five wards to be created: East; North; West; Waterside and South. After an inquiry, they got their way. But in the 1896 election, they lost not only the West ward, but also the South. However, the Unionists were able to hold on to three wards up to 1920 because the bulk of the ever-increasing Catholic majority was contained in the West and South wards.

When Sinn Féin swept the country in the 1918 British Parliament General Election, the British Government decided to make an attempt to curb that party's power in Ireland. It decided that local elections should be conducted by Proportional Representation (PR). The objective of the Act was stated as 'giving equal representation to all sections on the basis of population'. The British had two objectives: one was to ensure that Unionist minorities all over Ireland would gain representation on Local Government Authorities in proportion to their numbers; and two, it was hoped that PR would encourage small factions to contest elections and win seats off Sinn Féin, which they would have no chance of doing under the British 'first past the post' system of elections.

With, by 1920, a Catholic majority of 528 on the Municipal Register, it seemed certain that a Nationalist majority Corporation would be elected. But the Unionists made a bid to defeat even PR. They proposed a change in the ward boundaries, and a reduction in the number of wards to four. The Nationalists strongly opposed the scheme, which they said was an attempt to circumvent PR. After an official inquiry, the Unionist scheme was approved by the Tory-dominated Local Government Board. The 'fairness' of the Unionist scheme can be measured by the fact that their new boundaries gave the West ward such a colossal Nationalist majority that the Unionists did not even contest any seats there when the 1920 election took place. However, justice was done when, in spite of the Unionist mathematical gymnastics, the coalition of Nationalists and Sinn Féin won 21 seats to the Unionists' 19. Derry had a Nationalist majority Corporation for the first time in history, and the Nationalist Party's Hugh C O'Doherty was elected Mayor. It seemed certain that the Unionist hegemony over Derry's future was ended.

But within two years, partition had been ordained by the Treaty and the Stormont Parliament created. Hardly had King George V brushed the dust of Stormont from his feet than a catalogue of regulations, all with the purpose of re-entrenching Unionist rule throughout the Six Counties, were issued from the Ministry of Home Affairs. On 28 September 1922, Derry Corporation received intimation that the Ministry proposed to reinstate the five wards in operation before 1919, and to abolish Proportional Representation in all Local Government elections. The effect of the Stormont dictate was to restore a Unionist majority in Derry Corporation. In disgust, the Nationalists announced that they would not be participating in what they considered a farce and a gross denial of democracy.

The enactment of the Limited Companies Act by the Stormont Government was another ploy to combat increasing numbers of Nationalist voters throughout Northern Ireland. If any government anywhere brought forth such an outrageous piece of legislation today, it would be pilloried before the democratic world. But in the 1930s, with compliant British support, Stormont could do anything it liked. The Act gave all Limited Companies a Local Government vote, up to a maximum of six votes for every £10 valuation. This cynical ruse added 391 Unionist votes to the Derry electorate, but only 38 Nationalist votes (this again underlined the Unionist near-monopoly of business in the city). The Unionist business owners were happy to take the money off their Nationalist customers, while ruthlessly using the business vote to retain undemocratic minority political control of the city.

The original wards formed in 1896 were, of course, in use again; the Unionists retained a clear lead in the East and Waterside, the Nationalists were ahead in the West and South. But in spite of all the Unionist Party manoeuvring, its lead in the North continued to be eroded. So, at a meeting of Derry Corporation on 31 March 1936, the Unionists produced the plan for a new gerrymander. The plan was to eliminate the West and East wards, leaving the Waterside on the east bank of the river, and the South and North wards on the west bank. The areas in both discarded wards, where there were Protestant majorities, were added to the North, and the Catholic areas, much larger and more populous, put into the South.

The population at the 1926 census (the latest available at the time of the 1936 gerrymander proposal) showed that the city population then was: Catholics, 27,062; all others, 18,097, a Catholic majority of 8,965. But under the wards' system, 27,000 Catholics elected 16 corporators, while 18,000 all others elected 24 corporators. Would any sane person argue there was no gerrymander?

In 1936, there was a Catholic electoral majority of 1,189 in the South ward and a Catholic electoral majority of 2,971 in the West ward. The Unionist majority in the East was 831, in the Waterside, 964 and in the North, 492. The total Catholic electorate was approximately 9,400, the total of all others approximately 7,400. Who says there was no gerrymander?

The new wards proposed by the Unionists gave Catholics 5,738 votes in the South ward, Unionists 4,443 in the North and 2,298 in the Waterside. So, 6,700 Unionists in the North and Waterside could elect 24 corporators, while 5,700 Nationalists in the South could elect only 16. Glaring though these figures were, the real extent of how undemocratic they were was illustrated by the parliamentary figures. They showed the Nationalist number on that register at 16,947 and all others, 11,299.

The Stormont Government compounded the hypocrisy of the Derry Unionists by ordering an inquiry into the proposed gerrymander. That was unctuous window-dressing. But at the inquiry, one of the witnesses, an Englishman, Mr Arthur Halliday, principal of Skerries Commercial College, gave evidence strongly disapproving of the scheme. In answer to Mr Cyril Nicholson QC for the Nationalists, Mr Halliday, a Unionist, said:

> I think I should not say anything too strong if I say that it is really due to the fact that there is a fear that in a year or two the Unionist majority in the North ward will be wiped out.

The chairman of the inquiry, Vice-Admiral Archdale, expressed a desire to tour the proposed boundaries. But neither Alderman Samuel Orr, who had proposed the scheme at the meeting of the Corporation, nor any other Unionist member, volunteered to conduct the tour. The fact was that none of them knew the boundaries in detail. They had been worked out by senior Corporation officials who were all

Unionists. So, the Vice-Admiral had to be content with Mr Paddy Maxwell, leader of the Nationalist group on the Corporation, and the city surveyor, Mr Andy Hamilton, accompanying him.

In December 1936, the inquiry decision was announced. Naturally, it granted the Unionist request for the new wards. But the letter announcing the verdict was in fact an indictment of the whole scheme. It read:

> Very considerable opposition was offered to the scheme, while the evidence put forward in support was of a most unsatisfactory character. The new line proposed as a boundary between the two wards not separated by the river followed, in some parts, a course very difficult to define and no evidence was given in justification of this complication and none of the witnesses examined on behalf of the scheme had ascertained or was aware how the boundary would actually run.

However, with sublime lack of logic, the letter then added that the Ministry of Home Affairs was convinced that 40 members was too large a number for a body like Derry Corporation and it was reduced to 20, therefore no greater number of wards than three would be required. In 1938, the first Corporation election since the Stormont imprimatur on the 1936 gerrymander was held, and of course the Unionists won 12 seats to the Nationalists eight. Nationalist leader Paddy Maxwell told the silent Unionist benches at the first meeting of the Corporation:

> The eight members on my side of the House represent the majority of the people; the majority of Corporation electors, the majority of parliamentary electors, and 29,000 citizens against 18,000 all others. But numbers will tell in the end.

Immediately after World War Two, Derry's housing waiting list had reached a state of emergency. The Unionists resisted the pressure to tackle the problem. They simply could not afford to allow any building in the North ward, and when Creggan had been mentioned, even before the War, they had protested that expert opinion considered building on the hilly area would be far too difficult and expensive. But by the end of 1945, the position was becoming so embarrassing that something had to be done. So they decided that, after all, Creggan *was* suitable to accommodate many hundreds of houses. It was, of course, in the South ward, and anything was preferable to houses for Catholics in the North ward. Apart from that, the unwillingness to build in Creggan earlier had been sparked by a policy of not building houses at all anywhere in Derry. The Unionist hope was that lack of houses would drive Catholics to emigration and buttress their political hold. In the post-war years, the city was losing over 1,000 people each year through emigration. Creggan was literally the only large area left in the mammoth South ward which, by 1947, contained more Catholic voters than the total number of Unionist voters in the entire city. So the building of an estate, which at its peak accommodated 15,000 citizens, was reluctantly agreed to.

It was truly ironic; if the Unionist proposal to extend the city boundary in 1896 to include the areas already mentioned like Culmore, Shantallow, Ballymagroarty and so on had been acted on, estates would have been built there before any consideration of Creggan would have been entertained. Consequently, as I mentioned at the start, Derry's Creggan is an estate which was built many years before it should have been, yet long after it was desperately needed. Apart from all its other claims to fame, Creggan can be described as the estate built as a monument to squalid Unionist political expediency. That its people played a big role in the post-1969 years in the Civil Rights campaign which swept away the Unionist Corporation is also a truly ironic aspect of Derry's history.

Landlords and Tenants

The *Derry Journal* of 10 January 1944 announced the approval by the Derry Corporation of plans for the erection of up to 1,000 houses at Creggan where there would be a shopping centre and all modern facilities including recreational spaces. Contour surveys had already been completed and preparations of other plans were well in hand. In October of the same year, lack of urgency on the Corporation's part in a housing situation which required immediate remedies is evident in the edition of 13 October under the headline, *Derry Corporation's Housing Delay – Indictment by Stormont Minister:*

> The Minister of Health and Local Government said an allocation of 250 houses for Derry was accepted by the Corporation on 6 June. He visited Derry on 30 June and urged the Corporation to do all in its power to expedite the situation. Little progress having been made, officers went to Derry in August and made certain concrete suggestions with the view to expediting matters. The Corporation was requested to give the matter urgent and serious consideration but the Minister was afraid he could give no indication as to when it was likely building would commence.

It was November before the order vesting the necessary building lands required in the townlands of Creggan, Edenballymore and Ballymagowan was published. In May 1945, a new development saw the entry of the Stormont Trust, better known now as the Housing Trust. By June, an agreement was reached whereby the Trust would build 500 houses, of which 250 would remain the property of the Trust and the remainder would be handed over to the Corporation. The portion to be administered by the Corporation included Central Drive, Westway, Broadway and the streets in between the last two. These included all the gardens, Dunree, Melmore, Leenan, Malin, Dunmore and Inishowen. Beechwood Avenue and Beechwood Crescent completed the Corporation list. All other housing on the new estate was to be administered by the Housing Trust.

Maeve Kelly, a very civil servant, 2000. (Larry Doherty)

Maeve Kelly, now retired, began working for the Housing Trust in 1957. Her reminiscences give us an insight into the workings of the Trust in its dealings with its Creggan tenants. Staff were given training by the Society of Housing Managers. In charge was a Miss McCullagh who had arrived with a formidable reputation, having been previously employed as a lawyer at the Nuremberg Trials. Although beyond her brief while in the employ of the Housing Trust, she was known to have given legal advice discreetly, freely and informally to many who found themselves in need of direction. Maeve remembers her fondly as a stern but fair supervisor who demanded strict adherence to the rules, some of which would hardly command allegiance today.

A first priority was attitude to other members of staff and to tenants. Staff were obliged to address each other and members of the public formally. Maeve, then single, was always referred to as Miss Boyle. Tenants were to be accorded similar treatment. Rights and sensibilities were to be respected at all times. When visiting tenants, employees were expected to follow a strict code. When they entered through garden gates, these were to be closed after entry and closed again after departure. No short cuts were allowed. The walk between front doors of adjoining houses with front gardens had to be negotiated, entering and exiting through gates and walking the garden paths. The shorter route, which involved passing living room windows, was regarded as a potential invasion of privacy. There was also a strong insistence that access to a home should be effected only after an invitation to do so.

Maeve was at pains to stress that awards of tenancies were fair, using a points system based on need. To qualify for inclusion on the housing list, prospective tenants were required to fill in an application form which was designed to identify their current housing difficulties. Questions were asked about family size and gender breakdown, number and condition of rooms and bath/toilet/kitchen facilities. This was followed by a visit by a member of staff to confirm details. The next step was to place the applicant on the appropriate list, a process which gave rise to much misunderstanding, as the appropriate list depended on each applicant's particular circumstances. As accommodation ranged between two-room flats to four-bedroom houses, a range of differing demands could be met. If a family were large enough and fulfilled other relevant criteria, they would expect to go on the waiting list for four-bedroom houses. A dilemma arose when a smaller house became available and such a family could show that the smaller house, while not ideal, could improve their circumstances dramatically. Various factors were considered. Families with younger children, who required much less space than teenagers or older family members, might qualify for a house smaller than the ideal, depending on the urgency of their needs. Medical problems were also an important consideration. Management of competing claims was to be further complicated when redevelopment created an urgent demand for re-housing former inhabitants of redeveloped areas. Pensioners were a special category. Pains were taken to ensure that as far as possible only pensioners were in houses designed and built for pensioners. There were special cases when a widowed pensioner might share with a son or daughter if that was in the best interests of the pensioner.

While the points system could be expected to ensure fair allocation in the vast majority of cases, there were always situations the system did not cover. In such instances, the information gained from visits to applicants was vitally important. Final decisions on allocations were always made exclusively by Miss McCullagh who, in Maeve's opinion, never departed from the highest standards of fairness. She holds this opinion despite discovering the origins of a code which appeared at the top right hand corner of the forms issued to staff who went to inspect the living conditions of applicants. On the corner of each form was written either 1/3 or 2/3. Observations and a few questions soon revealed that these were indicators of religious denomination. Whatever use was made of information gathered from this code, Maeve was not able to determine, but she is fairly sure that the forms came from outside the Derry offices with the code already included with applicants' details. She is also sure that Miss McCullagh's allocations were made in response to need, rather than sectarian considerations.

High standards were expected to prevail throughout the service and measures were taken to ensure their application openly. Acceptance of even the smallest gift by an individual, while pursuing his/her duties, was frowned upon in case it could be construed as a bribe. A cup of tea was permitted while gifts like boxes of chocolates had to be brought back to the office. A 'thank you' letter was then sent out on behalf of the whole department.

However, Maeve, on a few occasions, fell below the high standards expected when she became an accomplice in a mild form of blackmail. Knowing her clients well, she agreed, more than once, to accompany a supposedly irate and desperate wife to the pub to demand the rent money from a supposedly feckless husband. Faced with the threat of public humiliation, the abashed husband unfailingly paid up. These incidents were always good-humoured and part of a contrived pantomime which nevertheless held out the threat of potential tactics to be used against errant husbands should the need have arisen. Maeve is reticent about details of the time taken in negotiations in the pub or whether refreshment was partaken as part of the proceedings.

Housing Trust staff members were assured of varied contacts with the public. Applications were received and processed at all times. Rent was collected on Monday, Tuesday and Wednesday mornings. Thursdays and Fridays were interview days. Some interviews were harrowing and adapting to new surroundings were sometimes puzzling for tenants. Maeve recalls one incident.

> I was sent to a house where a large family was living in one room. When I got there I found the mother pregnant and in labour. The room was full of children and there were indications that they would remain there throughout the labour, a prospect I considered undesirable for all concerned. I put them in my car and took them for a run, knowing that this was exceeding my responsibilities, but also anticipating that Miss McCullagh would have agreed with my motives, if not my wisdom, in ignoring the rules. I was relieved when I returned to find a successful delivery and gratified that I had been able to treat the children to a few hours entertainment in the country. I resolved there and then to press the case for re-housing the family in more appropriate surroundings. Their case was strong and soon, much to my satisfaction, they were given a four-bedroom house. A few months later, I decided to check on their progress and arranged a visit. I was shocked to find that the whole family was living in just one room of their new four-bedroom house. Perhaps poverty and previous experiences had ill-prepared them for the relative luxury of their new surroundings.

There were strict rules about the keeping of livestock. The keeping of dogs was discouraged, but this rule was more observed in the breaking than in the keeping. On occasion, dogs were bred and kept in bedrooms, but perhaps the most flagrant breach of the rules was the occasion when Maeve was sent to investigate a most unusual query. The Housing Trust office received a complaint that a woman had observed a horse looking out of a neighbour's window. Convinced she was the victim of a hoax, Maeve called at the address and stated the nature of the complaint. Much to Maeve's astonishment, the resident went upstairs and coolly led a pony downstairs from the bedroom and out on to the street. No explanation was given and no further action taken. It was enough that the practice stopped; no more complaints were lodged about tenant horses.

When another resident complained of a blocked toilet, he was given the standard reply in the circumstances, namely that such a problem was the tenant's responsibility. As the complaints continued, however, investigation seemed the wisest option. Maeve was given the task and set off in some trepidation. On arrival, she was admitted to the complainant's house and was more than a little surprised to find no light bulbs in any of the light-fittings. The relevance of this situation would become apparent later. Having made a mental note, Maeve decided to bring a professional attitude to the process of investigation by embarking on a process of elimination. In answer to the most obvious and the simplest query about regular flushing, she was assured that this was done regularly with little obvious success. After more questions, which were asked as much to postpone the inevitable as for information, she asked for a demonstration. Steeling herself, Maeve followed the tenant to the toilet and waited. The explanation came in a blinding flash when he pulled the light-switch cord and fixed the trusty investigator with a 'see what I mean' look, as the toilet remained unflushed. A chastened Maeve left, reflecting on the conditions which had produced someone whose previous living conditions had left them so ill-prepared for the basic comforts provided in their new home.

The general acceptance of the Trust's integrity is evident in the responses of its tenants. Remarkably, and without fail, the books at the end of each financial year were closed without a penny owing. Even more remarkably, this continued over the period of the Rent and Rates Strike, which says much for the general abhorrence of unpaid debt held by many, and the primacy of ensuring that the home was secure. Budgetary planning emphasised this priority. It was common practice to pay the collector a little more than the weekly amount each week. This allowed a surplus to build up so that at selected times a number of weeks could be missed out. More money from the weekly budget thus became available during these few weeks. It was no surprise to discover that the most popular periods for suspending payment were the annual summer holidays and Christmas.

One ingenious method of fulfilling the legal demand for rent on the one hand, and of avoiding public scrutiny on the other during the Rent and Rates Strike of the early '70s, was employed by a small number of women who had paid their rents in Maeve's office. Regularly, one of the women would call and present her with a folded newspaper, inviting her to have an interesting read. Already part of the conspiracy, Maeve would carry the newspaper away and open it discreetly to expose several rent books and accompanying rents.

While she witnessed cases of poverty and hardship, her abiding impression is that of serving a population in Creggan where honesty and integrity prevailed and where good humour helped the community surmount many difficulties.

Creggan's Unpaid Social Workers

Mickey Durey was one of the earliest settlers on the new housing estate, arriving there with his family on 8 December 1948. As a self-employed builder, he would have had some experience in dealing with bureaucratic bodies and was soon to put his acquired knowledge at the service of other tenants. It wasn't long before he had a steady stream of callers seeking his advice on a range of housing problems. As early as 1953, he was conducting the Electricity Room Charge campaign. In November of that year the *Derry Journal*, under the Chronicle and Comment column, reported:

> The question 'is a scullery a kitchen?' is causing quite a stir in Creggan and has already been the subject of a Corporation debate at which no satisfactory answer has been given by those responsible for the definition of a scullery that has created so much trouble. The Corporation has imposed on houses in Creggan and other estates, an electricity domestic rate room charge for sculleries that, in the opinion of someone described as a 'minor official', are 'kitchens' and financially must be so treated. It is stated that no notification of the charge was made until it was actually clapped on the householders and naturally they are up in arms as they say that their sculleries are not kitchens.

The *Derry Journal* also reported that:

> A unanimously passed motion to refer the whole matter back to the sub-committee to hear the views of the Creggan Welfare Committee was, contrary to all procedure, perfunctorily set aside in favour of an amendment by Councillor Gerry Glover that it be referred back 'without any governing reference'.

The Corporation initiated a test case against Durey who formed a committee to solicit financial support from the community to defend their stance in court. The tenants' case, which would have little relevance today, was eventually lost, but an important legacy was left. An able adversary for community issues had emerged as had a committee dedicated to improving the lot of Creggan residents.

As Mickey Durey became immersed in giving advice, his activities were to impact on his home life. His son, also Mickey, described the house as looking at times like a doctor's surgery, with one room designated a waiting room as prospective 'clients' awaited their turn for consultation. Nobody was turned away, even those who arrived in the early hours of the morning. When Mickey junior expressed annoyance at the intrusion, he was told firmly: 'This is my house'. Mickey's time was always given willingly, right up until the last few years of his life, when illness prevented him from doing so. His activities were all the more remarkable as they were conducted in his spare time. He was self-employed until he started with the Corporation in 1966, after which he worked with the Commission it replaced; he then worked with the Housing Executive until his retirement.

There is no doubting his sense of mission, having given up a large part of his life to the service of others without any monetary return. He was even reluctant to claim his pension. His son recalls the occasion when the family discovered that for three years he had not collected the pension. To this day he is convinced that part of his father's hesitation was his reluctance to admit to retirement and partly that he somehow felt that he had not earned it. Mickey junior does not specify which member of the family took on the problem, but admits that certain steps were taken to ensure their father could receive the money due to him. A year's back pension and a lump sum were negotiated as a solution to a problem which would not have arisen had it belonged to one of Mickey's clients.

Paddy McKeever, unpaid social worker, 2000. (Larry Doherty)

Paddy McKeever joined Mickey as an unpaid adviser to individuals in their dealings with statutory bodies. Apart from trying to solve the day-to-day problems which beset individuals, Paddy believed that communities should have an input on issues which affected their everyday lives. He was to serve on the Creggan Estate Tenants' Association and, from 1981, on the Lower Creggan Neighbourhood Association. Foyle Hill was well served by its Foyle Hill Tenants' Association and all three took on a variety of housing issues. He remembers one campaign over the right of tenants to have a choice in the type of heating installed in their houses. He recalls the occasion when he, John McChrystal and Joe Moran, each of them supporting differing strands of Nationalism, amicably conducted a survey of the whole estate on the heating issue. He is quick to point out that community advice workers, without fail, dealt fairly with all appeals for help from whatever quarter they issued.

Similarly, bodies with useful information were not to be ignored because of their religious beliefs or political persuasions. Paddy recounts details of a trip to the Shankhill to compare notes with their community group on home-heating problems. Here, information was exchanged and great care taken for their safety. The Creggan minibus was met outside the Shankhill, escorted to the meeting place and afterwards checked, with the aid of a mirror, to ensure that no explosives had been attached in their absence.

The *Troubles* added a new dimension as communities sought to overcome serious communal and individual problems. Mickey and Paddy continued to respond to individual appeals and spent many nights in British Army encampments trying to have someone's son or husband released. A particular difficulty with these negotiations was the dissension between parties and individuals on how much liaison, if any, should be maintained with security forces in the interest of finding solutions. Probably because of his high profile and his willingness to deal with requests from any quarter, Paddy was the victim of regular raids by the British Army. One incident illustrates the Army's hostility on one hand and the respect he was held in by members of his own community on the other. A parcel which had been handed in to the Essex Army camp had blown up, killing a major. The same evening, Paddy found himself under arrest in Liam McLaughlin's house in Creggan Heights on suspicion of causing the explosion. Fr Rooney was well aware of Paddy's good work and made his way through heavy rioting to Liam's house. When the Army decided to take Liam and Paddy to their camp at Piggery Ridge, Fr Rooney insisted on going too. All were released wihout charge before the morning.

Paddy blamed his deteriorating health on the pressures put on him. Even in his moments of relaxation, calls for his expertise continued unabated. Criticism by some who read political bias into his efforts did not help. He acknowledges the sterling work of many who gave of their talents, time and energy for the benefit of others. Apart from Mickey Durey, other notables were, Tom Doherty, Joe Moran, John McChrystal and Bridget Bond.

The value to the community of the work done by Mickey Durey, Paddy McKeever and others was eventually recognised by government, and resources were made available for the employment of full-time paid advisers with proper administrative back up. Their valuable work continues, but the extent of the selfless work of their unpaid predecessors remains to be fully recorded and properly acknowledged.

'Mother of Creggan'

Doris Kyle, who moved into the newly built number 9 Greenwalk on 11 May 1949, was arguably Creggan's longest-standing resident when first interviewed in 1997. She reared 14 children in her three-bedroom home – ten of them were born there in the same bed. There is an ongoing family debate over the exact number of her grandchildren and great-grandchildren. But Doris Kyle might never have become the unofficial 'Mother of Creggan' or got her house if not for a little fib and the help of God.

Back in 1949, the then mother of 'three-and-a-half' was living with her family in the back bedroom of her husband's parents' home on Strand Road. As there was no backyard, they hung the washing across the room and they washed in a tin bath on the floor. Everybody, it seemed, wanted a new house in Creggan. But the Northern Ireland Housing Trust had a rule that the head of the household had to be working. Unfortunately, Doris's husband Robert was unemployed. So taking fate in her own hands, Doris decided to declare on the application form that Robert was a wage earner. Then, to cover the angles, she gave money to a local priest to say a special Mass. Sure enough, by the time the Kyles had been allocated a house, Robert had a new job as an electrician at Lisahally and Doris's conscience was clear. She recalled:

> The new homes were like palaces. Many houses in Derry were in poor condition and overcrowded. I myself was brought up in a two-up, two-down house in Sloan's Terrace with eight other children. But Creggan was like paradise. People would come from all over Derry to see the houses. They'd knock on your door and ask you: 'Please show us round.'

Despite all this luxury, not to mention the built-in bathroom, it took the Kyles some time to furnish their new home. In the early days, they had to make do with orange boxes for chairs. There were no grants in those days; the Northern Ireland Housing Trust, who were landlords for about half the estate – Derry Corporation administering the other half – were strict taskmasters. Doris explained:

> They were very cheeky. They would march in and walk around the rooms to ensure that we were keeping the place properly. Then, say if there was rubbish in a grating, they would tell you to remove it or they would have to send a man out to do it and would charge you a fortune, though I don't think anyone was ever evicted.

The Kyles' original tenancy agreement bears testimony to just how strict the conditions were. There were clauses banning pigs, poultry, pigeons and rabbits (except one domestic pet), and according to other Creggan residents, there were regular checks to ensure the laws weren't ignored. Tenants weren't allowed to let ivy grow on the house walls, nor were they permitted to put up a shed in the garden or a wireless aerial without the written consent of the Trust. And they had to keep a close supervising eye on their children. One particular clause of the agreement stated:

> The tenant shall be responsible for seeing that his or her children behave properly on all parts of the Trust's estate, of which the premises form a part, and so as not to cause a nuisance or annoyance to other tenants or to the public and that his or her children do not spoil or damage any buildings, walls, fences, gates, trees, shrubs, plants, turf, or anything on the property of and belonging to the Trust, and shall repay to the Trust the cost of making good any damage or spoliation so caused.

Originally, Creggan was a more mixed neighbourhood and quite a high proportion of the first settlers were ex-servicemen and their families, according to Doris:

> There was no sectarianism then. There were B-Specials and Orangemen living in the neighbourhood, but nobody bothered them. When the trouble started, a lot of families left. It was very regrettable. Later Greenwalk neighbours were to include Rosemary Brown, a beautiful girl, who went on to become Dana.

When the Kyles first arrived in Creggan, Greenwalk marked the estate's boundary. Beyond it lay farmland. There was a big wall, separating the estate from Rosemount, which residents dismantled over the years, brick by brick, until it became known as the 'Hole in the Wall'.

> There were no shops, nor was there a bus service into the town. Back in the 1960s, a big placard went up on Westway announcing that there was to be a new cinema. We were all delighted – but they built St Joseph's School there instead.

Before St Mary's Church was built, people living in Creggan went to Mass at either St Eugene's Cathedral or the Long Tower Chapel. The Kyles went to the Cathedral, where, with hundreds of others, they would be forced to stand on the altar – such was the dearth of space. The new Creggan Chapel was built in 1959 and Doris's daughter Rosemary was one of the first babies to be christened there. Nurse Thomas, midwife to Creggan, was a regular visitor to the Kyle household during the '50s and '60s – delivering ten babies in the upstairs room 'on the same bed'.

Doris had the rare privilege of being the first customer in Rainey's new shop on Beechwood – before it opened. She was actually on her way down to Marlborough Terrace when she saw the van outside Rainey's, stopped to ask what was happening and walked away with a free bar of chocolate for her daughter.

When it came to rearing her 14-strong brood, Doris had to be well-organised.

> There were so many that some of them would have to eat their dinner on the stairs. Creggan was a good area for the children to be growing up. But I always had them up in bed at eight o'clock at night. None of them ever dared come in late.

The *Troubles* were to change things, however. Her main fear then was that the youngfellas would join the IRA. Like most houses in Creggan, the Kyles were raided regularly and there was a bucket of water mixed with vinegar permanently outside the front door to counteract the effects of CS gas. Gun battles were a frequent feature in the neighbourhood. One night in the early '70s, Doris had a lucky escape when a trigger-happy British soldier fired off a round. The *Journal* report of the incident ran:

> The bullet broke a front window and seemed to shatter. Some of it went out through another window, and some of it rebounded off two walls in the front living room, ripped a dress Mrs Kyle was wearing and lodged in an apple. She said an Army patrol then came along and she told them what had happened. One of the soldiers admitted firing the shot and said he had been fired on twice already that day and that he had an 'itchy finger' as a result.

All but one of the Kyle children have now left Creggan. There's now an American branch, a Scottish contingent and even a Strabane element. It is Doris's dream, if she ever wins the Lottery, to buy a private housing estate where she and her family could all live together. However, daughter Kathleen still lives nearby and the clan keeps a close eye on their matriarch.

'LANDED' IN INISCARN

One of the leading lights of the Creggan 50th Festival was community worker Eamon Baker, whose family has lived in Iniscarn Road for almost half a century. Here, Eamon recalls his halcyon days as a fledgling cub in the fledgling estate.

When we first moved to Creggan in April 1952, to an upstairs flat at 75 Iniscarn Road, I was 14 months; my big sister Ann was four and a bit. My father Joe originally lived at 6 Thomas Street, off Rossville Street; my mother Nellie came from Speenogue, Burt. They had been married since 1947 and had struggled like many others to find suitable accommodation for themselves and their young and growing family. This flat, upstairs and all, was a breakthrough, with the hope that somewhere down the line we would have our first 'real house' – rented of course – as Iniscarn Road and Creggan Estate itself grew and grew around us. My mother remembers Father McGonagle from the Long Tower Parish coming up to bless our flat that April springtime, for then, 'Upper Creggan' was part of the Long Tower Parish, just as 'Lower Creggan' was part of St Eugene's Parish. The ancient dividing line between the two parishes was, I think, Bligh's Lane.

I have a few vague early memories of 75 Iniscarn then: of my father on his bike cycling off down the town to his workplace in the Castle Laundry, throwing his leg over his bike, like some cloth-capped cowboy, the bicycle wheel ticking round; of an uneven brown-painted gate blocking my route down the high oilcloth stairs, saving me from taking a tumble. As well as low pay and poor enough working conditions, these were still days of post-war scrimping and of ration books.

Recently, my mother 'magicked' baby Eamon's very own ration book out of a circular black leather handbag I don't remember seeing since I was a wane. Stamped beside 'Meat' is 'James Doherty, Waterloo Place', and beside 'Fats, cheese, bacon and sugar' is 'The Imperial Stores, 43 William Street'. Presumably these stores redeemed the coupons torn from the ration book for government cash.

Our Ann was of an age to go to primary school before the Holy Child School opened its doors at Central Drive in 1956. She would walk all the way down to the Long Tower, sometimes with Ann Cox from lower down Iniscarn (number 33), sometimes with Sheila Gillespie from on up the top (number 101). She remembers a Miss Glenn as her teacher in 'baby infants', a Miss Friel in 'senior infants', and speaks with great affection of Mamie Pederson, her P6 and P7 teacher.

I remember walking up Iniscarn from what now is the roundabout; this must have been sometime in late summer or early autumn of 1954; I would have been three-and-a-half. I remember taking in the rich aroma of tar, as workmen forked the glittering treacly stuff down – Iniscarn Road was being completed – and a baby elephant of a steamroller flattened out and dulled the shine of the tar even as the men continued to spread. There was excitement that we were going to have a house, one of those just to my left, one of the ones we were passing; it was that gable end one, somebody said. I can't remember who I was with; my mammy, maybe with my new wee sister,

Bernadette, born up in 75; and the baby, Desmond (our Dessie) in the high black pram; perhaps our Ann and my father. Maybe we had 'walked it' from Thomas Street where my grandfather and all my uncles lived.

Of the actual flitting I remember little: the pale green po, perched unaccountably on one of the kitchen shelves alongside cups and bowls and dinner plates; our sewing machine, brown and hooded, stood stock-still on the back of Joe Deeney's coal lorry when whatever else we had was shifted already into our new house. (Joe was our coalman and my father had got him to help us move. Joe worked out of Fox's Yard and the Castle Laundry backed onto Fox's Yard). The bedrooms, three of them, were upstairs all right, but the downstairs was ours as well and we had our own separate front door instead of a shared hallway. We were 'landed', for the minute anyway.

In October 1954, my mother and father, Anne, me, Brendan and Dessie, who was three-months-young, moved into number 7 Iniscarn Road, Creggan Estate. Our Maire, Brian and Ciaran were born there. The youngest in our family, Claire, was born in Altnagelvin. My mother still lives there today (Iniscarn, not Altnagelvin).

They Were Happy Days in Creggan

Mary Walmsley was born in rooms above a flour mill at Foyle Street. With seven children crammed into the small city-centre flat, the Walmsleys were offered a three-bedroom 'palace' at 1 Greenwalk in Creggan. In this account, Mary, the daughter of an RUC man, tells Creggan man and local historian Tony McCourt of her happy childhood in the new estate.

By the time we were offered the house at 1 Greenwalk – which had a big bay window – there were seven of us living above the flour mill. With no running water in the flat, my mother was obliged to run up and down three flights of stairs to fetch and carry water in a big metal bucket. We were all delighted, especially my mother, when we moved to Greenwalk. To a child, it meant green fields far from the hustle and bustle of Foyle Street.

George and Isobel, my younger brother and sister, were born at Greenwalk. The rest of the children were born at the City and County Hospital. The Ferrys lived next door. We called Mrs Ferry 'Ma' Ferry – she was like a second mother to us. She helped out when any children were born. Likewise, my mother would help out around the Ferry household.

Religion was never a sticking point among the neighbours; other Protestant families lived at Greenwalk. My father wasn't the only policeman living in Creggan. There was no ill feeling whatsoever. In fact, when my friends made their First Communion, I remember crying my eyes out and asking why I couldn't do the same. Creggan in a child's eyes meant big, big, open spaces. I particularly recall the gardens. My father used to grow spuds, cabbage and rhubarb. There was always plenty of rhubarb.

I have five brothers and sisters older than me, and five who are younger. Billy went to Stranmillis, Ella trained as a nurse, and Davy worked as a barber at Waterloo Street before joining the army. My father, whose nickname was 'Wamble', worked at the old Victoria RUC Barracks at Strand Road. He was from Co Fermanagh. He served for a time in Coleraine where my mother Nellie was born.

All the children played in a big field on which St Joseph's Secondary School now stands. I think it belonged to the Thompsons who kept pigs there. I remember my brothers, Billy, David and Lawrence, playing cricket with the Breslins, the McCauleys and other neighbours. All 11 Walmsleys were schooled at First Derry PS. Each morning we made our way down Beechwood Avenue, past the big ravine, to catch the Lone Moor bus to Bishop Street. We went to Sunday School at St Augustine's on the city walls. Each year, St Augustine's organised an excursion to Portrush. My mother was given six tickets for the train, but when she arrived at the railway station she might have 12 children with her – neighbours from Creggan. I clearly remember sitting on the East Strand, behind Barry's Amusements, devouring a bag of buns. It was a happy childhood. We never had much, but everybody was in the same boat.

Although my father was a policeman, money was scarce. No matter how little people had, Catholic or Protestant, you always had a Sunday coat, hat and shoes. I can remember putting pieces of cardboard inside my shoes to cover the holes in the soles.

Then, when my father got a few pence together, he'd make his way to McKeown's shoe shop at William Street to buy strips of leather to mend the shoes.

As a teenager, I was friendly with Geraldine and Moya Ferry. Moya worked at the Rainbow Cafe, while Geraldine worked at the Melville Hotel on Foyle Street. We went to the Embassy together. We had moved to Moat Street by that stage, but I spent most of my time running up and down to Creggan. We left Creggan long before the *Troubles* started. There were 11 of us by this time and we needed a bigger house. That's why we moved to a five-bedroom house in Moat Street. 'Ma' Ferry was up and down to Moat Street while my mother Ella and I visited Creggan as often as possible.

I met my husband, Jimmy Plummer from Creggan Heights, towards the end of the 1950s. We weren't quite sure of the difficulties, if any, of a Catholic marrying a Protestant. We'd been going out for about five years when my mother came right out with it: 'Do you not think it's about time you and Jimmy saw about getting married?'

Before we were married, Father McKenna of the Long Tower called to see my father. God only knows what they talked about – they were in the living room for two hours – because my father never discussed it with me. Jimmy and I were married on 4 April 1964 at St Mary's, Creggan. We've been married ever since.

When my father died in 1970, all our old neighbours from Creggan came to the wake. By this stage he had retired from the police and was working as a lollipop man at Pump Street. He used to tend the nuns' plants there. The first visitor to the house when my father died was a nun. She said to my mother: 'Do you mind if I come in?' My mother replied: 'Religion doesn't come into it. It's never talked about in this house and you're very welcome.'

The younger generation could learn a few lessons from us because we lived and let live. To this day, I would say no wrong about anyone. My mother had an old saying: 'Never hurt anyone by word or deed, or you'll be paid back tenfold.' They were happy days. You might not have thought so at the time, but when you look back, they were.

The Creggan Bungalows

Eddie Blee was born in the Brandywell and moved to Creggan when he was three. For a quarter of a century he lived in Tremone Gardens in a prefabricated bungalow – similar to those still standing in the Glen estate. The bungalows, four streets in all, were torn down in 1974 and the aluminium sold for scrap. Here, Eddie recalls the highs and lows of growing up in the bungalows in the '50s and '60s.

When I thought about writing this piece on the bungalows, I started to recall so many fond memories. So many, in fact, that I could end up doing a book. When my parents and my sister Maureen and myself moved up into 15 Tremone Gardens, it was on 3 October 1949. I was three years old at the time, my sister was five, and the rent was 12s 6d (62p)-a-week. We had been born in 32 Deanery Street, in the Brandywell, in my Granny's house. The bungalows were erected around 1948 or so.

The new house had three massive bedrooms, a bathroom, a long hallway, a kitchen and the one great luxury, an inside coalhouse. We also had two very large gardens. Growing up in Tremone was an experience I'm sure many of us who lived there will always cherish. I remember my childhood days very clearly. Those days of the brilliant summers and the school holidays that we enjoyed so much.

During those times, the gang would get together and see what we were doing. Was it a walk out the road to the 'Black Hut', or down into the 'swinging tree' in the 'rest'? Well, those journeys were the choices we had then, having no TVs, videos or computers to play with. We never were bored as we had to make our own craic.

In the years before the Creggan Chapel was built, my sister and I attended the Long Tower Schools, and also the Long Tower Chapel. Mass in those days meant children had to fast from midnight on Saturday until ten o'clock Mass on Sunday morning. As soon as Mass was over, our first stop was down the steps to Florrie Kelly's shop for a bar of Cowan's toffee (3d), or something else to revive us. Then we'd beat the trail, along with my old pal Noel McFeely, up Stanley's Walk, up Bligh's Lane, run like hell past Kildea's, in case the dogs there came after you. We rested at the Brickfield.

I remember the many times, summer and winter, we travelled that route to school and chapel. Like many other children from that area, we all took part in whatever games were being played. If it was football, we had our own game called 'hitting the lamppost', which was outside Coll's or down at Bo O'Donnell's. We had a Sports Day when we challenged our neighbours from Swilly Gardens. As I recall, big Jimmy McDermott was their leader, along with Christy Barrett. Those Sports Days were something else. Dessie McLoone was our fastest runner. Some say he could outrun Champion the Wonder Horse, and he easily beat anything Swilly had to offer.

It was not all sunshine and happy days all the time. There were some sad moments when a friend or parent died in Tremone. The death threw a sadness that at that time none of us were aware of. However, in 1953, a great thing was happening in Tremone. A grotto was to be built by two former residents of the street who told me how this came about. Molly Cassidy (12 Tremone) explained how various people were approached about this project and how money was collected from the bungalows in Tremone, Swilly, Mulroy and the four at Central Drive, and the others in the Lower Heights. Mrs McLoone remembers that it was the Marian year, and she named her daughter in its honour. The three main men who did the work then were: a stonesmason called Shiels from Rosemount; another was from the Waterside; the third, a plasterer from Rinmore, the late Sean McGill. It was a great day when Bishop Farren arrived up to bless the grotto. For many years after that, it became the hiding place for Geronimo, Japs and Marines, and for our favourite game, 'Whoever falls the best'. That game created many a dramatic death scene.

Some years later, another dramatic project was undertaken by the Tremone faithful. It was the year of the 'Big Wedding'. Grace Kelly, the famous American actress, was to be married to Prince Rainier of Monaco. At that time, there was an annual parade of floats in Derry and the parents of Tremone decided to put forward as their theme this 'Big Wedding'. I can remember May O'Donnell dressed up as Prince Rainier. I think Grace Kelly was portrayed by a Sally McGilloway who was a friend of the O'Donnells. All the children in the street were scrubbed and cleaned and sat all around the lorry, which either belonged to Joe McGlinchey or Willie Gillen, coalmen at the time. I would say we had good times then, although my own children might not agree with me. When I start to talk about the good old days in Creggan, they usually say: 'Ah naw, Da, not again.' I wonder what memories they will have.

My father was in the Irish Army for some time, then he got a job in the Gasyard in the Lecky Road; he was a stoker there. The wages were terrible, but I suppose it was the best job around, or the only one. I can recall the many long nights that my late mother spent doing cuffs/collars for 'Sledgies' factory in Foyle Street which was just above where the 'Doll's Hospital' used to be. Most of the men in Tremone were fortunate enough to be working then, as some had big families to feed and clothe.

Christmas was a big occasion. My mother had a catalogue; *Samuel Drivers* it was called. Looking through it and seeing all that was on offer for Christmas was magic. Of course we didn't realise that's where our toys came from as we still believed in Santa. Going down the town around that time of year was exciting, seeing the train sets in the window of Edmiston & Keys at the foot of Shipquay Street.

No memories of Tremone Gardens, Swilly or Mulroy would be complete without a mention of the girls of those streets. In my own street there were plenty of fine young ladies indeed. They enjoyed life then as much as we did. We'd be heading off to the Black Hut and they'd want to tag along for the fun. As we got into our teens, I remember we once bunched up for a packet of fags. There was a debate as to who was going to ask the lady in the shop as she knew most of us and our parents. I was elected. I went up and asked for a packet of Peter Stuyvesant's, Yankee fags of course, and a penny box of matches. We waited till we were out of sight of Lily in the Black Hut. We climbed up one of the big trees where no one would see us. Lighting up that first fag made us feel ten-feet-tall, but we were as sick as pigs afterwards. The ground below us was coming up to meet us very quickly.

After I left school, I got a job in a leather goods factory in Foyle Street; it was called Halliday's. They made handbags and all types of leather goods. Of course the thing then was that when you reached the grand age of 18, you were paid off, because the firm would have to put on a big stamp. The wages were around £3-a-week. I then had to sign on the dole in Bishop Street; that was something else. If you hadn't enough stamps on, you got the dreaded National Assistance, a mere 32s 6d-a-week. The job scene then wasn't great. I worked with the Council Relief Schemes. If you leant on the shovel, you were sacked. (Did they want me to work?)

As we got older, and maybe a little wiser, we started going to the dances. Borderland was the 'in' place, but our favourite place was the Castle in Dungiven. After a few quiet pints of Porter, at 2s 1d per pint in Mulhern's, it was over to the bus depot across the road and on to the dance. The craic in the bus was fantastic. The resident singer would stand up and walk up and down the aisle murdering the latest pop song; you only hoped it wasn't your favourite. If you 'got off' and were courting on the way back, the 'stick' was worse than the singer.

The bungalows were good to live in. Sadly, for some unknown reason, they were pulled down. One story that I heard was that they had to make way for a new supermarket, but that never happened. As all my good friends and neighbours started to drift to new pastures, the old homestead was looking sadder each day we stayed. My father and I moved to a new place called Glenowen. It took me a long time to get used to it, but gradually it grew on me.

Those Were the Days

Another early resident of Tremone was Richard Doherty, who was later to become a military historian and acclaimed author. As Richard recalls here, his very street had quite a military history of its own.

There are new houses there now, but for more than 20 years all that remained was a stump, as if Fanad Drive had had a limb amputated. In a sense that is what did happen. Tremone Gardens was a limb and the scar of its removal was there for over two decades after the last bungalows were demolished.

For those of us who lived there, and especially for the generation who grew up in Tremone, there will always be some evidence of the street's life from the building of the Hawksley bungalows back in 1949 until soil was piled over the tarmac to commit 'our street' to memory. Just as an amputee feels sensation in a limb that is no longer there we will always feel something of the street in which we grew up.

My family moved into Tremone in October 1949. We lived there until December 1970 and, in the years between, my brother and sister were born in the street and my father died there. For me the memories are both good and bad: of happy days in warm summer sunshine; of those sad, shredded days in June 1964 when we bade farewell to a much-loved father.

As Creggan moves into its second half-century, and I likewise, my memories of Creggan are not so much of the estate as of that short strip of tarmac street, about 150 yards in length, with its 20 aluminium bungalows, and the many people who lived there. Of course, I also remember the friends in neighbouring streets, the characters – some pleasant, some very unpleasant – and the nearby Rosemount Boys' School. The latter's correct title was St Eugene's Boys' Public Elementary School, but to us, and to generations before and after us, it was always *The Rosemount.*

My earliest memories are tangled and the chronology would be almost impossible to unmesh. I can still recall that, initially, the street ran through from Fanad Drive to Bligh's Lane so that it was possible to drive in one end and out the other – if you had a car, that is. Then Bligh's Lane between Central Drive and Creggan Heights was turned into a footpath and our street, as well as Swilly Gardens, was closed off at the hammerhead in front of our house to become a cul-de-sac. When we moved in, the street was bare earth and it must have been 1951 before it was surfaced with tarmac, one of the few streets in Creggan that was not of reinforced concrete.

Watching the street being tarmacked was great fun. Getting myself clattered with tar wasn't: at least not the cleaning of the tar. The surface was actually rolled by a genuine steamroller, not one of your modern diesel jobs, and the driver, Bobby Simpson, was a friend of my father. Bobby later moved to live in Scotland.

The bungalows themselves were made of aluminium and factory-built by a subsidiary of the Hawker Siddeley Aircraft Company, which used the brand name Hawksley. They were spacious but cold in the winter, although there was supposed to be a system for blowing warm air from the chimney into the bedrooms; it never worked. In an earlier life, the bungalows had been aeroplanes, scrapped at the end of the war. I often wonder how many times my old home had been over Berlin. Or perhaps it had a more pedestrian existence as a training or transport aircraft. Might I be the only former resident who still has the original owner's 'handbook' for a Hawksley?

From its earliest days, Tremone Gardens enjoyed a great sense of community, exemplified by the building of the granite Lourdes grotto at the south end of the street in the Marian year of 1953. All the menfolk worked together to build it. The statue was painted by Brendan O'Donnell, who lived in number 7, while my father made the wooden stand on which it stood; and he also spent many hours lovingly French-polishing the wood. There was a light above the statue, electricity for which was drawn from Joe Blee's house, number 15, the last bungalow on the other side of the street. Communal pride in the grotto was tremendous and lasted for many years.

I can still rhyme off the names of all the original families in Tremone. It's hard to credit now that almost all the fathers were in work. If my memory serves me properly, there were only two, or maybe three, unemployed. About half the fathers were also ex-servicemen, having fought during the Second World War. Some, including my father, were old soldiers whose service went back to the 1920s. In an age when Creggan is perceived as a Republican area, it is worth recalling the number of men in British uniform in those days four decades ago: TA soldiers, Home Guardsmen, sea, Army and air cadets were all to be seen as they walked to or from their training sessions. And on Remembrance Sunday each year, the UTA had to lay on extra buses for the Creggan service to bring home all those who had been at the cenotaph in the Diamond.

In our first decade there, our immediate neighbours on either side were also ex-servicemen. One, Jimmy 'Toby' McFeely, who worked for the old Londonderry Gaslight Company, had been in North Africa and Italy with my father. On the other side, Joe Radcliffe had also soldiered in Italy and had an Italian wife, Lucia, to prove it. Mrs Radcliffe presented me with one of my life's earliest enigmas: there were times when I could hear her call 'piano' to her daughter and son and this vexed me greatly, since I knew that there wasn't a piano in the house. I didn't like to ask why she talked about a piano so often when she didn't own one, and it wasn't until years later that I realised that she was hushing her children – in her native tongue. The Radcliffes left Tremone, and the city, in 1959 to move to Antrim and later to England.

Next door to the Radcliffes lived the Colls. Tommy Coll drove for the Lough Swilly Company and often brought a bus home with him. The sight of such a huge vehicle in the street had all of us children flocking around. For some reason the Swilly buses had a smell that was distinctively different from the old UTA buses that operated on the Creggan route. In retrospect it amazes me how Tommy Coll managed to turn a bus in the street's tiny hammerhead. (One of his sons, Damien, followed in his late father's wheel tracks and now drives for Ulsterbus.)

Buses weren't the only unusual vehicles that could be found parked in Tremone Gardens. Ferret scout cars and Daimler armoured cars were also occasional visitors. They came courtesy of Jimmy McFeely, who was a TA soldier with the North Irish Horse, and he sometimes came home at lunchtime from the regiment's weekend training sessions, bringing the vehicle that he was driving that day with him.

My father cycled to work, and farther afield, for most of his life, although he bought a small motorcycle just three years before his death. For most people, transport was the UTA or shank's pony. In the street's early days, the only car was owned by Freddy Gallagher in number 10. It was probably a pre-war model and I remember that it had wire-spoked wheels which Freddy once painted green. That I can recall quite clearly, because I knocked over his tin of paint and the green patch was still visible on the kerb more than a decade later.

Even visiting motor vehicles were rare. Several breadmen, now an almost vanished breed, called in the street. One was my uncle, Bill Coyle, who worked for Brewster's in Little James's Street, later to become Milanda. His was an electric-powered van, a Morrison Electricar, which moved very slowly, thus allowing youngsters to hang on the back; the wonder is that no one was killed as a result of such practices. But when the back of the bread van was opened, there was a wonderful smell of freshly-baked bread that still comes to mind as the sweet smell of nostalgia and is but poorly-mimicked by the smells that waft through supermarkets.

We had a milkman, Willy Ferry, who still used a horse and cart. He had been my maternal grandparents' milkman in Rosemount and found a new generation of customers in Creggan. Occasionally he would give some of us children a ride on his cart, and the view of the world was marvellous from the driving seat. Mind you, the view of the horse's backside was something else, as was the ammoniac smell when it decided to relieve itself. But its solid waste didn't go to waste and helped plants to prosper in many gardens.

Until we left Tremone in 1970, James Campbell, who farmed at Creggan Farm just behind the estate, was still delivering vegetables by horse and cart. James, who died in March 1997, was a horse fanatic, as his late brother Sam had also been. And he was a good neighbour: at my father's wake he arrived at our door with a large pail of fresh milk. By 'fresh', I mean that it was still warm, the cow having been milked only minutes before.

We also had the oilman who made his weekly rounds. This wasn't a modern oil tanker pumping hundreds of litres of heating oil into storage tanks but a small van from which a few gallons of paraffin oil could be bought – and you supplied your own container. In those days no one had central heating and, with only one coal fire to heat a house, there was always a need for some form of supplementary heating. For many that meant an oil-burning, freestanding heater. We had a 'Fyrside' which, although efficient, was, on reflection, a very dangerous form of heating. Such heaters are probably banned today. There were coalmen and blockmen and turfmen; there were rag-and-bone merchants; there were brock collectors; there were fresh herring vendors; and there were the various 'tick' collectors from shops all over the town and every Friday the Nazareth nuns came around, collecting for their charges.

In the midst of all this, we children got on with the serious business of growing up and playing all sorts of children's games. We kicked football in the street, we played cricket and rounders and some even played tennis. Frequently, we were chased by someone's parents. On occasions we took ourselves off to the big field – we didn't know it as the Bishop's Field then – across from the Central Drive shops and there we had more space to play football or cricket. Other times we walked the roads behind Creggan, taking for granted the closeness of the countryside to our homes.

We were cowboys and Indians, goodies and baddies, cops and robbers, British and Germans, Japs and Marines. Davy Crockett, Audie Murphy, Gabby Hayes and big John Wayne; they were all among our heroes and we didn't know enough to always distinguish the characters from the actors. But we did know about some of the heroes of the war that had but recently ended and we lapped up films and 'comics' about that war. Our imaginations ran riot in the long days of summer and through the dark days and evenings of winter.

One of my earliest memories is that of our neighbour Paddy Nash, of number 24, sitting and chatting to us youngsters at his front door. The same Paddy Nash brought my brother Daniel home when he had gone round to visit Paddy with a 'piece and jam' clutched in his fist and a swarm of bees (or were they wasps?) had taken a liking to the jam. It was that same Paddy Nash who was the street's first death in my memory and gave me my first sight of a funeral. He was a lovely man and a very good neighbour.

Paddy Nash's was not to be the only death in the street. Although births far outnumbered deaths, it is the latter that stand out more clearly in the memory. Not until 1962, when Kathleen Blee died, did the street have another death, although Mrs Wasson who, with her husband Alex, had been the first tenants of number 4, died after their move to Westway. Another former resident to die in those years was Mrs Whitehouse who had lived in number 11. Then, in late 1963, Willy Barr died. The Barrs had only lived in the street a few years, taking over number 12 after the original occupants, Jack and Molly Cassidy, had moved to Westway. My own father was the next to die, in June 1964. Sad days whose memory never fades.

But there was happiness too, and friendships that lasted through the years. The children of the street went to a variety of schools, often those their parents had attended. So some went to the Rosemount Boys' or Girls', some the Long Tower schools, some the Brow o' the Hill, some even the Waterside schools. Then Creggan's first school opened in Central Drive in the late 1950s. This was Holy Child Infants' School from which, after their first three years, the pupils all transferred to a primary school.

Eleven-plus time, 1959 for me, sent many on differing paths. The first St Columb's College boy in our street was Peter McLoone; Pat Healy and I followed in '59; and there was a constant stream thereafter, as there was of girls to Thornhill. Others went to the Municipal Technical College, the Tech as it was and continues to be better known as, in spite of its current North West Institute title; or the Christian Brothers' Tech, or stayed at primary school until aged 14. Some girls went to St Mary's when it opened on Fanad Drive in 1959 and boys began attending St Joseph's on Westway when it opened two years later.

Believe it or not, there was also a dividing line for attending church. Almost all the original tenants of Tremone were Roman Catholic with the exception of the Wassons, who were Church of Ireland. One original family, who moved out quite early, was the Watts of number 5, of whose denomination I have no idea. But the dividing line was not between denominations: it was between St Eugene's Cathedral and the Long Tower. Much of Creggan went to the Cathedral but a large proportion attended the Long Tower, including our next-door neighbours, the McFeely family. Special buses were laid on for both churches on Sunday mornings; long before the Creggan bus service routinely used Linsfort Drive, buses for the Long Tower could be seen there on Sundays.

Sometime in the mid-1950s, there was a huge fuss and a large crowd, with me jammed in there somewhere, when Bishop Farren cut the first sod for the new church in Creggan. In May 1959, that church was dedicated as St Mary's with Father, later Monsignor, Martin Rooney as priest-in-charge, and Fathers Joe Carolan and George McLaughlin as hardworking and popular curates.

Another bit of building that I remember vividly was that of Creggan Heights. The site was guarded by a watchman whom we took delight in baiting so that he would chase us and wave his stick at us. The poor man had a club foot – hence the stick – and, as I look back, I still feel pangs of guilt for the way we annoyed him. There was one occasion, however, when we used his absence to perform a burial service. Some of us had found a dead cat and so we made our way into the building site, behind McLoones' back garden, and solemnly buried the unfortunate moggy in one of the foundation trenches. Shades of Tom Sawyer and Huckleberry Finn.

The building of Creggan Heights meant that we no longer looked out from our back windows onto countryside, but we were still very close to the country and walks out by Sarah Mitchell's cottage and up to Sheriff's Mountain and even to the 'Black Hut' were always adventures for us. My parents took us out to see, at close quarters, the huge silver barrage balloon that was flown at Sheriff's Mountain in 1955 to ascertain its suitability as the site for a TV mast. The alternative, as I learned many years later, was at Ardmore, but Sheriff's Mountain won and a new landmark was constructed, visible from our back garden.

From our front windows we could see another landmark going up: Altnagelvin Hospital. It provided us with a wonderful fireworks display one day when, still a steel skeleton, it was struck by lightning during an electrical storm. My father loved watching electrical storms and so we grew up not fearing thunder and lightning, although we were aware that others did: one neighbour sometimes took refuge with my mother in our house during such storms if her husband was out at work.

Looking back on the '50s, there is the inevitable tendency to see things in a rosy glow; but it wasn't so. There may have been magical times for us children, but our parents surely had a tough time making ends meet and there were few luxuries. Rationing was still in force in the early '50s and clothing styles for children had changed little since the '30s, although we were much better off than the children of that decade. Some of my clothes – and those of my brother and sister – were made by my mother, cut down from old coats and other garments to make practicable everyday wear for us. There were no branded 'image' shirts or tops in those days.

One former neighbour summed up the '50s for me when she described the decade as seeming to have been in black and white. Monochrome those years may well have been, but when they gave way to the '60s something ended for me. Perhaps it was the end of the innocence of childhood, for that time also marked my transfer out of primary school. Perhaps, too, there was a growing sense of worldliness about our little community. Whatever it was, life was never again quite as it had been in the '50s, in Creggan's first decade. Now I know the meaning of some words that I recall from a reading book at school in about 1957:

> Lost yesterday, somewhere between sunrise and sunset,
> Two golden hours, each inset with sixty diamond minutes
> No reward is offered, for they are gone forever.

The new houses recently built on the site of Tremone Gardens now bear the name Swilly Gardens. When I first saw the name, I was disappointed at what had been done, but I now think that, for we who lived there, it would have been a mistake to have used the original name. After all, those days are gone forever and we have our memories, which remain precious and personal.

The Special Years

Gerry Murray wears many hats: accountant, lecturer, industrialist, business journalist, radio commentator and political pundit, to name just a few. But in the following memoir, Gerry reveals that his favourite hat is that of 'son of Creggan'.

For almost the first 30 years of my life, I lived in Creggan, the only child of Johnnie and Mary Murray. My first few years were spent in a flat in Lislane Drive, followed by about five years in Carrickreagh Gardens. In 1962, we moved to 26 Fanad Drive and there I lived until I married in 1982.

Among my earliest memories are happy days at the Holy Child School. It was an infants' school and was an excellent preparation for more formal, more arduous schooling. In those days, there was such a demand for places that we were divided into two groups, the 'morning children' and the 'evening children', and each group had a half day of lessons. I was a 'morning child', as my mother thought it would be better to start school life by having to get up early in the morning. Our first teacher was Miss Daly, a sister of the city's future Bishop. Our days as 'Holy Children' were to be the only ones during our entire school life that we were to spend in a co-educational environment. Many of the children I met almost 40 years ago have remained friends. For the following 20 years, Nigel Cooke and I together went through the Holy Child and the Christian Brothers', St Columb's and Trinity College, Dublin, but we all retain a special affection for our first school and, in particular, its principal, the late Miss Mary Duffy.

We learned to read from a series of books which might seem archaic to modern educationalists, the *Dick and Dora* series, which also featured their dog, Nip, and their cat, Fluff. We were well grounded in arithmetic through counting in hundreds, tens and units. As First Communion approached, we learned the *Catechism* by heart. My reading was supplemented by my father making me read the headline of the *Belfast Telegraph* every night – without really knowing what it meant. As children, the assembly hall seemed massive to us, whereas now it seems so small.

Those idyllic days were followed by the long trek to the Brow o' the Hill, where we met boys from outlandish places such as Waterside and Pennyburn. However, I soon became a member of an elite religious group in Creggan – I was initiated into the altar boys. We were Plato's philosopher-kings and could now converse in Latin (*Dominus Vobiscum . . . et cum spiritu tuo*) and chant *Tantum Ergo* during Benediction. As nine-year-olds, we were far removed from using body sprays, but we compensated for this lack of French perfume by holding the incense-filled thurible under our soutanes and letting its sweet odours seep through our clothes. As we dressed like younger versions of priests, it was inevitable that some of our friends would ask us what Mass we were saying each Sunday. The mothers of altar boys were akin to the 'Feis mothers' and had a great and genuine pride in their sons. It was the mothers who ensured we turned up for the early Masses such as the half-six-in-the-morning during the Retreats. We were excused from the sermons of hellfire and brimstone preached by the Missionary Fathers and in their place played football outside the sacristy. Often we were told to play silently, as our shouts might disturb the congregation inside. We were stunned on the Sunday of the closing of the Women's Retreat as we viewed the display of hats that would have put Ascot to shame. We were fortified on the closing day of the Men's Retreat with the hearty rendering of *Faith of our Fathers.*

Our mentor was Fr George McLaughlin, now parish priest of Moville. We were marshalled with military discipline and efficiency, especially for the big ceremonies such as the 'Forty Hours' and 'High Masses'. Fr George had a great rapport with all the altar boys throughout his many years in Creggan and took a personal interest in all of us throughout the subsequent years. He has remained a great friend to generations of Creggan people. The highlight of the year was the altar boys' excursion to Portrush. The bus left St Mary's after ten o'clock Mass. It was the worst Mass of the year if you were one of the unfortunate altar boys who had to clerk it, as the eyes of all your fellow altar boys monitored your every movement hoping you would make a mistake. Mistakes were seldom made, not because of the peer pressure, but because of the good training!

A striking point about Creggan in the '60s was that football was played on almost every available green space. The ground on which the community centre and youth club on Fanad Drive now stand was once four football pitches. The boys from Dunree, Greenwalk, Melmore and Fanad played as often as possible, and the democratic approach to playing, once the match had started, was that you only got a side when two boys arrived, otherwise you sat on the sidelines waiting for the arrival of another would-be player.

Sadly, some of the stalwarts of those matches died while still young men and are still remembered fondly: Gerry McDaid, Artie Palmer and Sean (Jock) McDevitt. The usual game was 'ten, half, twenty, the winner', meaning that half time was reached when one team had scored ten goals, and twenty goals were required for outright victory. If the game was becoming too long, the simple solution was 'next goal, the winner'. Our main interest in newspapers was reading the *Ireland's Saturday Night*, and we often queued outside McCool's shop at Central Drive waiting to read of the exploits of Manchester United and Celtic, as well as Derry City.

The '60s saw Derry City win the Irish League for the first time in the club's history, and Nigel Cooke and I regularly headed down to the Brandywell through the cemetery. My mother always told me she could tell the result by standing at the sitting-room window and looking at the faces of the men and boys as they made their way home. Tony O'Doherty, also from Creggan, was a stylish player, but all his qualities were overlooked by the partisan home supporters during the local Derbies with Coleraine as Tony donned the jersey of the Bannsiders. Ironically, it was at Brandywell I heard one of the first political rallying calls. During a closely contested Boxing Day match against Coleraine, one wit roared: 'Come on Derry, and get stuck into the university thieves!' This was one of the few memories I have of politics in Creggan before the deluge of 1968 changed the political horizon forever.

In the '60s, politics was confined to periodic contests between the Nationalist Party and a motley collection of Labour supporters. Shortly after I had made my

Confirmation in 1962, there was one such electoral contest. Eddie McAteer, the sitting Nationalist MP at Stormont, was opposed by Stephen McGonagle, who stood as Independent Labour; my parents both supported McGonagle. St Mary's Secondary School in Fanad Drive was one of the polling stations and, after teatime, two groups, mainly made up of youngsters, gathered on the two walls outside the main entrance. The occupants of one wall chanted Nationalist slogans and were faced by cheering McGonagle supporters. Neither group seemed to know what they were cheering, and it was a mere distraction to us, the apathetic football-playing gang across the street. For the record, McAteer won, outpolling McGonagle by 8,720 votes to a very respectable 5,476. Within seven years, John Hume would beat McAteer by almost the same margin.

There was little interest in the politics of Westminster. The absentee MP had the grand-sounding name of Robin Chichester-Clark; he never came campaigning in Creggan. Easter 1966 was the 50th anniversary of the Easter Rising and I was nearing the end of my first year at St Columb's. John Hume was my history teacher and he divided us into groups to prepare projects. Our project was the Easter Rising and we found a lot of material from the Christian Brothers' monthly paper, *Our Boys*, which many of us still received. The only Republican that we actually knew in Creggan was Tommy Carlin, who flew the Tricolour outside his bungalow at Central Drive every Easter. There was a Westminster election, also in 1966, and Neil GIllespie stood as a Republican polling a mere 2,860 votes, indicating that there was no great support for the Republican cause even in the year of the high-profile Easter Commemoration. For most of us, 1966 was memorable because it was the first World Cup we watched on television. Even though it was in black-and-white, it was exciting to see Pele and Eusebio and the little North Koreans every night. Looking back, those were days summed up in the words of one of Val Doonican's songs, *The Special Years.*

> From pig-tails to wedding veils,
> From pinafores to lace,
> And in between are the special years,
> Time never can erase.
> From play toys to college boys,
> From little girl to wife,
> And in between are the special years,
> You remember all of your life.

The painful and tragic events of the subsequent 25 years can never erase those magical days of childhood in Creggan. I am proud to say I come from Creggan.

Creggan or Foyle Hill Estate?

The social cachet of living in Creggan was somewhat damaged by the advent of the Troubles. *Or at least that's what erstwhile Rathkeele resident John Thompson seems to reckon. John, as he recounts here, would allow the cock to crow three times and tell passing foot patrols that he came from Foyle Hill – which he suggests is a different estate entirely. Though interestingly, he's allowing us to publish his recollections in this book about Creggan . . .*

Let me begin by correcting the popular misconception that Rathkeele Way is part of Creggan. We in Rathkeele Way were, in fact, residents of Foyle Hill Estate. Where is Foyle Hill Estate and what connection, if any, does Foyle Hill Estate have with Creggan? Ah, how answering those geopolitical questions taxed the minds of even the keenest social science graduates of the British Army and RUC footpatrols' finishing schools. Such patrols had to be social scientists under cover. Who else could be so devoted to their daily task of on-the-street-into-your-face interviews with residents of Creggan?

> *Name?*
> Thompson (with such a surname you were erroneously presumed to be a Protestant visitor, evangelist even, but more likely a Dole man in Catholic Creggan).
> *Address?*
> Rathkeele Way (quietly mumbled), Foyle Hill Estate (clearly articulated).

With such an address your erroneously presumed non-Catholic, non-Creggan credentials were misleadingly established. More practically, you were spared the lengthy, oft repeated 'This is your Nationalist life' discussions with social scientists so committed they carried out their research at gunpoint. Indeed, if your life were really interesting, colleagues would arrive and whisk you away to secluded remote places for continued overnight discussions about people and players in your little street.

Otherwise, life in Rathkeele Way was simple. There was no talk of class. To be well off in Rathkeele way was to have a father who had a job, any job. After the closure of the BSR, some fathers lost jobs never to get another; thus, for an increasing number, work was more a memory that a reality. Several such men secretly cleaned house and prepared dinners while wives secretly worked longer part-time hours until something better turned up.

Rathkeele, now a one-way street, is a narrow street, originally built with no thought for car parking as no-one thought its intended inhabitants would ever own cars in sufficient quantities for parking to be a problem. Rathkeele was a children's street. One media report, much and proudly quoted by the residents, declared Rathkeele to have the highest number of under-fives of any single street in Europe. We played football, rounders, cricket (our variety), tennis, 'kerby', 1-2-3 red lights and knick-knock.

McLaughlin's new fence was twice 'kicked to bits' (his words), not out of malice, but by football-mad wanes who took advantage of the relative ease with which a goal could be scored at the McLaughlin's goal post. Scores of 15-0 were not uncommon.

Maurice Cooper, aged 13, made a 'wipe' (technical term) at the ball, missed and sent his shoe flying through my bedroom window; unfortunately for him, and me, the window was closed. Those were the days when if your friend got 'hit' for some impropriety, you also got hit; 'hit' being another technical term meaning 'parentally, or even next-door-neighbourly, thumped'.

Ah, those were the days; the summer sun was hotter, the winter snow stayed longer, ice-cream pokes (cones) were bigger and a penny 'bubbly' lasted all day (even all night if your mother didn't find it), and we played without a care in the world and so it should have been, for we were children.

Who could have predicted that of those children one would be murdered as a British soldier, and another would fast to death in his search for Irish freedom? Of the mothers and fathers who took care that we children might play without a care, who would have predicted that one mother would become a Sinn Féin member of a devolved Northern Ireland Assembly and that one father would die when his own bomb exploded?

Many girls would follow their mothers into shirt factories while many sons would face the same unemployment of their fathers. My own mother Mary would die, aged 51, never to know the joy of being a grandmother. Our family home would become a house allocated to another family for their home. A few, a lucky few, would attempt to follow childhood dreams only to find that fulfilled ambitions were pale shadows compared with childhood memories of long hot summers.

Chapter 3

Saints and Scholars

The fledgling estate grew quickly, and by the early '50s it was apparent that greater provision would have to be made for the residents' spiritual and educational needs.

Creggan, contrary to folklore, was always very largely Catholic. And the dynamic for development came substantially from the Catholic Church, which over a period of two decades established a chapel, two primary schools and four secondary schools. The Church was also involved in setting up the youth clubs, about which we will hear more in later chapters. The Godly triumvirate responsible for much of the initial spadework were Monsignor Martin Rooney, Fr Joe Carolan, (both of whom are recently deceased), and Fr George McLaughlin. All three were assigned to St Mary's Church when it opened in May 1959 and were together there until 1974.

It wasn't always easy to be a priest or a teacher in Creggan. Up until the early '70s, the Holy Child Primary School was so over-subscribed it had to take two separate lots of pupils every day under the auspices of a Morning School and an Evening School. Later, during the *Troubles*, schools were regularly caught up in the conflict. All the schools bear marks of gun battles, and most were to lose pupils or past pupils. St Peter's playground was commandeered as a rifle range by the Official and the Provisional IRA, while the pitches at St Joseph's could be as dangerous as any minefield, situated as they were right in the firing line between Westway and the Army base at Rosemount.

The clergy meanwhile were forced to try and guide the community through some of the worst moments of the *Troubles*. Six of the men and boys killed on Bloody Sunday were from Creggan, prompting the largest common funeral ever held in Derry, when the 13 coffins of the dead lined the rails of St Mary's altar.

Fr George McLaughlin, one of those who officiated at the Bloody Sunday funerals, is now a parish priest in Co Donegal. In this chapter he recounts his experiences in Creggan – as do the principals of the Creggan schools.

The Triumph and Turmoil of St Mary's Parish

> People say it was a mixed estate, but that's not really accurate. It only had a small percentage of Protestants, though relations between the religions were very good. Protestants were very involved in the community and with parish activities – and if they saw us out on our house visits, they would call us in to see them. We often would sit and have tea with them. And when the Troubles came, we'd make a particular point of doing it. – Fr George McLaughlin, Creggan Parish 1958-78.

St Mary's Church was due to open in December 1958, but hiccups in construction meant that 'Derry time' was duly observed, and the chapel didn't host its first Mass until 31 May 1959. Up until then, the estate was split into two parishes; those who lived north of Bligh's Lane attended St Eugene's Cathedral, while residents south of the line went to Long Tower. This meant that Mass-going was actually quite a complicated affair, requiring teams of buses – organised by Ben Scampton and Sam Cox – to ferry the hordes to and from the town.

The Catholic Church was aware of the need to service the city's newest suburb properly, however, and laid the founds for St Mary's in the mid-'50s. And two years later, Fr George McLaughlin, who had spent the two years since his ordination assigned to Belfast and Strabane, was sent to minister in the estate, a role he was to fulfil for 20 years.

> The opening of the chapel was a cause for great jubilation. There were marvellous decorations put up and there was a sense of great joviality in the community. The day of the opening, the chapel was jammed, with many more outside. Cardinal Dalton was in attendance and the preacher was William Conway, who later himself became Cardinal. The principal concelebrant was Bishop Farren. Initially, Fr Martin Rooney was the priest in charge, while I was curate. I didn't actually know I was going to be assigned there until it opened. A third priest, Joe Carolan, then joined us that same year. The three of us were together in Creggan until 1974 and had a great relationship. Back in the early days, Creggan was an easy enough parish. You could walk round it in about an hour. And the houses were virtually all Catholic.

Unemployment blighted Creggan, even in its early days. The high percentage of men out of work led to mass emigration with husbands leaving home. But despite the relative poverty and the onset of overcrowding which rapidly dogged the estate, there were few complaints.

> People had been so used to being treated like second-class citizens, they were quite delighted just to have got a house. When the new homes were

being built, women would push their prams up from the town and hide holy medals in the sites – in prayer that they'd be allocated a Creggan house. You would later hear them saying: 'I even got the house I put the medal into.' But the area did have its problems. Although the houses were new, there was soon overcrowding. Young couples couldn't get public housing so they ended up staying with parents. Before I went up to Creggan, I heard wild stories about families burning all the wooden fittings from inside their homes and about people keeping coal in their baths. But there was no foundation in these. People treasured getting a house.

Many people in the new estate came from the Lecky Road and Long Tower areas and would settle down very quickly among old friends.

People got on well – there was a great community spirit. The Waterside people tended to hanker a bit for home and found it a bit more difficult. But other than that, people put down roots very quickly.

For the first decade after the settlers landed, facilities in Creggan were non-existent. The estate consisted of nothing but houses; shopping was very limited and there wasn't even a playing field laid out for children. A school, the Holy Child, had opened in 1956, but it only catered for infants under the age of eight. And it was so heavily subscribed that it had to run two separate sets of classes every day – the 'Morning School' from 9.00am-1.00pm, and the 'Evening School' from 1.00pm-4.00pm – to accommodate the demand.

The Church was very concerned about the lack of amenities, so in the mid-'50s, Fr Des Mullan, who'd a great interest in youth organisations, started up the Boys' Club in the big hut that had formerly been used by the Housing Trust to collect rents. The club, which could pack in about 200 people, was to become the main social outlet for youth. Fr Joe Carolan later became very involved, and it hosted all sorts of activities including regular concerts, dances and film-shows. At the time, it was the only social outlet in the area, and many of the events were run on a completely voluntary basis by people like Kevin McCaul and Brendan O'Donnell.

A Girls' Club was to start in St Mary's School in the early '50s and the two clubs later merged into the Youth Club currently operating on Fanad Drive. The Boys' Club remained based in the old Housing Trust hut until 1971 when the new community centre and youth club were built opposite St Mary's Church. The new centres, which became great rallying places for the community, were part-paid for by 'sales of work' organised by local women who would spend the summers knitting, and baking wares for the big Autumn Fair.

> The Church helped put the heart into Creggan; it helped develop the area's identity; it cemented the community.

The arrival of St Mary's Church in Creggan would also herald an upturn in the area's educational provision. The advent of intermediate schooling in 1959 – in the form of St Mary's Secondary School for girls – was a major step up for a community whose post-primary educational scope had until then been very limited. St Joseph's School for boys opened on Thompson's Field in the early 1960s with John Maultsaid as its first principal. Then in 1967, Creggan got a second intermediate school for girls in the form of St Cecilia's; Theresa Cunningham was its first head. But the reason for the apparent glut of new schools in the area was less than altruistic, as Fr George explains:

> The whole issue centred on the availability of sites. As sites were controlled by the old Corporation, it was very difficulty to get permission to build anywhere in the city except in Creggan. They were intent on maintaining an enclave there. So, when the Christian Brothers' moved up to St Peter's in 1971, all secondary education on the cityside for Catholics, with the exception of the grammar schools, was based in Creggan. Pupils were bussed in from all over the city. But while there was some resentment because of this, people were glad to have got something.

Primary schooling was, however, still proving very problematic. The Holy Child catered for children until they were eight, at which stage they were presumed hardy enough to make their way down to the Christian Brothers', Rosemount or the Long Tower.

> At one stage in the early '70s, numbers at the Rosemount Boys' got so big that a full class from Holy Child couldn't be transferred. So they had to be kept on an extra year. And ultimately Holy Child became an all-age primary school. Then in 1972, a second primary school, St John's, opened up under Hugh Kelly's stewardship.

Housing problems, in the form of overcrowding and discrimination against Catholics applying for Corporation-controlled homes, led to unrest in Derry in the mid-'60s. On the day the lower deck of Craigavon Bridge was due to be officially opened by a Stormont minister, the Housing Action Committee blocked it off with a caravan.

> I think we realised change was coming when the Housing Action Committee led by Eamonn Melaugh started its activities. At the time, Eamonn had little popular support, although I had great regard for him and the way he attempted to improve things in his quiet way. Creggan was relatively unaffected by the initial rioting in the late '60s, because it

> was a good distance from the city centre. But once Bloody Sunday happened, the estate became the focal point of the trouble in Derry.

When the soldiers first arrived in Derry in August 1969, they got a rousing welcome from Catholics. In Creggan, local people, including Republicans, would invite them in for tea. Wiser heads like Fr George were more muted in their celebrations:

> The day the soldiers first came into the city, I'd a gut feeling that things would go wrong and I remember feeling very sad. I was standing in the grounds of St Mary's as hordes of people marched up from the town in triumph, saying that they'd beaten the police and that the Army would now look after them. But I remember talking to groups of them and telling them that this was only the beginning of trouble.

The Army decided to billet soldiers in a block at St Cecilia's School and knocked at the Parochial House at five o'clock one morning to demand the keys. The priests told them they had no keys. But the Army were in by breakfast time, 'hiding behind the wanes', as Fr McLaughlin put it. Relations with the Army and the Creggan community were to degenerate within months, as soldiers became involved in riots and searches. Yet despite the high levels of conflict, it wasn't until 8 July 1971 that Creggan suffered its first civilian fatality of the new *Troubles*. Seamus Cusack, a 28-year-old welder from Melmore Gardens, was shot in the thigh on William Street. He was taken to Letterkenny Hospital for fear he'd be arrested if he were taken to Altnagelvin. But he died of blood loss shortly after being admitted. The Army claimed that Cusack was an IRA man, but this was strongly denied by eyewitnesses who insist he was unarmed when he was shot. A second man, Dessie Beattie, was shot dead by soldiers in a riot the following day. The two deaths led to a huge influx in support for the IRA, and, later that week, an estimated 1,500 people attended a recruiting rally for the organisation in the Bogside. The local clergy was on full alert.

> A couple of weeks later, the IRA grabbed a young policeman at the Rossville Flats and brought him up to St Mary's School; the plan was to shoot him. But we succeeded in talking them out of taking action and the man was freed. On another occasion, a soldier was caught by a crowd in Creggan. His story was he'd been leaving a girl home. But it was after a particularly wild day of rioting and the crowd was going to hang him. A local Republican intervened and we managed to escort the soldier back to Bligh's Lane and to safety.

On 9 August 1971, houses throughout Creggan were raided as the Army began its Internment swoop. Resentment was heightened to such an extent that barricades sprung up at every exit and the estate sealed itself off from the world. Similar defences were erected in the Bogside, and 'Free Derry' was born. Then on 18 August, British troops launched their first attempt to clear the no-go areas. But they met stout resistance in Creggan. As soon as the Army dismantled one barricade and moved on, the residents erected it again. A fierce gun battle between the Army and the IRA broke out close to the Kildrum Gardens entrance of the City Cemetery and a 19-year-old IRA man, Eamon Lafferty, was killed. Fr McLaughlin gave him the last rites where he fell in the cemetery, but Lafferty was already dead.

Back in the early *Troubles*, priests, who were mindful of not wanting to further inflame the situation, refrained from making homilies at funerals, other than to appeal for no retaliation. In some cases, there would be a full IRA guard of honour inside St Mary's Church; this provoked little excitement – many in the community would have sympathised with those early victims.

> Bloody Sunday completely changed the landscape and is really the starting point of the *Troubles* proper. Up until then, the bother had been spasmodic. Bloody Sunday was a declaration of war.

Fr McLaughlin and Fr Martin Rooney joined what is now known as the Bloody Sunday march in Creggan. They were there, in a personal capacity, as members of the local community, protesting against Internment without trial.

> You would never have imagined what was going to happen. I was called in to a house in Glenfada Park to tend to a woman who'd had a turn, when I heard the first firing. We knew it wasn't the IRA because the weaponry was so heavy. By the time I got out of the house, there were boys lying dead outside – everywhere, it seemed. I anointed three or four of them. Fellows whose faces you knew well, parishioners and friends. I was shocked, unable to take it in. The walk back to Creggan was the longest of my life. I went from there directly to the hospital and then went round the homes of the people in the parish who'd lost loved ones.

While all of Ireland and beyond was stunned by the 13 deaths, Creggan, in particular, was left devastated. Six of the victims were sons of the estate. All 13 coffins were carried into St Mary's Church the Tuesday night after the killings. And the following day, thousands of people from all over the world, including Irish government ministers, packed into the grounds for the funeral. Cardinal Conway presided at the Mass.

> St Mary's Church holds nearly 2,000 people, but there were thousands more outside and there were tears in every eye. The community was in shock. Disbelieving. Numb. Creggan, and indeed Derry, would take a long time to recover. We tried to keep in touch with the families, put a bit of heart back into them. But some never recovered. The clergy of the Derry diocese held a news conference in the City Hotel and issued a statement condemning the Bloody Sunday murders. But the Provos took off, thanks to Bloody Sunday; after the funerals, there were boys queuing up to join the IRA.

The Widgery Inquiry into the killings was to provide the people of Creggan with further grief.

> The inquiry was very insulting. A number of priests made statements and attended the hearing in Coleraine, but we felt it wasn't going to make any difference. I wasn't called to give evidence, though I do think I should have been.

The growth in the Provos was followed in July 1972 by Operation Motorman, when the British Army cleared away the barricades and set up camp at Piggery Ridge, behind Creggan Heights. And as the conflict grew, with more shootings, bombings, raids and arrests, so too the life of the local priest became busier and busier.

> I was called out regularly every night. I slept in a chair, half-listening to the shooting and waiting for the knock. I could be called out to tend to people who'd been shot, or asked to go down to the barracks on behalf of a parent whose son had been lifted. One night I was called to see a fellow who'd been shot on Broadway. My suit ended up clattered in blood so I threw it in the bin. The following night, there was a bomb in Rinmore. And my spare suit also got covered in blood. The next morning, before I could leave the house, I had to ring down to a friend to bring me up another suit as I'd nothing left to wear.

Parents whose children became caught up in the conflict frequently called on the clergy to intervene and help them.

> The police and Brits would occasionally give a fellow a second chance if you put in a word for them, though it would only be if they'd been caught doing something relatively minor. Likewise, it was possible to do business with the Provos. If, for example, the parents wanted their son out, you might say to the IRA 'You'd be far better without that fellow there', and they'd put him out.

Fr McLaughlin remained in Creggan until 1978, by which time the *Troubles* were beginning to settle down a bit. But the unreality of the situation would leave its legacy on the estate for years to come.

> The people have weathered the *Troubles* well, but there was a lot of heartbreak. Families were broken up, and there were some bad partnerships thrown together because of the pressure of the times. The estate still has its problems; but, all things considered, it has survived very well. It's now perhaps the hardest area in the city to get a house in. And at times it was difficult for us. But all you could do was be kind and be reasonable and attempt to direct people in a Christian way.

Above: Bishop Farren cutting the first sod for St Mary's Church, December 1954. (*Derry Journal*)
Below: Spectators at the sod-cutting ceremony. (*Derry Journal*)

Above: Dedication of St Mary's Church at Creggan, June 1959; Architect FM Corr makes a symbolic presentation of a gold key to Bishop of Derry, Dr Farren. (*Derry Journal*)

Dedication ceremonies;
Dr Farren, accompanied by Fr Rooney, June 1959. (*Derry Journal*)

Above: Fr Des Mullan and Nationalist MP Eddie McAteer with organisers of 'sales of work', which raised funds for St Mary's, December 1955. (*Derry Journal*)
Below: Fr George McLaughlin officiating at the Bloody Sunday funerals. (*Derry Journal*)

Society of St Vincent de Paul

The St Vincent de Paul Society (SVP), which is one of Ireland's leading charities, has had a presence in Creggan from its earliest days, when there were two conferences, St Anthony's and St Mary's, and meetings took place in the old Boys' Club hut. Presently there is one, St Mary's, which covers the Creggan parish.

Jimmy Clifford, currently vice-president of the St Mary's Conference, has vivid memories of his first contact with the Society. His brother had died in England and Jimmy's circumstances did not allow for sudden demands on his slender purse. At the time, he was the father of three children and his unemployment benefit was £9.00 per week. In desperation, he turned to the SVP who paid his fare to England and the expenses for his brother's funeral. Impressed by their reaction to his plight, and the manner in which they conducted the whole transaction, he later joined the St Mary's Conference, where he became aware of the historic background and the philosophy of the movement.

The St Vincent de Paul Society was founded in Paris in 1833 by Frederic Ozanam, a young French student. Seven men formed the membership of the first Conference of Charity in Paris in 1833. A year later Ozanam proposed that the work be placed under the patronage of St Vincent de Paul, whose name was adopted by the Society whose declared aims were:

> . . . to help its members grow in the love of God and their fellow men and women through direct personal service of people in need.

Jimmy soon learned how the SVP put this 'service of people in need' into practice. A pamphlet on the movement expands on its philosophy, declaring:

> Need is the only criterion used in deciding whether or not Society support should be offered. There are no double standards in our giving. Society friendship and support are available to everyone who is in need or who is disadvantaged, regardless of race, colour, creed, class or group in the community to which they may belong. Prejudice, whether political, religious, moral or personal has no place in the work of our Society.

The first practical step is to identify the need. To do this, St Mary's Conference meets on Mondays, when individual cases are considered and the utmost confidentiality is observed. Visits are then planned for Friday nights. There are clear guidelines:

> Vincentian visitation, which includes home, hospital and prison visitation, is the cornerstone of our work. Confidentiality is always respected and maintained. Creating friendship, listening sympathetically and avoiding judgemental and patronising attitudes are key aspects of visitation.

For sound practical reasons, visits are always in pairs. Some cases are clearer than others. Jimmy tells of a visit when an elderly man swathed in a blanket answered a knock at the door. As it turned out there was no food in the house and no fuel. The situation was quickly rectified by arranging a quick delivery of coal and food. This case was one of those, not easily detected, where an elderly person living alone found it difficult to ask for help and neighbours were not aware of his plight.

Other difficulties arise through alcohol-related problems and some through mismanagement of household budgets. For the latter, advice is given or classes made available. Care is taken, as far as possible, to ensure that aid gets to the needy and help in kind is favoured, although money payments are made when more appropriate. Assistance depends on circumstances. Where appropriate, food, fuel or furnishings are purchased directly from suppliers. There have also been arrangements with local retailers. An account was kept with travel agent Des McLaughlin so that he could deal with approved cases with minimum fuss. McLaughlin's clothes shop, at the behest of the Conference, also supplied clothes discreetly in an arrangement where the Society later picked up the bill. A regular need is beds and some ex-factory beds have been provided, where the supplier, knowing the circumstances, does a special deal. Ulster Ceramics has also donated material to the Society.

Regular supplies of clothes and furnishings are also ensured through the operations of the SVP shop which accepts donations of both. On clothes, the Society, aware of the people it helps, advises that as a general rule people should not give what they would be ashamed to wear themselves. In the Strand Road shop, a number of washing machines are on hand to ensure that items emerge spotless. Donors of furniture and utensils are also encouraged to donate items in reasonable condition.

It is always stressed that the support offered, practical or material, is never seen as a substitute for a person's statutory entitlement; it is always supplementary to it. A former president and member for 42 years, Pat McCallion, speaks in glowing terms of the good relationship set up with Tom Villa, manager of Social Services. As a result, statutory responsibilities could be identified and processed, leaving the Society to deal with those who had escaped the Social Security safety net. Jimmy Clifford, the only SDLP Councillor for the Creggan area, finds himself wearing two hats. He has the experience to discriminate between statutory and voluntary responsibilities and is in the position to offer solutions on both levels without compromising the principles of the Society.

While these workings of the Creggan Conference are pursued under the strictest confidence, there is also a public face. Pat McCallion talks of 27 years of annual bus runs for pensioners. Each year, five buses head off to Inishowen. One year the route takes them to McNamara's [hotel]in Moville and the following year to the Lake of Shadows [hotel] in Buncrana. Another pensioners' event is the Christmas Dinner in the Community Centre.

All of the activities need funding. The major sources are the Sunday 'church door' collections and the annual collection. In Creggan, funds are raised by the Parish Welfare Committee. The Society is also grateful for the funds that John Hume directed their way when he was awarded large donations to disburse to worthy causes.

Because of the confidential nature of the activities of the Creggan Conference, the general public has little appreciation of the Society's contribution to those in need. The path cannot always be easy but they have the philosophy of St Vincent de Paul to guide them:

> You will find that charity is a heavy burden to carry, heavier than the bowl of soup or the full basket, but you will keep your generosity and your smile. It is not enough to give bread and soup, this the rich can do. You are servants of the poor, always sincere and always good-humoured. They are your masters and the more difficult they will be, the more love you must give them. For it is only by your love that they forgive you for offering them the bread.

War and an Irish School: St Peter's High School

Despite applying for a job at St Peter's when it first opened in Creggan in 1971, it took Creggan man Martin Bowen 18 years to get a position at the school – as headmaster! Back in the early days, there were suspicions that the Christian Brothers' favoured 'Old Boys', and young Bowen, a former Rosemount Boys' and St Columb's man, didn't even get a reply.

> I was in the final year of my teacher-training in Manchester, and several of my peers from Derry, like Paul Elder and Seamus Bonner, who had been at the Brothers', applied to the new school and were immediately accepted; I'm still waiting for my letter.

Undeterred, Bowen wasn't long getting a post teaching PE and French at St Joseph's, courtesy of his eagle-eyed granny who spotted the job advertised in the *Derry Journal.*

> The routine back then was you were supposed to go to the Bishop and he told you where you were teaching. But I was so naive that I rang Willie John Maultsaid, the then St Joseph's principal, directly. He said to me: 'Do I know you?' I told him I was at the College. So he asked me had I been a swimmer along with Liam Ball. And I told him I had. So then he said: 'You left my daughter home one night – and had the good sense never to come back!' And sure enough, I'd left her home from a gala. So then he said to me: 'Would your granny be Brady?' I said she was. Well that clinched it, and he told me that I was to start work on 1 September. That was the end of the interview.

But it wasn't the end of the story. Maultsaid needed another PE teacher, so while he still had Bowen on the line, he asked him was there anyone else there looking for a job. So Bowen passed the phone to a pal, who was standing beside him in the Students' Union, a big fellow called Eamonn Timoney, from County Down. And sure enough, he too got a job.

> For the first year we were at St Joseph's, myself and Timoney would jog up to the school from Princes Street. It was a very abnormal situation. One morning we arrived just after two policemen were shot dead in their car at Helen Street. Throughout the early '70s, St Joseph's lay sandwiched between two checkpoints. So to get into the school by road, you had either to pass through a British Army checkpoint, at what's now the top of Creggan Hill, or an IRA checkpoint on Westway. Once, one of the teachers, who had been pulled up about being late, objected to the British

> checkpoint and told the soldiers to 'For Christ's sake, hurry up'. The next morning, the soldiers 'found' a round of ammunition in his car and arrested him. He was held until 4.30pm that day, until the Bishop got involved. But we all learned a lesson from that – keep your mouth shut.

The schools themselves, as all Creggan teachers such as Martin Bowen will tell you, were largely oases of calm in the midst of all the mayhem.

> The youngsters could maybe have been up all night because of house raids, or they could have been out rioting to the wee hours, but when they came into the school, all that was forgotten. We would meet the youngsters at the weekends, when they were out rioting, and they'd be shouting over greetings to you as you walked past; but they weren't abusive.

St Joseph's itself, caught in no-man's-land, could be a dangerous place; there was an unwritten agreement that what were rather euphemistically referred to as 'engagements' had to wait until after school-time. One afternoon, however, Bowen was unlucky enough to ask his PE class to stay in after hours for some extra practice.

> While we were out on the pitches, someone emptied a magazine at Rosemount Barracks. Now, the youngsters' natural instincts might have been to run, but in PE we had trained them on a 'Command and Do' system, and they were very good at it. So when I said 'Hit the dirt', everyone did. Otherwise we'd have been caught in crossfire, no doubt. The Army later said they spent two hours returning fire at 'identified targets'. But what happened was someone had driven up to the corner of the school, fired at the barracks and driven off again. There was a lull – possibly the Army had seen us and were giving us a chance to go – so we took off. But as soon as we were gone, it started up again. Then people from the other side started landing down and shooting back again. The school's wooden art-block was virtually demolished in the firing.

The rules of engagement in Upper Creggan were a lot looser than on Westway. In the early '70s, the Officials and the Provisionals shared a firing range in the grounds of St Peter's, and they would practise, with both rifles and pistols, while classes were on. Martin Bowen says the school still bears the scars.

> Apparently the grounds were ideal, because there were two courses: one for long-range practice, the other for shorter distances. The Officials and the Provos had a timetable for the place – one lot would practise for an hour or two in the morning, the others for an hour or two in the afternoon; not every day though. But one day, as one crowd were leaving and the others were arriving, a British Army helicopter landed nearby and

> a massive gun battle broke out with both lots shooting at the Army. It went on for three hours, during which time the children all hid under their desks. The whole side of the school was demolished, and there's still some bullet tracks around.
>
> We stayed clear of politics in the classroom, except perhaps to teach the youngsters about self-preservation. If someone was injured by a rubber bullet, we might take the opportunity to explain to the class that if you throw stones, expect what you get. Some of the boys in the senior classes at St Joseph's were tied up in the political situation, though it was never mentioned. Many past pupils went to jail. Other pupils had fathers or brothers in prison. Occasionally, if a child was a bit upset and we couldn't identify the cause, we'd ask the mother to come in. She would tell us that the father was in Portlaoise and the child was wrecked-tired from travelling to the jail. So we'd make allowances.

Bowen, like many young teachers in Creggan, took part in the Bloody Sunday march. Many pupils from St Joseph's were also there, including Don Mullan, who went on to write *Eyewitness Bloody Sunday.*

> My memory of that day is of escorting pupils back from the march. Some of them were big hard men, who would have been offering you outside the classroom for a fight. But that day, we were leaving them home, and the tears blinding them. I remember taking home Gerry Duddy, knowing that his brother Jackie had been killed. He hadn't heard, and I wasn't brave enough to tell him.

Many teachers, including Bowen, spent the days after Bloody Sunday taking statements from civilian eyewitnesses. Many of these appear in Don Mullan's book and he recalls:

> A few of us were awfully tempted to get involved. We sat down and thought hard about it. We knew murder had been committed.

Bowen, however, stuck with the road less travelled.

When Creggan man Bowen went to St Columb's College as a pupil, he was aware of the elitism that existed there. He himself was a successful swimmer and so escaped the worst vagaries of the system. But now, as principal of St Peter's, his views on grammar school streaming are more critical.

> If it wasn't for schools like this, schools like St Columb's would be in hellish trouble. The idea of having grammar schools, and the elitism that goes with them, is wrong. I'm not saying the solution is comprehensive schooling, but the very business of leaving grammar schools to deal with the elite, and leaving everyone else outside, isn't right. I do think the circle's turning in schools like ours, however. Nowadays, we're getting a

St Peter's High School, 2000. (Larry Doherty)

lot more parents involved in the management of the school. Moreover, our system here isn't punishment-based. Rather, we reward achievement. The school is a 'No Put Down' zone. And there's a young brand of teacher coming back into areas like this. They're professional and full of enthusiasm and verve. I hope they don't burn out in 25 years, like many of those who started in the early '70s. The natural life span of a teaching career should be 40 years. And principals and the authorities have a responsibility to see that teachers see their terms out.

Caught Up in Conflict: St Cecilia's College

St Cecilia's opened in 1967 with an intake of 369; it now houses over 950 girls from all parts of the city. Grainne McCafferty has taught at the school since 1971 and became its principal in 1991.

St Cecilia's first principal, Terry Cunningham, came to work on the morning of 13 October 1969 only to be told that the British Army was going to requisition half her school as a billet. Indeed, the school still has a special entrance known as the 'Army Door' which was built by soldiers to their block to keep them away from the pupils. In those early days of the *Troubles*, relations between Creggan people and the newly arrived Grenadier Guards were fairly good. However, by the time the Army had moved out of St Cecilia's and into Essex Factory across the street, matters had degenerated. The area was to become a nightmare, and any action taken against the Army post in Bligh's Lane affected the school.

In September 1971, soldiers shot dead St Cecilia's pupil Annette McGavigan. They tried to claim she had been killed in crossfire, but local witnesses say no shots had been fired at the Army. Over 10,000 people were to attend the funeral. A very moving account of the incident was published in *St Cecilia's: A Celebration of 25 years* in which Terry Cunningham recalled how the entire school was left 'stunned and heart-broken'.

> Mr Hunter, the local inspector, came to offer his condolences, and wept when he saw the wreaths in the office. Most of us cried at Assembly the next morning – little realising that two years later we would cry again when 14-year-old Kathleen Feeney was shot dead on 14 November 1973. Another pupil, Celine Jarvis, was shot and left paralysed on 9 December 1971.

According to Cunningham, riots were a daily feature of life on Bligh's Lane, and she spent many afternoons negotiating cease-fires so the girls could get home. Bomb-scares were another common occurrence. Virtually all the major funeral processions and protest marches passed outside the school. And, of course, there were gun battles.

> On 16 March 1972, shots were fired by the Army into a classroom where children were doing drama with Mrs Grainne McCafferty. When I was told, I ran upstairs to find the children crouched under the desks. After evacuating the children, I met with an Army officer. Even though I showed him the scorch marks of the bullet on the floor, where it had ricocheted between the feet of a child, he was adamant that there had been a gunman shooting from the window and that he had bullet marks in the camp to prove it.

St Cecilia's College, 2000. (Larry Doherty)

Grainne McCafferty, who is now principal of St Cecilia's, believes the teachers' main aim during that time was to provide a haven for the pupils.

> The children wanted and needed normality, a place where they could do their work and play with their friends. They were coming from houses that were regularly raided and had to cross barricades to get into the school. Children are always resilient – and largely unaffected – but they were less buoyant and youthful than they are now. What was happening outside rarely, if ever, spilled into the classroom. Children were so glad to get away from it all.

Tensions arose when pupils wanted to go on protest marches. The teachers were worried about the dangers of such outings and tried to keep them in. However, some of the girls were from politically-involved families.

> If there were political discussions in class, you'd let them run their natural course. But I remember one coming to a sudden end after a girl, whose brother had been sentenced to over 100 years in jail, got upset. If there was a bomb in the town, after you'd hear the bang there'd be a frisson throughout the school. We attended the funerals of relatives of quite a few girls. The circumstances of the deaths weren't a factor. We went on behalf of the child.

At the height of the first Hunger Strike in 1980, St Cecilia's hit the headlines when the British Ministry of Education decided to use the school in what was widely regarded by Nationalists as a cynical propaganda exercise. The then headmistress was given twenty-four hours' notice that a VIP would be arriving at the school and was warned not to tell anyone. The following day, Secretary of State Humphrey Atkins's wife landed at the school, where Special Branch escorted her on a grand tour of the premises. Mrs Atkins was then photographed taking tea in the Home Economics class in a bid to assure a British audience that they had the situation, and indeed Creggan, under full control. Needless to say, when the children told their parents who had been at the school, there was uproar. Scores of pupils had relatives in the H-Blocks, jailed under the authority of Mrs Atkins's husband.

That night, the school was daubed with paint and the following day a picket sprang up at the school gate. The principals of all the schools in the area were also very angry and publicly accused the British Ministry of 'hijacking' St Cecilia's and of endangering the lives of the pupils in the school. The Northern Ireland Office subsequently apologised and the photos of Mrs Atkins taking tea at the school were never published.

A very strong and innovative system of pastoral care was to grow up in St Cecilia's during the '70s – a system which survives to this day and which has recently caught the eye of the Department of Education in London.

> In those days, parents didn't come in to see teachers in schools, so we went out into their homes to meet them. Each form teacher is given timetabled time to visit the homes of the pupils in his or her class on a regular basis – not only when the child may be in bother. The idea is that it is much more comfortable for parents to talk to the teachers and discuss various problems on their own turf. This also means that we understand problems a lot better and gives the teacher a greater empathy and closeness with the child. The scheme, while expensive, has paid dividends too in improving school attendances and raising pupils' self-esteem.

Another key strategy promoted at St Cecilia's is the need for children to achieve. Back when the school opened in the 1960s, non-grammar pupils weren't expected to do exams. But that has never been the case at Bligh's Lane. Approximately a third of the school's fifth-years now stay on after the age of 16. And over 80% of sixth-years go on to higher education.

> Not everyone achieves GCSE or 'A' levels, but we don't recognise there is such a thing as failure. The selection process really harms children in that it brands 65% of children failures. It damages their confidence hugely. We motivate and encourage our children to achieve all they can; we teach them to value themselves; we try and instil them with confidence. Obviously there's no point saying to a child 'You're wonderful' and then telling them they're not going to do any exams. The world market demands qualifications, so we also lay on other courses in fields such as childcare, IT, and Leisure and Tourism. I didn't come into teaching to be a businesswoman. Education isn't a product to be sold and bartered with; essentially, you're dealing with people's souls. There are many things we do here that you can't enumerate in School League Tables. How do you measure self-esteem? Only the parents, the children and the staff really know what we're doing here.

THE BUSINESS OF EDUCATING FOR BUSINESS: ST MARY'S COLLEGE

Dame Geraldine Keegan is principal of St Mary's College. Under her stewardship, the school has achieved many national and international accolades. In 1992, it was the first in Northern Ireland to win the Charter Mark Award; in 1996 it became the first public sector organisation to win the Northern Ireland Quality Award, and in November this year became the holders of the coveted UK Business Excellence Award 2000.

St Mary's, which opened on Fanad Drive in 1959, is now the most over-subscribed of all secondary schools in Derry. The school has more than 900 pupils, increasing numbers of whom are staying on after the age of 16. Keegan explains why:

> We do everything possible to provide as many choices as possible for the children. We also feel that a crucial factor of education here is to get parents and the local community involved. So you'll find at St Mary's that parents take GCSEs along with their children; they help out teachers in the classroom; there's a Parents' Writing Group; and we run a 'Teach Your Child Maths' class.

The Sisters of Mercy, who ran the school from its inception and through most of the *Troubles*, were hugely successful in placing their pupils in the workplace after they left school. However, in recent years the emphasis has changed and now more and more girls want to enter further and higher education.

> The focus is different now. Nowadays, we would expect every pupil to leave school with an externally validated qualification. Thirty-four per cent of girls now get five or more GCSE grades 'A' to 'C'.

Keegan ascribes the school's part in its success to the decision to implement 'Total Quality Management' (TQM) in 1992. TQM is a system of management that originated in the United States and which is used in business corporations throughout the world to improve performance.

> The main focus of TQM is on the customer – which in our case is the pupil. The system gets you to maximise the potential of people in your organisation. It aims to reduce hierarchies and get everyone involved in the decision-making process. In many schools, a lot of junior staff are left out of management, but we find that many of our best ideas come from our youngest colleagues. TQM also places a big emphasis on staff training. Other schools are now adopting similar ideas, which is very flattering to us, though we always attempt to stay one step ahead. This is a very innovative school.

St Mary's College, 2000. (Larry Doherty)

Keegan sees competition between schools as important, as she says it ensures standards are constantly kept high.

> You can't stand still, it keeps you on your toes. And ultimately the main beneficiaries are the children.

Keegan wants to see even more involvement from the local community and businesses in her school. Among the initiatives she has implemented are a School Industry Partnership, a Higher Education Liaison Programme and a Role Model Week, where women who are leaders in their fields hold talks in the school.

> The vast majority of pupils in the school are highly motivated; apathy is not a factor and many are keen to go on into Higher Education. The spirit here is very pro-achievement.

Educating for a New Era: St Joseph's Secondary School

Sarah Kelly spent 24 years teaching at St Mary's in Creggan, before becoming principal of St Joseph's in September 1997.

The collapse in 1997 of Creggan's biggest industry, United Technologies, had a very strong effect on school children in the area. Sarah Kelly was 'devastated', and she admits to having become obsessed with the failures of industry in the North West.

> Parents here have always given education a very high priority, but it is becoming increasingly difficult to give pupils, particularly boys, an incentive to work if there are no jobs for them when they're coming out. Boys need something to aim for. In its early days, this school helped many boys get apprenticeships, and you'll now find that many former pupils are running their own companies, but these apprenticeships don't exist any more. The lack of jobs leads to us putting perhaps an over-emphasis on higher and further education. But a large percentage of our boys just want to work. And they're very good workers, as you'll see when they're organising social events or functions at the schools. It's just that the openings for them don't seem to exist any more.

There are currently 940 boys at St Joseph's, making it one of the largest boys' secondary schools in the North. And the numbers who want to stay on after 16 are growing ever year. In 1997, 60 remained to do post-GCSE courses. And GNVQ vocational courses are becoming very popular.

> If I could run the courses, I could fill the school. We're constantly adapting the curriculum to meet the boys' needs. And I'm also a great believer in getting them involved in extra-curricular activities. And next year, we hope to run even more vocational courses alongside 'A' levels.

Recent government research suggests that girls are outstripping boys in pre-16 educational achievement. The gulf, if anything, is wider in Derry. Boys, however, tend to narrow the gap again after 16, according to Sarah Kelly.

> The add-on factor for boys is much greater and we find that after 16 they're starting to set their sights higher. Girls want to please more – they'll generally do what they're told. But it's harder to get girls genuinely interested in something than it is boys. Boys listen to news more. They pick up more.

Kelly has also noticed a great yearning for success on the part of her Creggan pupils.

> They take great pleasure in credit. We carried out our own research into what sort of rewards they want. They like getting notes in their daybooks. And they like their parents to be informed when they're doing well.

Kelly is another principal who wants to see the current transfer procedure scrapped.

> The 11-plus is devastating for boys who don't get places at grammar schools. Afterwards, many think that the only way they can assert their individuality is through 'laddishness'. Half our time is spent trying to improve their confidence after the 11-plus knock-back. Every year, however, we are getting pupils who passed the exam – and this year, we have two classes who got Cs and above.

As in other Creggan schools, it's not uncommon for pupils at St Joseph's to have relatives in jail.

> At a parents' night, shortly after the first IRA cease-fire, one parent was bemoaning the lack of opportunities for young people in the area. And she started complaining that now, with the cease-fire, the youngfella wouldn't even be able to join the IRA!

In recent years, St Joseph's has adopted a pastoral system of getting to know pupils' parents and of involving them more in the school. And when, for example, a father or a sibling of a boy is in prison, the school is keen to foster very close links with the mother.

> You'll find that there is an external back-up for the families of political offenders. We also like to encourage the mothers in such cases to get involved in projects we're running in the school.

Several past pupils of St Joseph's were to become victims of the *Troubles*, including Jack Duddy, who died on Bloody Sunday, and Ranger William Best, who was shot dead by the Official IRA. A Mass is said every November at the school for deceased alumni – and it's always packed. Other children became involved in the IRA and ended up in jail. And still, very occasionally, Creggan children do become involved in rioting, though, according to Kelly these tend to be largely primary school pupils.

> Without fail, we found that the parents didn't want their children involved. Parents look to you to provide security for their children, to keep them out of it.

St Joseph's Secondary School, 2000. (Larry Doherty)

On 'Gaza Strip': The Holy Child Primary School

The Holy Child Primary School on Central Drive is Creggan's oldest school and for a long time was the estate's most hard-pressed. After it opened, it had to cater for so many pupils that it split the intake into halves with one group being taught in the morning, the other in the evening.

During the *Troubles*, life on Creggan's so-called 'Gaza Strip' was difficult for children and teachers alike. The school was to lose many ex-pupils in the conflict and many more were jailed. But the emphasis within the walls of the schools was always on providing an oasis of normality.

Currently, there are just under 400 pupils on the roll, the intake largely drawn from St Mary's Parish, although relatives of former pupils also commute to the school. Principal Charlie O'Donnell says partnership with parents is a key priority for his staff:

> We feel that the achievement of our aims depends on a relationship between parents, staff and pupils which is firmly based on mutual respect and understanding. The parents of our pupils are collaborators in the educational process, and the school strives to promote co-operation by developing closer links between home and school.

Parents are encouraged to promote school as an enjoyable experience – and asked never to use the school or the teacher as a threat to the child. Another key aim promoted by the school is that of tolerance. Teachers aim to instil that virtue in each child and encourage respect for difference whether religious, social or political. To this end, the staff run an anti-bullying project and indeed the year 1999/2000 was set aside as Anti-Bullying Year at the school. Charlie O'Donnell:

> Our objective is to create a safe and happy environment where a child can feel free from bullying and enjoy coming to school. We consider bullying to be a most serious problem and recognise that every single person in the school has a part to play in eradicating it. To date we have asked all pupils and parents to sign an Anti-Bullying Pledge, and we are encouraged by the great response to this.

Another initiative introduced has been that of teaching pupils modern languages. A second language isn't normally taught in primary schools, but the Holy Child has tutors for German, Spanish, French and Irish. The school hopes to develop a fifth language club, Italian, and to look at providing other after-school activities for the children.

Above: The Holy Child Primary School, 2000. (Larry Doherty)
Below: The 'Gaza Strip', Central Drive in the early '70s. The Holy Child School is on the right. (Eamonn Melaugh)

A Haven of Peace: St John's Primary School

For over a decade, the Holy Child Infants' was the only primary school in Creggan. Then in 1971, St John's Primary School opened on Bligh's Lane in the grounds of St Cecilia's Secondary School. Catherine Bradley, who has taught in St John's since it opened, is now its principal.

Catherine Bradley commented on the early days:

> Looking back, you notice that the children in the early days were always tired. You can tell that a lot has changed from what they write and draw. Back then, the children would draw tanks and soldiers. But, as teachers at the school, it was always our priority to keep the *Troubles* at bay and keep the school a haven of peace and stability.

St John's, however, was also to see its share of the *Troubles*. In its first year, attendance figures rose and dipped 'like the Alps', varying from 722 down to four. The school's retired headmaster, HV Kelly, says both staff and children deserve great credit for coming to school every day 'in a war zone', where CS gas was 'more plentiful than air' in the playground. Writing in the school's 25th anniversary booklet, Kelly recalled:

> Every morning, about 9.00am, someone at the cemetery end of the school would fire a couple of rifle shots at the Army base in Bligh's Lane. The Army, of course, reacted, and a number of parents appeared in my office and demanded transfer certificates for their children. I was told they didn't want a new Catholic school in Creggan. I found myself standing in the playground writing out transfer certificates while a group stood around me giving me the names of the children for whom they were required. The rifleman, whom I had met previously, was prominent among them.

The school was also to lose two of its number through *Troubles*-related incidents. Gordon Gallagher, who was eight, was killed when he triggered a bomb in a garden. Catherine Bradley:

> I remember that his Wellington boot was found in a tree. Later, we were to lose Stephen McConomy, who was killed when he was hit by a plastic bullet.

Despite what some might consider extreme difficulties, St John's flourished as a centre of educational excellence. Jim McChrystal, who chairs the school's Board of Governors, believes that it is the best of its kind in the entire Western Board area. He commented:

St John's Primary School, 2000. (Larry Doherty)

> Our record of achievement proves it. If you take the country as a whole, the percentage of pupils who pass the 11-plus is 23% to 25%. But in its worst year, this school had a 45% pass rate. And the rate has varied from 55% to 60% over the past few years. Exceptional! It says a lot for the dedication of the teaching staff that in the 25 years I've been here, I've never heard a teacher discuss the intake or the area. They get down to work and do an excellent job.

Catherine Bradley believes part of the success is down to high expectations on the part of both the teachers and the parents. But she doesn't think that children should just be channelled for academic success. She says it's also important that they achieve in extra-curricular fields. Nor is Bradley a fan of the selection process.

> I don't like it, though I toe the line and get on with it. I've seen children devastated at getting low grades. I've seen their confidence badly damaged in some cases. The 11-plus is not and should not be the be-all and end-all. It's only part of the curriculum. Our philosophy is child-centred; we believe that every child will achieve, and has achieved, in some area. It is important the child leaves school feeling good about themselves and knowing that they can do something.

To this end, St John's puts a high value on excellence in sport, music and drama – sometimes with unexpected dividends. At the time of Taoiseach Bertie Ahern's visit in January 1998, the school choir was called upon to perform *Danny Boy* for him at only an hour's notice, a task they conducted with relish, and, according to Mr Ahern, very tunefully. New initiatives such as a reading centre and a facility to train parents in teaching their children how to read have been set up in recent years. Closer links have also been fostered with local secondary schools. A recent multi-million-pound redevelopment has presented children and staff with greatly improved facilities to carry this ambitious work forward into the new millennium.

Naíscoil na Rinne

Naíscoil na Rinne is an Irish Language, social care, educational and cultural development organisation which has been established in the Creggan area since 1984. The organisation started life more than 16 years ago as an Irish Language playgroup, where pre-school children received their early education in an atmosphere devoted to Gaelic speaking and teaching – allowing the children to acquire their language and childcare skills in a natural learning environment. In the late 1980s, as the Naíscoil's work expanded to take in Irish language tuition for local schools and the wider community, it adopted a central role in generating community activity in the Creggan area and became the focus for some of Creggan's local development groups.

Based in Cromore Gardens, in the heart of the Creggan community, Naíscoil na Rinne is housed in what were once three derelict garages and a block of four disused flats, both of which are now converted into an early-years centre and a multi-purpose parents' cultural resource centre. Over £250,000 was raised from bodies such as the National Lotteries Charity Board, Children in Need, the local Derry Development Office of the DOE and from the local community to assist in the refurbishment programme. Over the years, the Naíscoil's energy, ideas and enthusiasm have also helped to spawn other groups in the area – such as the Creggan Community Initiative, a body which was established to promote social, economic and environmental projects in the estate, and the Creggan Early Years Network, a partnership of both statutory and voluntary childcare providers.

However, the core work of the Naíscoil during its 16-year history has been the development and delivery of a range of Irish Language social care and educational services to improve the quality of life for the Irish Language community. The staff and committee of the Naíscoil view the encouragement and development of the Irish Language and culture – not just in Creggan, but all over Derry – as the fundamental basis of its work.

Despite funding problems in the early years of its existence, the Naíscoil has grown considerably, providing a comprehensive service, which meets the needs of parents and children from the Irish Language community in Creggan and the surrounding areas. At the present time, the Naíscoil offers a range of activities which cater for over 40 children and their parents on a daily basis. These activities include an early years project, an out-of-school activity group, a community outreach programme and a parental support programme. In addition to the social care and educational services, and to cope with a demand for suitable Irish Language materials, the Naíscoil, with the support of the District Partnership, has recently opened an Irish Language Early Years Resource Unit. In the Unit, staff and volunteers from the Naíscoil write and design Irish Language nursery books, parents' language programmes and children's songbooks. Many of these publications are combined with specially recorded cassette tapes that children and their parents can use to encourage and develop their Irish Language learning. The parents' language programme has proved to be particularly successful and is extensively used in other areas in the North of Ireland and in the Irish-speaking regions of Donegal.

Minister of Education, Martin McGuinness MLA, visits Naíscoil in Creggan. (courtesy Naíscoil)

With the recent opening of Gaelscoil Éadan Mhór, Creggan's first Irish Language primary school, which is situated in the grounds of the Seán Dolan's GAA Park, the Irish Language situation in the Creggan area is rapidly expanding, mainly due to the high demand that currently exists, and also because local Creggan residents welcome and support its development. In fact, a measure of the demand that exists is the number of children who currently wish to avail of the Naíscoil services. Presently, pre-school places at Naíscoil na Rinne are at an all-time high. From the response of the local community, the Naíscoil is certain that this growth will continue on an annual basis, which in turn will ensure the preservation of the national language and culture for future generations.

In addition to its local work, Naíscoil na Rinne, in co-operation with other Irish Language providers from Belfast, Newry and Armagh, has been responsible for the formation of Altram, which is an Irish Language pre-school organisation. The main aims of Altram are to provide a voice for Irish medium pre-schools, promote high-quality pre-school provision and create access to the Irish Language for all sections of the community. Altram has offices in both Derry and Belfast and has recently gained recognition as an NVQ training centre.

Naíscoil na Rinne's work is mainly in the language and culture field; however, as a community it does not feel isolated. The Irish Language community is an important part of the entire community, and by being seen to help others and work with them, it helps to get its message across that the Irish Language and culture can play a positive role and enrich the entire Creggan community. Naíscoil na Rinne, which is now the oldest community organisation in the Creggan area, has proved to be a success story. It has been to the fore in shaping the future of the Creggan area and has helped to address issues, such as high unemployment and social deprivation, which have existed in Creggan for many years. For the future, the Naíscoil intends to play its part in ensuring that Creggan and the Irish Language community within it will continue to develop and prosper.

CHAPTER 4

Ceol, Craic and Culture

They made their own entertainment in those days. No, really. They did. And look where it got them. Creggan gave life to some of the finest musicians in Ireland, including a Eurovision winner and its own Top Ten rock band. Creggan can also boast an actress who starred in an Oscar-winning film and, indeed, if we stretch to Beechwood Avenue, the lead player in one of the world's most successful TV shows. As one contributor suggests, the estate bred a writer or dramatist on every street corner – and it fashioned at least one award-winning filmmaker. And let's not forget of course, the legendary radio comic who once asked the EC's most senior politician, deadpan, where he would get directions to the European wine lake.

So what exactly did people do before the advent of television and Gameboy? Sports commentator John Dunne got in some early practice reporting on lollipop-stick races at one of Creggan's many streams. Brian Devlin and hundreds of other street urchins would pound their feet on the floor of the Boys' Club while a hapless projectionist tried to get the film going again. Meanwhile, over at the Girls' Club, Dana would be dragged to the stage for a song. Joe Mahon fished for sticklebacks and newts – always mindful of the crocodiles lurking below, while newer generations, as Mickey Bradley will remind you, had entertainment of a whole different sort entirely laid-on in the summers of long riots and short raids . . .

The Stream

Creggan may have lost its dog track when the houses started going up, but the locals were, for a while, still able to pursue their love of 'live racing' thanks to the ingenuity of young John Dunne and his friends. John, who later taught at St Joseph's and became a sports broadcaster of repute, recalls here those innocent days in Creggan's Garden of Eden.

A great roar went up in the imaginary grandstand as Caughoo crossed the finishing line ahead of Zucchero and Dante. This was not Aintree, Sandown or Goodwood – no – this was a humble little stream that flowed down Bligh's Lane behind St Mary's Church and School and the contestants weren't thoroughbreed horses but simple wooden lollipop sticks. There must have been 500 excited punters at the meeting and those with winning dockets lined up to be paid out, while others studied form for the next race.

I cannot remember how it all started – after all this was the early '50s and children with imagination could manufacture their own fun. I suppose my friend and I bought two ice pops one day and finished them off as we met the stream. The obvious happened and the first 'horse' race took place. The rest is history.

We gathered ice pop sticks by the hundred and used every name of every horse we could remember. Flat sprinters, stayers, Classic winners, hurdlers, steeplechasers – what did it matter? Arthur looked after the runners. My friend had a very methodical mind and he spent some of his college-free time writing out the lists of runners at Ayr, Beverly, Brighton, Kempton or Hurst Park. We usually had three meetings-a-day and Arthur's job was to have the runners ready and neatly separated in numbered elastic bands.

Attendances were small to begin with, but word soon spread and the boys of Rinmore, Central Drive and Creggan Heights soon joined their counterparts in Malin, Dunmore and Leenan. The late, much-loved Johnny Irvine was a great enthusiast and he made sure that good order was maintained. I suppose the craic must have lasted for a few months, but things were to go very wrong in dramatic fashion.

By accident or design, someone discovered that if you slit an ice pop stick with a razor blade, it would sink. I think the culprit exiled himself to England years after – perhaps he couldn't live with his guilt. Anyway, Caughoo, which had won eight races straight off the reel, was 'nobbled'. The boys of Rinmore were on; the race went off. Caughoo stuttered to a halt and the sods and stones rained down. God rest him, Johnny Irvine threw the last sod and led his disgruntled troops home. We all knew the game was over and, with a sourness of regret burning in mouths and throats, we too trooped silently and guiltily away.

Creggan – Before it Was Trendy

Nostalgia can sometimes paint the world rose-coloured. And while most people, like Brian Devlin, have many happy memories of the Creggan craic in the early days, they also had to endure poverty and tougher times as well. As Brian explains here, it wasn't always fashionable to live in Derry's politically inspired estate.

My first memory of Creggan is of me scurrying up the steps of our home in Melmore Gardens and exploring the vast rooms with their cavernous echoes as our excited voices filled the void. I was born in number 2a Chamberlain Street and in 1950 my parents were allocated a house on the new estate. I spent my childhood and youth there from the age of five. My father was a docker and my mother remained at home rearing eight sons and a daughter.

In that sprawling estate, with its criss-cross streets that stretched from Piggery Ridge and sloped down into the Lone Moor Road and beyond, I remember the bleakness of mid-winter and the welcome rays of the sun in high summer. Those desolate patches of arid ground became our playground long before television consigned Dan Dare, Dick Barton and the McCooeys to float in the ether for eternity.

It was no hardship at all walking to the 'Wee Nuns' [St Eugene's Infants] on school days, or making the same journey each Sunday to St Eugene's Cathedral to attend Mass. I made that trek many times, and a million times since in my mind. Walk to the middle of Melmore ('the circle'), left into Greenwalk and right into Leenan, left into Broadway, turn right down Beechwood Crescent then down Beechwood Avenue. Left into Marlborough Terrace, past the 'Frying Pan' pub and O'Hare's Chemist at the corner, sharp right turn into Creggan Street past number 43, my father's family home, and left across the street where the diminutive figure of Fr Mulvey could be seen standing sentinel at the chapel doors. After Mass, maybe go to Jack McDaid's on the corner of Creggan Road and Windsor Terrace for some cigarettes for my father. Ten Gallagher's Blues for 1s 11½d and a long luxurious ice pop with the ha'penny change out of a 2s piece [10p].

One of the high points of the weekend was the films shown in the Boys' Club beside the parochial house at Beechwood Crescent. I would stand in the pouring rain or the freezing snow with other children to gain entrance to the tiny, dingy wooden hut where we would sit on hard benches. The cacophony of excited children and the unsuccessful attempts of the adults to restore order ended only when the flicker of black-and-white images speckled the screen. If the film broke down, which happened frequently, the small structure trembled in the uproar and din. The younger children booed and hissed while the older ones stamped their feet. Each week seemed like an ordeal or cruel initiation to be endured for the privilege of seeing Superman, or Marvelman, or The Three Stooges. Sheer bliss!

I attended Mass and other religious services in the Cathedral until 1959 when St Mary's was built at Fanad Drive. By then, the Holy Child Infants' School had been completed and a secondary school would follow to meet the needs of Creggan's

The Devlin family, from left to right: Michael, Brian, Richard, Brendan, Damian, Anne, Molly, Eamonn, Richard (jnr). Missing from photograph, Tony and Seamus, circa 1953. (courtesy Brian Devlin)

burgeoning population. I remember my Uncle Michael, who worked in the offices of Farran's the contractor, being laid off when the new chapel was completed. He suffered the same fate of many in the town who were forced to leave to find employment elsewhere.

The pattern was to be repeated for many others in 1967 when Monarch Electric shut out its workforce. Situated in Eastway, this company, which produced record changers and recording equipment, employed about 2,000. I remember, too, a cold winter day in January 1961 when I began work there. I sold my birthright by signing a 'no-union' contract. Such a shameful action was conditional to getting a job in my own home town in those days. Despite inducements, blandishments, threats, promises, I would never, for the rest of my working life, repeat the exercise. Later, thanks to the excellent efforts of a number of the workers, the Birmingham-based Company was obliged to recognise the negotiating rights of its employees. It would be easy to draw parallels between this experience and some modern employment practices.

The work there was dull and tedious and, for the most part, unskilled. A great camaraderie masked the fact that pay and conditions were poor and that working overtime was a prerequisite for a decent living wage. Many families, including my own, depended on it for its greatest single source of male employment. When the factory closed, I was working there with three of my other brothers – I remember one family with five sons there. The impact of such a loss was felt in nearly every street on the estate. That same year, my father was made redundant when the Liverpool-Heysham shipping line stopped trading at the Derry port. My mother was devastated. Months later, at the age of 58, she went back to work in a local shirt factory. Twelve years later she left work to nurse my father in the months before he died.

I remember when I was growing up in Creggan the unkind names it was called, the unfair reputation it had, and the dreadful slur cast upon the people who lived there. My parents had an ambivalent attitude to living in Creggan; they deeply resented the appalling social and political circumstances that brought the estate into being and the stigma of the early days, while at the same time they fiercely defended it and its people. In the years before her death, my mother often reminded me that we lived in Creggan long before it was trendy to do so. My only sister, Anne, still lives in the family home.

Melmore Memories

Creggan's first ever television set was to make its appearance on Broadway just round the corner from the Mahons' Melmore Gardens household. Small wonder then that the lure of the greasepaint was to prove so strong for young Joe Mahon who went on to become such a successful film-maker. Though, as Joe explains here, he did well to survive a childhood of mad dogs, hidden monsters and red water worms that could burrow from your feet to your very heart . . .

I was the first-born and we lived, my new-fangled parents and I, in a flat in Magazine Street for about 18 months. I was a privileged child from the outset because, whereas the other 36 tenants had to queue for the one lavatory, I had the exclusive use of a complete set of terry-cloth nappies, hand-washed and hung in diagonal permanence across the room, neatly dividing the sleeping area from the eating and cooking area. I also had an enormous chrome and lacquered pram which had a suspension like a Mercedes Benz, but my mother soon got sick of humping it up and down five flights of stairs and she also got sick of people asking her if she had adopted a wee Korean baby, so she stopped taking me out.

I remember none of this of course, but my mother recalls it as if it were yesterday. She also recalls the excitement with which she received the news that we were to be allocated a house in Creggan. Number 21 Melmore Gardens had a living room with a bay window, a kitchen and a larder, two bedrooms, a bathroom, a front hall, a back hall, a coal shed, a front garden with steps leading up to a front door, to which we had the one and only key, and a back garden that stretched away into the distance. House? It was a vast mansion set in rolling acres of upland pasture. My mother planted marigolds in the front garden and my father grew potatoes and blackcurrant bushes out the back. I dug them all up.

For people who had been reared in old terraced houses with large families, this was alien luxury. My mother came from Bishop Street. Not Bishop Street Within. Bishop Street Without. Without indoor toilets, without bathrooms, without hot running water, without anything resembling a garden. My father came from Deanery Street in the Brandywell, where houses were even smaller. Ten of them lived in Deanery Street. Twelve in Bishop Street. Dr Who's tardis didn't raise an eyebrow in our family circle.

Not having anything to which I could compare it, I took to Melmore Gardens as a duck takes to water – my mother's contentment washed over me as I trailed after her, and my father brought home sweets from 'down-the-town', a place where the air was always thick with cement dust and where they filled your pocket with huge handfuls of copper and silver coins. My father was a plasterer and most of my uncles were in the building trade, and our house was often filled with the sounds of hammering, clattering and whistling. Men didn't growl in those days when children appeared. They stopped working and bent down and told you that your da was only a bum and then winked and gave you a penny.

There is a black-and-white photograph somebody has of 21 Melmore Gardens on a summer day. A slim, dark-haired, young woman in a pale, figure-hugging suit is standing beside a huge pram with a tasselled parasol. She is holding a bonneted baby in her arms and she is smiling down at a scowling three-year-old boy in a sailor suit, complete with pocket whistle on a white cord. The boy could easily be mistaken for me, but he is, in fact, a junior cadet in the Korean Naval Corps. Soon there were four of us. The sun shone, the marigolds bloomed relentlessly and the blackcurrants survived my attempts to dye my entire body purple. My mother made jam and Magazine Street was seen as a short purgatorial diversion on the road to fulfilment.

Such idylls don't last. One day a black taxi arrived outside our door and chugged patiently while some of the neighbours gathered round with their arms folded. All five of them, my father and my uncle Tommy included, wore gabardine coats, belted round the waist, and carried brown suitcases, also belted round the middle. Only my father didn't wear a cap. Two joiners, two plasterers and a labourer were going to England to get work, to send money back. I resented the indignity of having my arm waved for me and shrugged free to watch in petulant silence as they drove off. My mother lay on the couch and told me to take my sister for a walk in the garden. I walked her round the garden until she wouldn't stop crying. I despaired of them both and went to pick the wallpaper off the bedroom wall.

For the next six years, the back garden grew docks and nettles and bred ladybirds and butterflies. The blackcurrants reappeared unbidden and potatoes popped up in strange corners. Every Friday night, my mother took us down to the phone box at the

Young Joe Mahon on left, with brother and Derry City Manager Kevin and sister Anne c.1955. (courtesy Joe Mahon)

corner of Greenwalk and Leenan Gardens. We queued alongside girls with bouffant hairstyles who were ringing guys called Chuck and Chester at the American Naval Base. I would tell my father what I'd had for my dinner and what I wanted for my birthday and he would pretend to get them mixed up. I thought this was hilarious.

One day my mother brought me in, put on my Sunday clothes, pulled a dripping wet comb across my hair and took me to a house in Broadway. The front door was open and people stood in the hallway. The front room was laid out with rows of benches and everyone sat quietly and watched a small black-and-white picture of a man playing a trumpet. This was a television. We watched the man playing the trumpet for about ten minutes and then gave up our seats to more people and went home. My mother said that we would get a television some day and I wondered what our house would look like with the front room filled with rows of benches, and people with their hair slicked down. For years after, I thought Broadway was Broadway.

School was the Wee Nuns in the Long Tower grounds, a double confusion for me since the nuns were disappointingly of average height and the tower was neither long nor even a tower. Mrs McGettigan was the infants' teacher and she was so old that she didn't bother asking you who your father was. She wanted to know your grandmother's name. I didn't know. It was a long walk from Melmore Gardens to the Long Tower and you went via Bligh's Lane, which we called Breeze Lane. It was a real country lane in those days – stone walls overhung with hawthorns and sycamores and deep sheughs running down each side. I was supposed to meet up with my cousin Kathleen Ramsey from Cromore Gardens, but often I missed her and went on my fearful way accompanied by the wee white woman, the whispering man and the red water worms that crawled out of the sheugh and burrowed through the soles of your shoes and up to your heart. The walk back up to Creggan was even longer.

The planners, if there were any in those days, must have reckoned that Creggan people wouldn't own cars because they made the streets too narrow for vehicles to pass each other comfortably. They were really access routes for milkfloats, bread vans and men who hawked fresh herring or collected rags. Micky O'Hagan, the Stewart twins and I would sit on our steps and collect UI numbers, and one day we didn't get a single new one. There was a grass, oval-shaped roundabout halfway down Melmore Gardens and we called it the 'Circle'. Marathon football matches were played there with scores frequently reaching the nineties. Bonfires were held there on 15 August every year, the culmination of weeks of foraging, scouring, raiding on neighbouring streets and careful storage round Doherty's back. Old tyres would mysteriously appear and black and red smoke would billow out into the night sky as we performed our pagan rites to the strains of a frenzied accordion. As the embers glowed later on, Frankie Mooney would sing *Story of a Starry Night* in a high tenor voice, and everyone would fall silent and stare into the fire. Next morning we would search the ashes for the blackened potatoes we had planted and pick the skin off and suck them in with cooling breaths. Everyone said they were lovely, but mine were always hard.

There were no schools in Creggan, no church and no community centre. There was simply a vast wilderness called the Bishop's Field, through which the continuation of Bligh's Lane eventually reached the Creggan Shops. Sam Ramsey's fish shop, McCool's newsagents, Harry Doherty's grocery shop, Hegarty's butchers, O'Hare's chemist and post office, Coyle's sweet shop – I got to know them all eventually and hated when I was sent a message, because the message was rarely straight-forward. For a start, you usually had to tell the shopkeeper who you were.

> Tell them your name and who your mother is and that I asked for a quarter-pound of tea, not a half-pound in the order, and that he charged me for a large packet of digestives instead of a small, and tell him to give you four baps, but only if they're fresh today.

You were expected to do this in a crowded shop and to a shopkeeper who had partial hearing and amnesia and who knew rightly that one of your parents at least was Chinese or Korean or something. You'd sooner be bitten by a mad dog, and in Creggan, that was a frequent occurrence.

All the dogs there had surnames. Rex McLaughlin. Darkie Doherty. Rover Carlin. I didn't know any of the dogs in Westway by name, but none of them had ever heard of the theory that barking dogs don't bite. Even now, I have the recurring vision of a black-haired, white-fanged cross between an Alsatian and a donkey galloping towards my throat, growling something about 'limb from limb', while his owner ambled along complacently 50 yards behind him shouting, 'Don't worry he won't touch you!' He didn't. Just as the dog was about to prove his owner a liar, a blackthorn stick landed right on his nose and a hoarse voice urged him to 'gwaytaehellathat!' The owner raised an objection when he finally caught up and Hooky gave him the same directions with quite specific instructions as to how he should carry the dog in the process.

Hooky Moore must have been in his seventies then. Some nights he would stand under a lamppost in Melmore, a bottle of stout in one hand, a stick in the other and tell ghost stories to Michael Stewart, Willie Carlin and me. Hooky was a wonderful yarn-spinner, a real dramatist who could make your hair crawl across your scalp and make you wish your mother would call you in for bed. He once took half-an-hour to take the top off a Guinness bottle because he kept pausing for effect to stare you in the eye and feign speechless amazement that you'd never seen the woman with the rat's face at the top of Westway or to warn you never to go near the Doctor's Dam during a full moon. When your mother did finally call you, it was a mad dash down the dark street past scaly claws that shot out of the hedges and snatched at your ankles, scuttling along the pavement in your wake.

The Doctor's Dam was a waterlogged quarry on the other side of Creggan Heights and it was living with tadpoles, frogs, sticklebacks and newts. We called the sticklebacks 'spricks', and a red-breasted specimen was a prize possession. We caught them in jam jars lowered into the muddy water on pieces of string. Paddy Doherty had convinced me that newts were really baby crocodiles and that lurking down there in the murky, fathomless depths were huge, spring-jawed parent newts that would break the surface some day and devour the lot of us for harassing their offspring. I fished with taut nerves, coiled muscles and watchful eyes, amazed at the foolishness of others who dangled incautiously over the edge shouting raucous invitations to the monsters below.

At the end of the '50s, my father came home and never went back to England to work. He saved enough money to buy us a television and that seemed to mark the beginning of a new era. By the time I was 11, there were four children and the house was getting smaller. I remember sitting on our front steps one day talking in sombre tones to Martin McLaughlin and Michael Stewart. I told them we were moving to a new house with more bedrooms up in Foyle Hill Estate. I felt the need to say something tough and unsentimental because us Melmore men were like that. 'I'll be glad to get out of this dump,' I said. They both looked at me and I could see the hurt in their eyes and I was instantly flooded with shame. I wanted to tell them that I had just told the worst lie of my life, that I would leave here with misery and fear in my heart. But I couldn't. Because us Melmore men were like that.

It's too late to tell Michael. Martin, it was a lie.

DANA: FROM EUROVISION TO EURO MP

Creggan people have never been known to let a little hard work and adversity stand in the way of success. Take Rosemary Brown, for example, the girl from Greenwalk. As a child, she decided she wanted to be a singer, so with typical single-mindedness, she put away childish things to concentrate on her craft. And by the time she was just 17, Rosemary, as 'Dana', was the toast of Europe.

Dana's Eurovision success with *All Kinds of Everything* sparked possibly the greatest celebrations Creggan and Derry have ever seen. However, the years to come were no rose garden for the singing star. Problems with her health weakened her voice and forced her to quit touring. And at one stage, there were suggestions that Dana might never sing again. Nevertheless, showing marked resilience, she bounced back and in 1979 topped the Irish charts for an entire year with her anthem for the Pope, *Totus Tuus.*

After moving to Birmingham, Alabama in 1991 with her husband Damien Scallan and four children, Dana became a presenter on a Christian TV channel, where she became known for her strong views against divorce and abortion. And it was these opinions that prompted pro-life activists in Ireland to write to her in 1997, asking her to consider running for the Irish presidency. Dana demurred, but after the approach was reported in the Irish papers she received floods of letters begging her to reconsider. So she did.

At first, the Establishment, as exemplified by the likes of the *Irish Times*, was sceptical to the point of laughing out loud – particularly as getting nominated for the presidency is so difficult. To run for the top office, you must have the backing of at least 20 members of the Oireachtas, or win the support of four county councils.

Unabashed, Dana headed out to rural Ireland and garnered enough support for her 'Family Values' crusade to secure the nominations of five local authorities: Donegal, Longford, Wicklow, Tipperary and Kerry. Her honest, almost naive style, and strong Catholic ethos, appealed to many 'traditional' voters who had felt disenfranchised. And come the day of the count, the Derry girl came in third out of five candidates, winning 14% of the vote; her critics were silenced – if not dumbstruck.

Dana's support base in the west of Ireland had been particularly strong, so in 1999 she declared she would run for the European Parliament in the Connaught-Ulster constituency. Despite approaches from some of the larger parties, Dana again ran as an independent and against all the odds took the third seat.

Yet for the people of Creggan, it is perhaps as a singer that Rosemary Brown will be best remembered – the smiling young girl who gave the area great hope in one of its most troubled times. The following interview, published in Creggan's *Latest* magazine shortly after her Eurovision triumph, gives an insight into young Dana's determined and talented character – a character formed and moulded in Greenwalk, Creggan.

Q. Winning the Eurovision Song Contest was a remarkable achievement for one so young. Did you ever, prior to the contest, feel confident about winning?
A. I was determined not to think of it as a contest, just another performance. No. I didn't think of winning.

Q. Mary Hopkins appeared to be genuinely delighted at your success. Did you have an opportunity to talk to her after the result was announced?
A. During the time of the voting, Mary Hopkins told me that I was going to win and afterwards she was delighted.

Q. What were your feelings when you were alone with your thoughts afterwards?
A. When finally left alone, I was only fit for sleep. It is only now that I am able to give any thought to my success.

Q. Were you at any time frightened by your success?
A. Success itself is never frightening. I felt the burden of the responsibility afterwards, responsibility to and for a lot of other people – for the people whom I might influence and towards the people to whom I owe a great deal.

Q. Many journalists reported that you intended to give up your education entirely. Others stated that you were going to continue privately with your studies even to the point of engaging a tutor. Do you intend to pursue your studies?
A. Music to me is now a way of life. It isn't an academic study. The point has been reached where I can take examinations towards diplomas. It's not separated from my life, it's a part of it. Now as for English – I find enjoyment in it. No, they aren't really studies any more.

Q. You find enjoyment in English?
A. Well, as an extension of the previous answer, during the recording of my LP, I read most of a book. It was a fantastic relief. Recordings are long and during the intervals I can be completely absorbed in reading – in the last recording I was engrossed in a book while the arranger was practising with the band. I didn't even hear the call for the break and I just caught the red light.

Q. What book were you reading?
A. *Three Old Shades* by Georgette Heyer, a 17th-century historical romance. That really was relief.

Q. Would you consider studying for a different career later, possibly teaching?
A. I think the possibility is always there – if I failed in show business. But that isn't a good way to start out in show business.

Q. You seem to be unaffected by your staggering success. To what do you attribute your composure?
A. I've always tried hard to take things as they come. We have to learn to take the knocks. They help us to overcome.

Q. How do your parents feel about you as an international star?
A. They don't look on me as an international star. To them, I'm Rosemary.

Q. Do you think that your mother and father would like you to lead a normal life?
A. They would like me to lead a life where I would be happy and do the things I would be happiest at.

Q. You realise that a normal life is almost impossible for you in the near future. Does this bother you?
A. To me it's really an attitude of mind. This is my way of life. It feels normal.

Q. Most girls would like to change places with you. Is there anyone with whom you would like to change places?
A. Again, this depends on a person's attitude of mind. There's no point in wanting to be someone else, or wanting to be somewhere else.

Q. Do you, for instance, look forward to the things that most girls want – marriage and a family?
A. It crosses my mind from time to time, but I have made up my mind that I would be in no position to get married. Show business has not effected this.

Q. What other show business stars to you admire?
A. I usually try and judge stars on overall standard, but there are so many good all-rounders that it would be impossible to single any out.

Q. What about Tom Jones?
A. Very dynamic!

Q. Mr Johnson, your manager, has obviously played a large part in your success. How much of your success to you attribute to his guidance?
A. As far as my musical training background is concerned, the spadework must be attributed to my parents, and in some cases to my relatives, but the channelling of this base into a commercial commodity must be entirely attributed to Mr Johnson. He persisted with my image in the face of adverse pressure at the beginning of my career.

Q. He named you Dana, which in Gaelic means 'The Bold One'. Any significance?
A. Entirely untrue! Well, maybe sometimes; I think I'm just about normal.

Q. Being one of the young generation, which is labelled rebellious and permissive or inquiring and charitable, what is your impression of them?
A. I think that precisely the same labels could be applied to both youth and adult. The younger generation is not self-contained.

Q. And the Derry youth?
A. They're not a bad bunch at all.

Q. Derry people are extremely proud of you. How do you feel about them?
A. To me there's no town like Derry. I have great affection for Derry and the people in it. I'm very proud that I've been able to make them happy. It was very touching the way they showed their affection and pride in me.

Q. You have achieved what is probably the ambition of many singers. Is there anything further you wish to achieve?
A. I'd like to be able to reach the position where I was considered a good entertainer as opposed to singer.

Q. Finally, Rosemary, has your stardom affected in any way your religious belief?
A. It might be better to ask me – has my religious belief affected my stardom? But in answer to your question – why should it?

Front cover of *The Latest* which features Dana, 1970. (courtesy *The Latest*)

Above: Artistes who appeared on the *Night of Memories* fund raising concert for St Mary's Boys' Club at the Guildha December 1970. It includes leading Irish tenors, Josef Locke, Patrick O'Hagan and Michael O'Duffy, with Phil Coulter, Dana, Majella Brady, 'Wee Willie', Johnny McCauley and Peter 'Boy' Roddy. Also included are: stage manager Jimmy Duffy; accompanist James MacCafferty; promoter Eddie Davis; Fr Joe Carolan. (*Derry Journal*)
Below: Dana receives a copy of *The Latest*, the St Mary's Boys' Club magazine which was to feature her in the following edition, 1970. (courtesy *The Latest*)

No Business Like Show Business: The Kerr Dynasty

Creggan playwright Eddie Kerr would love to have been a bandsman like his father 'Every Voice'. But, with typical self-effacing humour, he tells you the talent wasn't there, so he took up the pen instead of the microphone. Kerr Senior, who died in June 2000, was perhaps best known as the vocalist with the Johnny Quigley All Stars. But his career as a singer and mimic also saw him work with top musicians from all over Ireland and Britain. And, in his heyday, he topped the bills all over England, leaving the likes of Englebert Humperdinck so far down the running order that he could have got a job on an optician's chart. Eddie Kerr:

> My Da was from the old Foxes Corner on Gallagher's Square in the Bogside. The legend is that back then every corner had their own singing group, and they would hold singing competitions like the 'Back to Backs' you get nowadays.

The elder Kerr went on to become a leading light in the various choirs springing up through the city, especially the Derry Dockers' Choir which was renowned throughout Ireland, before graduating in the '50s to become the front man with a dance band.

> In those days dance bands didn't just provide music. You would have had string sections and brass sections giving their own mini-performances. And you would have had drama skits on the stage as well. My father was very good at impersonations, and he developed a routine which included Al Jolson, Frank Sinatra, Satchmo, Sammy Davis Junior and Dean Martin. In the 1970s, he would sing *What a Wonderful World* using all the different voices – thus Eddie 'Every Voice' Kerr.

In the '50s, Derry was to foster a very thriving showband scene, much of which centred on the Kerr household in Melmore Gardens.

> 'Every Voice' Kerr became the lead singer with the All Stars and later with the Creggan band, The Emperors, who were managed by the late Gordon Sweeney from Dunree Gardens. The reason they were so popular is that they were very good, very tight. None of them that I knew of could read music. But after hearing a song two or three times they would have it learned. And the musicians competed all round Ireland with the very best. There was immense talent in Derry; if you wanted to put together a showband, you just went up to the back room of the Rocking Chair on a Thursday afternoon and you'd have no bother recruiting yourself a drummer, a guitarist or whatever.

In the early '60s, 'Every Voice' Kerr and Gay McIntyre took a band to England and cleaned up on the circuit there, playing before crowds of 6,000 at venues such as the Bull Ring in Birmingham. But the day-in-day-out slog of travelling and performing was wearing and the singer came back to Derry.

> The public has no idea just how difficult life was for the showbands. They thought nothing of driving to Cork, playing a concert and then driving home to get up and head off to Dublin at nine o'clock the following morning. And they'd be travelling in an old van sitting on speakers or instruments, often having no money in their pockets until they were paid. Effectively – and I mean no disrespect by this – they were musical navvies.

The austere life of the bandsmen was to become the subject of one of Eddie Kerr's earliest plays, *One Night Stands.* The drama looks at how the musicians were exploited by a small group of ballroom owners who held a monopoly on the showband scene in Ireland.

> The owners were interested only in profit; they maintained their position by excluding groups who wouldn't conform to what they wanted or agree to their pay structures. They wouldn't pay for vans or travel, nor indeed instruments. You got a flat rate from the cartel regardless of whether the venue held 1,000 or 5,000 punters. And the owners particularly disliked the way Derry bands would challenge them. The Derry bands were more popular, and more articulate, and wouldn't bow to the cartel.

The author researched *One Night Stands* by taping interviews with former bandsmen, but found he could only use about five per cent of what he recorded.

> Suffice to say that the younger generation did not invent either drugs or sex. Most of what I discovered – while very entertaining stuff – was very libellous or unfit for public consumption!

The father's genius for music may have passed the son by, but breeding will out, and Kerr the Elder's talent for entertaining was to be passed on through the genes. What the father could do with the spoken word, the son found he could do with the written one. Eddie started writing at the time of the Hunger Strikes when he scripted a pub theatre piece for *Doire Eile* on the H-Block campaign. His first full-length drama, *Beatin' Docket,* was produced in 1984, and to date Kerr has completed 13 works – most of which have played to packed houses in Ireland and two of which have been resounding successes in the US as well. His speciality is black comedy – yet he doesn't shy away from serious issues like child abuse, alcoholism or domestic violence.

> It's sometimes difficult when you're writing and living in your own community. You have an audience that you want to bring with you – but if you push too much too soon, you damage the journey.

Eddie's day job – project manager in charge of the children's Artemis Programme at the Verbal Arts Centre – is ideal in that it affords him the opportunity both to develop new talent and nurture his own. He also travels to Louisville to host drama projects at the University of Kentucky every year. And he's never afraid to branch out into a new genre.

> I do some stand-up performance poetry when I'm in the States and I find it a useful sideline when I'm asked to speak to lecture groups or whatever. You can't exactly recite a play. I would be dicing with artistic death if I were to do it. So I've developed what amounts to a one-man show.

Success is unlikely ever to get the better of the playwright, however, thanks to his grounded Creggan upbringing. Though that's not to say that hard work doesn't bring its rewards.

> Last year, when we took *Packie's Wake* to New York, Kevin McCallion from Inishowen Gardens had the lead part. The audience loved it. And on the opening night they gave us a standing ovation – whooped it up big time. The reaction was terrific – beyond what you could have dreamed. As we were coming off the stage, Kevin grabbed me and said, 'Jesus, Eddie, this isn't bad for two Creggan men.' I'm very proud to be from Creggan. If people see that I can establish myself as a writer – someone they know, from the same estate – then they know they can do it too.

A One-Off Comedian: Tommy Kelly

Tommy Kelly at BSR reunion, mid-'70s. (Dan O'Donnell)

You can count on one hand the number of radio or TV interviews that are truly memorable: Jeremy Paxman's merciless hounding of Michael Howard when he asked him the same question 13 times; Terry Wogan's attempts to hush up George Best after the soccer star got loose in the 'Green Room' a bit too early; and maybe Michael Parkinson's first tête-à-tête with Billy Connolly.

But Tommy Kelly's interviews on the Gerry Anderson Show on BBC Radio Ulster in the late '80s and early '90s were always special. And the higher placed the target, the sharper his arrows would gleam.

John Cole, the BBC's political editor in London, earned his corn interrogating world leaders about the weightiest matters of state. But when Tommy got him on, his first questions were: 'D-do you ever get recognised in chip shops? And d-do you get into the pictures for free?' Later he was to ask him, deadpan: 'H-how do you remember the news?' Cole lapped it up, but the soft hissing of punctured egos was to become a standard feature of Anderson's Friday morning slot.

John Hume was another guest. Kelly was devoted to the MP as he'd helped swing him his first house in Creggan, but there was no resisting the opportunity to take the hand.

> T-tell me, Mr Hume, you know the w-way there's a European b-butter mountain?
> *I do, Tommy,* answered the SDLP leader.
> And you know the w-way there's a European b-beef mountain? continued Kelly.
> *A-ha,* said the MEP cautiously.
> And you know the w-way there's a European w-wine lake? said Kelly again.
> *I do, Tommy,* came the reply.
> Well, I wonder could you tell me where it is . . .

The great and the good gamely queued up to take the stand. Werner Hoybek was another victim. And singer Bridie Gallagher was flummoxed when Kelly wanted to know if she had a 'book in the credit union'. When he wasn't interviewing, Kelly had an 'Ask the Doctor' advice slot, which, you can imagine, was about as far from medicine as it was from sanity. He also presented a 'Cookery Corner' and regularly co-hosted 'Complaints Days'. The radio presenter Sean Coyle is credited with discovering Kelly – though it took considerable coaxing before Gerry Anderson agreed to give the comic a hearing.

> I was told about this extremely funny man with a stutter who was MC at Mailey's Bar for the Back to Backs [team talent competitions] on Wednesday nights. I went to hear him and thought immediately he was a must for Anderson. But when I told Gerry about him, he was a bit worried that people might think we were making fun of Tommy's stutter. But I eventually got Gerry to go down to Mailey's, and within five minutes, he said we had to have him on. He was very taken by the fact that Tommy never ever stuttered on the punchline of a joke.

The gravel-voiced Kelly may have modestly thought his humour would only carry in Creggan and the Bogside, but his droll wit travelled across the country. Sean Coyle:

> The show did a bus tour of the North, and everywhere we went, Tommy was recognised. We stopped one day so Tommy could visit the little boys' room at a pub in, I think it was, Broughshane. But after about half-an-hour there was no sign of him. The boys in the bar had spotted him and started buying him whiskey. Anderson and myself had to drag him out. Another time, we stopped at a hotel in Enniskillen where there was a wedding function going on. It was pretty noisy, with lots of people about – and I was wondering would Anderson be recognised. But when Tommy went up to the bar for his round and spoke a couple of words, the whole place went silent. Everyone in there knew his voice. All sorts of people then started coming up to him saying: 'You're Tommy Kelly off the radio.'

During that same trip to Fermanagh, the show visited a mansion house on an island in the middle of a lake. Sean Coyle:

> The lord of the manor offered us a drink and told Tommy to say 'when'. Tommy's eyes lit up as the host kept pouring the whiskey slowly into the big tumbler until it reached the very brim. Tommy never stopped him at all – and then explained: 'It's the stutter, you know.'

In previous lives, Kelly had worked as a merchant seaman and in the BSR factory on Bligh's Lane. He had also been an ice-cream man and was once accused by the police of playing his jingle loudly to warn the IRA when a raid was imminent.

The jingle was indeed a useful weapon. Legend has it that when Kelly was nearly out of ice cream, he would find a house where he knew there were about 15 youngsters inside, park his van and play the tune endlessly until some poor harassed parent came out to empty his stock.

Unfortunately, Kelly didn't enjoy good health and died at the relatively early age of 64. He fell asleep watching a Sunday football match on television and never woke up. Sean Coyle:

You often hear it said, but in Tommy's case it was true: he went before his time. Gerry [Anderson] was devastated. He had to go on air the following day and tell the public; it was very hard. The first Friday after that was terrible – but we decided never to try and repeat the act; Tommy was a one-off. He would have been great on the box had he lived. He was a very bright man. The punters absolutely loved him. They knew there was a real kindness there underneath the jokes.

The Undertones' Debt to Creggan

'There was music there in the Derry air' wrote the poet, who could well have been standing outside the Boys' Club where Mickey Bradley and his fellow Undertones played their first concert. The rock band – Derry's most popular ever, indeed arguably the North's most successful as well – went on to produce Top 20 anthems such as Teenage Kicks, Jimmy Jimmy *and* My Perfect Cousin. *But as Mickey explains here, none of this would have been possible without the help of the people of Creggan.*

If we were loose with our geographical boundaries and include the bottom of Beechwood Avenue as part of Creggan, you could safely say that The Undertones were a Creggan band. I wouldn't be so careless though, so we'll leave O'Neill's house, and what went on there, for another day (when is the next Lone Moor celebration?).

But The Undertones' story is certainly incomplete without a mention of at least three institutions in Creggan. I'll start with St Peter's School at the top of Southway. Don't tell me it's Foyle Hill and not Creggan – I refuse to draw such distinctions. St Peter's was where I went to school, *and* Feargal Sharkey, our singer, *and* Billy Doherty, our drummer. I learned guitar at the school, under the (after-school) tuition of Paul Elder – he also gave lessons to John O'Neill (the one who wrote *Teenage Kicks*, not the one who played football). The odd thing is we never played at St Peter's. In fact, the first big stage we appeared on was in St Joseph's School in Westway at the invitation of Pat McNabb, a teacher at 'St Joe's', who organised a variety show in March 1976.

The Undertones played six songs, but not under that name. For some reason, off the top of his head, Feargal called us 'The Hot Rods', as in Eddie and the Hot Rods. We could have been done for breach of copyright, but we weren't getting paid anyway so . . . A couple of years later, just after appearing on *Top of the Pops*, we made a return to St Joseph's, this time under our right name. That first appearance was only a few weeks after our real first-ever performance. That was also in Creggan, at the scout hall at the bottom of Creggan Broadway. In fact, it's probably better known as the Boys' Club, but by 1976, the local Catholic Boy Scouts of Ireland (CBSI) unit, under Mickey Fahey, had taken over the hall. Feargal was some sort of scout leader with the unit, and he managed to get us permission to rehearse in the old building, which used to belong to the Parochial House just further along Beechwood Avenue (anyone not familiar with the geography of Lower Creggan will probably have fallen asleep by this stage). And he also managed to get us an engagement, as they were called. Not a 'gig', never a 'gig'.

On February the something (I forget the exact date) 1976, the five of us got up on a stage, which was all of ten-inches-high, and played cover versions of songs by The Rolling Stones, Dr Feelgood, Eric Clapton and Them. The audience loved us; their average age was nine.

I was born on 13 August 1959, ten years and five days after the Bradleys moved into the new house in Creggan Broadway. I was born at home, number 36, weighed 12 pounds, and was christened next day at St Mary's Church at the top of the street. I was so big the priest thought I was a couple-of-months-old and questioned my aunt

Kathleen about why this baby was only now being brought for christening. Well, that's the story I was always told. I wasn't the only one in the street born that day. The Coyles, across the street at number 47, had a baby girl, Marie, born that morning. But the late '50s was a time for baby boys. A year-or-so earlier, Mrs McIntyre, down the street, had a son, Terry, about the same time, and Mrs Carlyle, next door to the Coyles, had twin boys, Trevor and Kevin. After I was born, Mrs Travers, around the corner, had Thomas, and right next door to us, Mrs Mellon had a son with curly red hair, Tony. Creggan was enjoying a baby boom, which began in the '40s and lasted a couple of decades, and that meant no shortage of friends to play football with, to fight with, to race with, to play Japs and Americans with, to build trolleys with and to simply hang around with.

At the risk of starting arguments, I have to say that Creggan Broadway was the best street in the whole estate. Not just because of the families who lived there (and still do), but because of the great space. Broadway is . . . broad. Not the roadway, as Creggan bus drivers will tell you as they manoeuvre past parked cars, but I suppose what you could call the pedestrian area. Outside our house, there was a footpath we raced on, ran trolleys on, played marbles on; then a grassed area we played football on; then a step down to another footpath, too near the road to play on, and we didn't need the space anyway. Across the street from us, Creggan Broadway – note the use of the correct full title – looped into an area we called 'The Green'.

The Green was where the bigger matches happened. On occasion, usually a Sunday evening, men would play football as well – when I say men, it's possible they were only in their late teens – but I remember them in their white shirts and good trousers; bigger, faster and stronger, but still letting us wee boys get a run at the ball. The black tar lines between the concrete slabs on the road around The Green meant it was the best place to play a 'tipture'. I've never seen that word written before so the spelling is irrelevant. I haven't room to explain all the rules, but it's a game for two to four players which could be described as a cross between football and tennis. The fact that it could be played on the road gives you an idea of how many people in Broadway had cars in the 1960s. We didn't need them as the Creggan bus was always a double decker, and there was a separate Westway service which came up and down our street. Today there's only a small minibus on the Creggan route, but I remember when the bus stop was around the corner from Magazine Gate, the queue would sometimes stretch right up Magazine Street, almost to Castle Street.

> Joke: What does CBS stand for?
> Creggan Bus Stop.

It wasn't even funny when I was nine and a pupil at the Christian Brothers' School – but how many other bus stops have you heard mentioned in a joke?

It was a Creggan bus driver, driving one of the new single deckers, with doors at the side as well as the front, who told people at the top of Broadway about the rioting which had broken out in William Street in August 1969. After that, the Creggan bus was sometimes an endangered species.

For the first couple of years of the *Troubles*, from 1968 until 1970, I don't recall much of any consequence happening in Creggan – I don't even remember much about the explosion in McCool's house in Dunree Gardens. Creggan seemed to be relatively unaffected by rioting or bombs for those first few years, especially compared to down-the-town. The first time I smelled CS gas was 1971, when the riots at Essex factory were happening; Essex was visible from Demesne Gardens, a street off Broadway. I sneaked down and stood with the crowd of spectators – there was always a crowd of spectators – when a gas canister landed not too far away. Pandemonium. As far as I was concerned anyway. I ran all the way home – just like Brendan Bowyer – only I was coughing and spluttering and thinking I was going to be sick.

It was also in 1971 that night-time raids on Creggan took place with Saracens making forays through the barricades in the early hours of the morning. As Creggan Broadway is one of the main streets into the estate, more often than not they parked outside our house. You couldn't exactly go back to sleep, with rubber bullets being fired and stones hitting shields, armour plating and lampposts. So while my mother went round the house tidying up (either to make the place more respectable if we were searched, or more likely, to give herself something to do while she worried, instead of sitting down and worrying), the rest of us tried to sneak a look out of the window to see what was happening. It would all be over with the Saracens pulling out before dawn, four o'clock in the summer, eight o'clock in the winter.

Someone once described summer as the season of long riots and short raids. I'm not sure if that phrase rang true for the summer of Operation Motorman when the Saracens came back and stayed. Before Motorman, the guns at the top of the street were held by the Provos at their daily checkpoint; after Motorman they were held by soldiers from the Coldstream Guards. Some child psychologists will probably disagree, but seeing all that military hardware, from whatever side, seemed to be as much entertainment for a 12-year-old in 1972 as playing football, or running around on trolleys, or watching *Animal Magic* on television. Of course, not everyone was as unaffected or uninvolved as I was, but I think that if you asked Tony, or Terry, or Kevin, or Trevor, or Thomas, they might just say the same.

The Undertones, circa 1977 in Creggan Street, just before redevelopment. (courtesy Paddy Simms)

The Traditional Heartbeat: Comhaltas an Chreagáin

Recent times have seen a massive revival in Irish music and dancing in Derry. And nowhere is this more apparent than in Creggan where Comhaltas is now running traditional classes, concerts and festivals. But as Vincent Strunks explains here, not only are the Creggan musicians keen to promote their culture at home in Derry, but they've also been taking it to every far flung corner of Europe.

Comhaltas an Chreagáin is a local branch of Comhaltas Ceoltóirí Éireann, an organisation formed in 1951. It is Ireland's premier cultural movement and its aim is to protect and promote our national heritage. Comhaltas an Chreagáin formed in 1986 to become the third branch of Comhaltas in Derry.

Traditional music and language classes first began in St Peter's School and then moved to the library in Central Drive. Ceilidhe and set dancing classes were also held in the 'Corned Beef Tin' for a number of years under the supervision of Frankie Roddy, but sadly died out a few years ago. Within a few years, in 1991, we moved to our own offices in Cromore and the classes are still running very successfully.

Since the classes started, great strides have been made in the progress of many of the young people coming through them. Over this time, children who have come through the classes have gone on to win numerous championships, Feiseanna Dhoire Cholmcille, County and Ulster Fleadhanna, and indeed Fleadh Ceol na hÉireann.

At the moment, those who have come up through our classes from a young age are now doing the tutoring. We feel that this is a very important aspect of our work; not only have we helped produce good musicians, but teachers as well. However, we can only play a small part in the teaching of the music. The main effort comes from the dedication of those learning and their parents who ensure that they practise at home. Other than music, classes include Celtic art and drama, with local schools, and participation in many local events and festivals.

One of the main features in our short history has been the link with Tory Island. Our first trip was in 1987 and they have continued over the years to this day. These visits led to a very special friendship between ourselves and the people of Tory, with many exchange visits taking place. Many famous people have visited Derry in recent years, but Creggan can boast that it was the first to play host to a King – Patsy Dan MacRuaraí, King of Tory.

During the past number of years, members have played in concerts in Wales and appeared in international festivals in Poland and Belgium; also included were trips to numerous fleadhanna throughout the country. Some of our young musicians played for President Mary McAleese during her visit to the Creggan Parents and Toddlers Association. The branch also hosted the County Fleadh in 1996, the first time it was ever held in a housing estate rather than a town or village.

Our most recent trip was to Islay in the Scottish Hebrides. This was to take part in a commemoration to mark the loss of over 200 people on the *Exmouth* who left Derry

Beginners' fiddle class with tutor Kathleen McGuinness, 2000. (courtesy Vincent Strunks)

Quay for Canada in 1847 and perished on the Islay coast. The Irish Consul General, local MSPs, MEPs and many local dignitaries attended the ceremony.

We would consider that our musical tradition and language is a link between the present day and those who have protected and fostered our national culture in generations gone by. It is therefore our duty to pass the heritage on to our children and to secure it for future generations. We feel that Comhaltas an Chreagáin has both the will, commitment and the ability to ensure that our heritage will flourish within the community and secure the link between our future generations and ourselves.

Le blianta anuas chluin muid ó na meáin chumársaide tuairsí ar náire Éireannaigh as ár nÉireannachas. Ach, fágfaidh muid fáthanna na dtuairsc sin ag na polaiteoirí. Bíodh sin mar atá, tá muidne i gComhaltas an Chreagáin den bharúil gur cearta é ag achan duine bheith bródúil as ár ndúchas chultúrtha agus go bhfuil traidisiún beo luachmhar againn i gceol, amhráin, rince agus teanga againn.

Ar an bharr sin, measann muid gurb iad ár dtraidisiún cheoil is teanga an ceangal idir sinne inniu agus iad súid a chuaigh romhainn.

Mar sin de, tá sé orainn uilig an oireacht a chóthú agus a thabhairt ar aghaidh dár bpáistí agus na glúnta atá le theacht.

AN ENDURING COMMITMENT

Bronagh Gallagher
(courtesy Bert Gallagher)

It takes a special talent to rise from doing a 'turn' on Creggan Broadway to performing a starring role on Broadway, New York. But Bronagh Gallagher, who began treading the boards at St Mary's Secondary School in the 1980s, is one of the few to make the transition and is now one of Ireland's leading young actresses. Bronagh, whose big break was in The Commitments *in 1991, went on to appear in the Oscar-winning thriller* Pulp Fiction *before landing roles in* Mary Reilly, Star Wars – The Phantom Menace *and most recently* The Most Fertile Man In Ireland. *But to this day, as she reveals here, Bronagh remains fiercely proud of her Derry roots.*

I have no hesitation in acknowledging that my time in Creggan helped motivate me to achieve my goals. When we are properly prepared for a job, the job is usually well done. When we have the right tools, be it education, support of loved ones, physical stamina or experience, we feel more confident to enter into it and tackle the job. This is how I feel about growing up in Creggan (and the Bogside) in Derry.

Many events and people impacted on my life: my family home; my education at St Mary's School; my involvement with the local dramatic productions in Creggan with Cora King and Tony O'Donnell. I had a growing awareness of the city's political, social and economic situation, and of the people's hopes for the future. My upbringing left me with a deep-rooted awareness of what life was like for people prior to being housed in Creggan – the continuous struggle to preserve their pride and dignity throughout all the hardship. This sense of reality is one I have always carried with me.

My dreams and ambitions were of becoming an actress and I received great support from my parents and the teachers at St Mary's. However, while I received such great support there was always the constant reminder that while my dreams were not impossible to achieve, things may not work out that way. My mother Maeve and my father Bert and the teachers, Mrs Marguerite Martin, Cora King, Mrs Sarah Kelly, Miss Hunt and Miss Keegan – all the teachers in fact – constantly pressed the point that my education was the greatest key of all, and how right they were.

Until that point in my life, I had no real interest in academia. I saw no reason to spend all my time learning about subjects I had no passion for. But after much encouragement, and not a few red faces, I came to realise that education was fundamental to whatever path I intended to pursue in life and was the foundation stone to acting, films and adulthood itself. When I began to concentrate more on my studies, I received fantastic emotional and financial support from my parents and my school for my acting. My grandparents Ruby and Jackie Drury from Broadway in Creggan, and Lily and Jackie Gallagher from Cable Street, were also so loving, strong and supportive.

My Granda Drury is a bit of an actor himself, having been involved in many productions in Derry in the '50s and '60s, and he was always very encouraging towards me. We still get up and do a 'wee turn' together at Christmas.

Wherever I go in the world I am always so proud to say where I am from and this pride is re-established every time I return home to Derry and visit St Mary's or the Ráth Mór Centre. At St Mary's I see how people have built up a unique facility that not only assures excellent educational standards, but one which also enjoys the full support of the community. The Ráth Mór Centre, meanwhile, has become such a focal point for Creggan people, a community-owned enterprise which provides employment and a social nucleus to the area. Even its design, that of the ancient Irish fort (Ráth) symbolises the strength and stamina of local people.

My experiences of Creggan have provided me with more than just memories. They have given me an understanding of reality which I shall continue to teach and carry with me through my own work and my own life.

CHAPTER 5

Sport

It's hard to imagine how an area so bereft of sporting facilities could produce such a wealth of athletic talent. But the narrow streets of Creggan sired a host of first-class footballers, a European boxing champion, an Olympic swimmer – not to mention the first Derryman to conquer the English Channel.

Amenities have improved significantly in the past few years with the development of the synthetic pitches, the Seán Dolan's GAA Complex and the Tar Abhaile fitness centre. That these facilities are there at all is down to hard work and more than a little craft from the locals. Back in the early '70s, for example, the area in front of the shops at Central Drive was no more than a grassy plain. Then one day a certain Northern Ireland soccer international borrowed a set of goal posts from a nearby pitch, dug four holes in the ground, and the legend of Bishop's Field was born. Wisely, however, for the first year or so, Tony O' would take the nets home and keep them in his back garden in case anyone would attempt to borrow them back. But more of this anon.

Throughout the area's development, sport was a high priority thanks largely to the dedication of the volunteers who ran the Boys' and Girls' Clubs. And it is with St Mary's Boys' Club that we start our look at Creggan's sporting successes.

From Little Acorns: St Mary's Boys' Club

The completion of the early phase of building development in Creggan left vacant the site offices which were situated at the top of Beechwood Avenue. Fr Des Mullan soon identified the premises as a potential centre for youth facilities in the new estate. As it turned out, it was to become, for a time, not only a boys' club, but also the hub of social life in Creggan. It was a sign of the times that provision for girls was not considered in the early days of planning activities for the youth of Creggan.

One of the first volunteers to give his time to preparing the newly acquired facility was Willie O'Connell. Willie was first recruited to youth work when Fr Des approached him at a concert in St Columb's Hall and invited him to become involved in running St Eugene's Boys' Club. The new club in Creggan was to be a branch of St Eugene's and it was as a member of this club that he found himself on the roof of the former site offices. Willie has fond memories of viewing a film taken by Fr Des of himself and AN Other tarring the same roof. Showings gave rise to much hilarity when the similarity to Laurel and Hardy of the two figures in outsize overalls was spotted. Grandiose titles were not to be accorded. Even in July 1951, when the premises were used for a meeting to hold draws for the semifinal of the Colmcille Cup, the venue was advertised as 'The Creggan Hut'.

In October, direct involvement of the members was assured when a meeting in the Boys' Club Hut at Creggan, presided over by spiritual director Fr Mullan, appointed the following boys' committee: chairman, William Kyle, 9 Donegal Street; vice-chairman, Michael Ennis, Creggan Terrace; secretary, Edmund O'Donnell, Leenan Gardens; and committee members Noel Barr, Alex McLaughlin, Alphonsus Campbell, James Shields and Patrick Loughrey.

By 14 November 1951, progress was such that the *Derry Journal*, under the heading *St Eugene's Boys' Club, Creggan Section*, was able to report that football activities were in full swing and that training was being taken by Jimmy McCann. Under his guidance, the newly formed Creggan team had, the previous Saturday, made its debut in the St Eugene's Boys' Club league, where it had earned a draw against the much-fancied Glen Stars. A billiards handicap was also under way. The club, however, did not restrict itself to sporting activities. William Bryson was instructor for the harmonica band, and Phil McCauley conductor of the choir. A precedent, which boded well for the club's development as a centre with wider social interests, was the formation of an energetic ladies committee.

The final seal of approval came when Bishop Farren came to bless the club's premises at the end of November. The accompanying *Derry Journal* report, that 'Fr Mullan showed film footage of last year's Boys' Club activities,' is a reminder that he was an enthusiastic recorder of club events. One can only hope that some of this valuable record survives.

The end of an era for one football venue and the shift of Boys' Club football activities to a Creggan base were heralded in club notes of 28 November 1952: 'With the removal of club property on Saturday last, St Eugene's reluctantly said goodbye to

Rock Park and brought to an end a seven-year connection with this well-known field.' The notes then begin to refer to Bishop's Field as the club pitch. Concerts also begin to feature in reports. In November 1951: 'After only three weeks training, Willie Bryson's troupe acquitted themselves extremely well at the club concert on Sunday night', and by March 1952 a further concert featured the choir and the harmonica band. A show in April included guest artistes William Traynor, Myra Brady, the Andre Sisters, Thomas McDermott, June McMonagle, Ann O'Hara and B McGuigan. The following October, a new management committee was elected. Gus Orr was to become the club's first full-time leader, and the first to hold such a post in Derry.

The first step towards the emergence of the Creggan club as a separate entity occurred in November with the announcement:

> The Catholic Boys' Clubs in Derry City have formed an Inter-Boys' Club Football League. The competition will consist of five clubs: Waterside, Long Tower, St Eugene's, Coleraine and the Creggan section of St Eugene's Boys' Club, who will enter as Don Bosco's.

As it turned out, Don Bosco's were to be first winners of this competition when, in the Inter-Boys' Club League decider, they defeated Long Tower 3-1 to lift the Bishop's Shield. The club's winning ways continued; in July 1953 they won the Father Browne Shield.

The public declaration of the club's emergence as an entity separate from St Eugene's appears in the *Derry Journal* of 16 November 1955 in the section *Around the Boys' Clubs*. Obviously, a new name had already been chosen, as the following report comes under the heading *St Mary's*:

> For numerous reasons, 68 of which are apparently known to St Eugene's Boys' Club, Orchard Street, the management committee has changed the name of the club. This step has been long overdue.

It is not surprising, given their track record and the autonomy they already operated under, that independence would be sought. The cryptic reason given needs explaining, however. Brendan O'Donnell, a long-time member and youth worker in Creggan, remembers the occasion when a row ensued involving the lodgement of £68 in the 'wrong' bank account. The row itself was not serious, but simply precipitated the inevitable move towards autonomy. St Mary's Boys' Club was under way.

Until the name change, the club had sponsored a wide range of activities. A comprehensive list of sports had been catered for. These included football, boxing, table tennis, gymnastics and athletics. The first annual road race, for the Father Mullan Cup, had taken place in April 1952. The three-mile circuit, which began at Club headquarters, took in Westway, Central Drive, Fanad Drive and Beechwood Crescent. A greater emphasis on boxing is suggested in the decision, taken at the meeting which confirmed the name change, to appoint a boxing coach.

Other activities, more social than sporting, had included joinery and leathercraft

Presentation of Boys' Club trophies with Dr Farren, Fr Mullan, members of committee and representatives of successful clubs, 1950s. (*Derry Journal*)

classes, chess, drama, debates and concert entertainment. July 1955 saw the first successful summer camp at Shrove. However, despite the new name, emphasis was to be on continuity rather than change as the club continued to cater for the community in Creggan.

Roger O'Doherty has treasured memories, first as a volunteer, then part-time paid worker and finally full-time paid club leader when he succeeded Gus Orr. The post received 75% funding from the Ministry of Education, the rest being raised by the club. During his time there the outhouses of the Morgan house had been commissioned to accommodate the growing needs of the club. The house itself served as the parochial house. The harmonica band still flourished, practising three times a week under tutor Willie Bryson who also ran the drama club. This club was very active, travelling to give performances and compete in youth club competitions run by the Northern Ireland Association of Boys' Clubs. Occasionally, concerts were organised where Waterside, St Eugene's, Long Tower and St Mary's clubs made contributions. The Hayseeds were prominent in these shows and in the regular Sunday night concerts in The Hut. Originally specialising in cowboy songs, or what would now be called country music, this very popular and talented group went on to win a skiffle contest. Skiffle was a re-invention of American folk music, popularised in the UK by Lonnie Donegan among others, where music was made using the humblest of instruments. Of the nine-man Hayseeds, four played guitar, one supplied rhythm on washboard and one played bass using the standard bass for skiffle, namely tea chest with broom handle and single string. A feature of their performance was their vocal arrangements. Although their formation owed a lot to country and skiffle music, the range of individual talents, within the group, allowed them to bring a varied musical programme to audiences in Creggan and beyond. Some went on to have careers in music. Members included Jim Toland, James McMonagle, Chuck McGuigan, Gerry Doherty, Victor O'Hagan, Sean Villa, Gerry Hegarty, the late Bosco Hegarty and Sean Coyle. They and other local talent continued to perform at the regular Sunday night concerts.

Other interests were also catered for. Wednesday nights were reserved for old-time dancing to Charlie Kelly's Ceilidhe band and weekends were for film-going. The Saturday matinees were packed regularly, as were the two showings on Sunday. Projectionist Chris O'Neill gave sterling service. The Christmas Funfair brightened the festive season for many and a few went home with the bonus of Christmas fare won at various draws on the rickety wheel. Comprehensive community involvement was assured with the decision in December 1955 to organise stalls, each the responsibility of a different Creggan street.

Roger O'Doherty recalls the first annual summer camp in Shrove. Although it set a precedent for many more successful camps, this first one was overshadowed by tragedy with the accidental death of Willie Kerr. A memorial Mass was said at Shrove the following year. Camps at Leenan, Rathmullan, Portnablagh and Portmarnock were to follow in later years. Up to 100 members were catered for in any year. Under-12s, under-14s and under-18s were allocated a fortnight each. The marquee was the camp headquarters. Morning and evening prayers were said here and Masses were offered on Sundays. Meals were cooked and served under the supervision of Bosco Hegarty and

Above: 'Wee Willie' performing at a Halloween party in the Boys' Club, October 1964. (*Derry Journal*)
Below: St Mary's Boys' Club Ceilidhe Band, Feis winners, 1955. (*Derry Journal*)

Boys' Club ballroom dance team, December 1961. (*Derry Journal*)

Clyde Sturgess and shows were put on to entertain local people, all under canvas.

During this era, football was easily the most popular activity. Competitions organised by the club drew many entries and spectators. During the summer, under-12, under-14, under-18 and open competitions attracted entries from 50 teams. Teams in the open competitions were sure to have a number of senior players in their ranks. Four matches might take place on summer weekdays and six on a Sunday, when they could start at 2.30pm and carry on until darkness fell. Initially, games were played in Thompson's field, later the site of St Joseph's School, and then moved to the chapel field, where St Mary's Church and School were eventually built. Their popularity can be gauged by the collections taken up during competitions when the day's take could reach £100.

While the committee had put tremendous energy into organising the orthodox, they were not afraid to embark on the unusual. They had planned a day when a variety of sports, competitions and entertainments could be catered for and were seeking a suitable name. Club leader Roger O'Doherty, with others, was mulling over the problem when Dick Gillespie supplied the apt title, which suited the terrain as much as the content, when he suggested 'The Highland Games'. Judging by the nature of events, the emphasis was on fun rather than serious competition. Duck races, balloon-blowing competitions, and tug-of-war were among the attractions. Gaelic football provided more serious competition.

During Roger's time as leader with St Mary's, the club flourished. Hard work and enthusiastic co-operation between youth leader, adult management team and a boys'

The Hayseeds skiffle group which won the Skiffle Championship at the Guildhall, December 1957. (*Derry Journal*)

committee had ensured this. The boys' committee had members who, although continuing with traditional activities, were to oversee a new era of development for the club. It included Brian Ball, Jackie Deeny, Phil McCallion, Kevin O'Donnell, Kevin McCaul and Brendan O'Donnell. After Roger's departure, the club was managed and run exclusively by voluntary workers. The Creggan club had been well served by its spiritual directors. In the early days they included Fr Des Mullan, Fr George McLaughlin and Fr Anthony Mulvey. It is generally agreed that the combined talents and energy of Fr Joe Carolan and Kevin McCaul, eventual full-time successor to Roger, ushered in a new dynamic. By the mid-'60s the club could take stock of a flourishing organisation. Change was also under way.

Under the title *St Mary's Boys' Club Keeps Abreast Of Modern Trends*, the *Derry Journal* of 17 September 1967 carried a report which paid tribute to past and current developments. It also promised improvement of physical facilities and administrative reorganisation. It began:

> Founded just 16 years ago to cater for the needs of the then developing Creggan Estate, St Mary's Boys' Club, an organisation which has grown from modest beginnings in pace with the area it was designed to serve, can now rightly claim to be one of the big success stories of the Boys' Club movement in Derry City.
>
> The work that the club has done in the intervening years has more than justified the efforts entailed in its establishment. Under the guidance of Spiritual Director Rev Joseph Carolan, a 12-man management

> committee and a senior boys' committee, all of whom have given voluntarily of their services, the club has provided a wide variety of activities for boys of the estate such as football, boxing, physical training, snooker, table tennis, darts, discussion groups, debates, weightlifting, swimming and an annual camp.
>
> Up to the commencement of the current season, the club catered for boys in the 12-20 age groups and had a total membership of 150 with an annual nightly attendance of 100. All in all, a pretty progressive establishment by any standards. While satisfaction with previous accomplishments is evident, eagerness to modernise and confidence in the most recent measures becomes apparent. But the Spiritual Director and management committee still felt that not enough was being done to provide a comprehensive organisation fully geared to the needs of a changing society. Plans were laid and, after extensive research and debate, a campaign was launched at the start of the present season aimed at rejuvenating the club and extending its scope to include all the boys in the district in the 5-21 age groups, numbering about 600 in all. The campaign, designed to keep the club abreast of the modern trend, took the form of a drive to give the club a new look.

Under the heading *First Phase*, the report of a new function for the old 'Hut' appears, which probably represents the club's response to competition from similar attractions:

> Phase one of the plan entailed the improvement of the physical facilities afforded by the present structure and here the committee decided to extend the existing canteen facilities incorporating the main body of the central hall. This portion of the building was completely redecorated, new fluorescent ceiling and wall lighting was installed. Cafeteria-type tables and easy chairs were acquired and the end product was a spacious, well-lighted and tastefully decorated canteen/coffee bar. Here, at nominal charges, club members can entertain their friends, both male and female, to tea coffee, sandwiches, minerals, hamburgers or hot dogs served by an efficient ladies' committee working from a superbly fitted modern kitchen.
>
> Entertainment-wise, the coffee bar is very much 'with it', boasting a resident disc jockey who nightly plays record requests. There is also a bandstand complete with microphone and amplification equipment to encourage club members, whether individuals or groups, to try their hand as amateur entertainers.
>
> To say that the innovation has been a success would be something of an understatement. It has surpassed the expectations of the administrators with an average nightly attendance of 300, the majority of whom also avail themselves of the club's other activities.

Restructuring of management is described under the heading *Revolutionary Change*:

> Phase two of the campaign involved a revolutionary change on the administrative side of affairs and the removal of entrance fees and weekly subscriptions. In the past, boys paid a subscription of between 15/- and 30/- annually, according to their age. Now every boy who is a member of the confraternity can take part in the club free of charge.
>
> Phase three in the process of re-organisation also involved administration. The total membership was divided into four sections of about 150 boys in each for the purpose of engendering the competitive aspect in sport. Each section runs four football teams, four table tennis teams, four snooker teams and four darts teams. The top teams in each sport go forward to meet their counterparts from the other sections in semifinals and finals.

Sporting activities seem to have dominated, judging by the rest of the report:

> The one activity which will undoubtedly derive most benefit from the changes is football, which is certain to attract many from the large influx of new members. The football side of affairs is flourishing just now, mainly due to the fact that the club has had the use for the first time of the all-weather pitches at Oakland Park on Tuesday and Thursday evenings and on Saturdays and Sundays. The instructors in this activity are Messrs Hubert Hamilton and Billy O'Donnell.
>
> Another highly popular activity is swimming, with sessions at the city baths from 7.00pm to 8.00pm on Monday evenings. Under the instruction of Messrs B O'Donnell and P Canning, this activity attracts about 60 boys and here, too, more recruits are expected.
>
> The boxing sessions have never had it so good with the attendance figure now over the 60 mark. Such has been the popularity of this activity of late that the committee had found it necessary to increase the number of nights devoted to boxing to four per week. The regular instructor on Tuesday and Thursday evenings is Mr T Donnelly and he will be assisted on Monday and Wednesday evenings by long-time club helper Bosco Hegarty.
>
> The club camp project, first started in 1955, has visited all four provinces in Ireland in its time. It attracts about 60 campers each year and is self-run by the boys under the supervision of Mr Brendan O'Donnell. Last year the camp was held at Enniscrone, Co Sligo.
>
> These are just some of the activities which have combined to make the club one of the most successful in the city. The programme arranged for the current season was a mammoth one, but the results attended to date have been gratifying, particularly to Fr Carolan, the prime mover in the re-organisational drive.

Harmonica band, St Mary's Boys' Club, 1959. (*Derry Journal*)

> The office-bearers and management committee of the club are: chairman, Mr Hugh Doherty; vice-chairman, Mr George Kilkie; organiser, Mr Brendan O'Donnell; secretary, Mr Kevin McCaul; committee members, Messrs Bill Doherty, Tony Carlin, Tommy Conaghan, Paddy McCoy, George McKinney, Kevin Helferty and Lawrence McLaughlin.

Religious affiliation was all-important. The evidence is in the final paragraph:

> To become a member of the club, it is necessary to be a member of the young men's confraternity, which includes every youth in the estate between 15 and 21 years.

Continuing expansion was to be facilitated by the granting of access to St Joseph's School for Boys' Club activities. In September 1967, the club management thanked the school for putting the school facilities at its disposal and announced its plans that were to include contributions from teachers:

> The club's programme of activities for the season is: art, craft, metalwork and woodwork, St Joseph's Intermediate School (instructors are qualified teachers); drama (instructor, Mr Leo Marshall); physical training, basketball, St Joseph's Intermediate School (qualified teachers); Gaelic football at Oakland Park (instructor to be appointed); soccer at same venue

Above: St Mary's boxers with trainer Bosco Hegarty, 1963. (*Derry Journal*)
Below: St Mary's Boys' Club members with leader, Roger O'Doherty, 1959. (*Derry Journal*)

> (Hubert Hamilton, coach and Neil Barr, assistant coach); swimming at the municipal baths each Monday, 8.00pm-9.00pm, (organiser, Patrick Canning); athletics (John Downey); boxing in the club gymnasium (Tommy Donnelly); weightlifting (Jack McCann); judo (Hugh McCann); snooker, billiards, chess, darts and draughts in the general games room; table tennis at same venue (P Begley); debates, discussions, folk group, pop group, disc jockeys, Question Time, Quiz Ball and dancing; seasonal activities – camping, canoeing and cycling.

Ahead were the great days when Damien McDermott, Charlie Nash, and others would bring glory to St Mary's. Under the driving force of Father Joe Carolan, Kevin McCaul, Brendan O'Donnell and many more, it was to go from strength to strength until, eventually, a purpose-built youth club was constructed to cater for the youth of Creggan. With this expansion into other and more suitable venues, the role of The Hut declined. In the intervening years, since the founding of the Boys' Club in Creggan, it had provided a venue which had not only housed an incredibly varied programme for boys, but was also the centre of social activity for the estate. That such a humble headquarters could host such an array of valuable work is a tribute to the efforts of numerous workers and volunteers who contributed significantly to the making of a community in Creggan.

St Mary's Boys' Club PT team, 1959. (*Derry Journal*)

Don Bosco's FC, winners of under-17 league and cup for second successive year in St Eugene's Boys' Club football competitions, October 1955. (*Derry Journal*)

The Carlyles: The Legend and the Legacy

Hughie Carlyle, who came to live in Creggan Broadway in 1949, was one of Derry City Football Club's long-established heroes. A Scot, he had played for Motherwell against St Mirren in the cup semifinal of 1933 in what was to be an unfortunate game for him. A free kick and penalty had been awarded against Carlyle for two tackles, and St Mirren scored from both opportunities. Motherwell were beaten 3-1 and, even though it was generally agreed that the refereeing decisions were unfair, some directors felt he had let the club down. As a result he was placed on the free transfer list. But Motherwell's loss was to be Derry City's gain. When he was not included in Motherwell's tour of South Africa, Hughie decided to seek his fortune with Derry City. He was never to return and remained in Derry for the rest of his life. Motherwell were to regret their decision. After one of his early games for Derry, the Motherwell manager appeared with an offer to transfer him back to Motherwell. Billy Gillespie, City's famous manager, was in favour of a transfer, but director George Sidebottom, himself a Motherwell man, insisted he should stay. In spite of the lure of much-needed cash, board and management agreed with Sidebottom. His influence soon became apparent. *Belfast Telegraph* sports columnist Malcolm Brodie describes the early days:

> Derry won the City Cup in Carlyle's first season with them, were runners up the following season and won it again in 1936. This shows the tremendous consistency of the side in those years, and there is another pointer to it. In that period Derry had a run of 42 home games without defeat. It was brought to an end when Bangor beat them 2-1. Derry continued to be a power in Irish football even after their unbroken run of home wins ended. In the 1936-37 season, they were beaten in the final of the Irish Cup by Linfield (after a replay) and the following year, they lost the Irish League after a test match and replay with Belfast Celtic.

Hughie's first match against the legendary Belfast Celtic provided a real test as he was destined to mark the brilliant Davy 'Boy' Martin. Frank Curran describes Carlyle's contribution and the observation of another Derry character:

> The Hughie Carlyle legend probably began that day. In a wonderful game, City won 2-1, and though Martin slipped through once to score the Celtic goal, he was so totally blotted out by Hughie otherwise that local wit Eddie 'Hawker' Lynch quipped: 'Martin was bound for Wolverhampton but couldn't get past Carlyle.' Davy Martin was in fact transferred to the English club that same season.

Such performances did not go unnoticed and representative honours were to come his way before long; in his second season, he was chosen to play for the Irish League. Eleven more appearances followed and on each occasion Hughie captained the Irish

Above: Irish League selection which defeated the English League 3-2 in 1936 at Windsor Park, when Jimmy Kelly scored all three Irish goals and Hughie Carlyle captained the team. Derry City players (front row, from right); J Kelly, J Duffy, EDR Shearer, H Carlyle. (courtesy Carlyle family)

Hughie Carlyle, wearing IFA Inter-League jersey, circa 1935. (Carlyle family)

League selection. His greatest memory was the historic game at Windsor Park in 1936 when the Irish League beat the English league and Derry City favourite Jimmy Kelly scored all three Irish goals. Two other Derry players, EDR Shearer and Harry Duffy, shared in the historic victory.

Hughie played 14 seasons with the City during which he played over 500 first team games, scored 52 goals and left behind a host of great memories. Former *Derry Journal* editor Frank Curran sums up his contribution:

> Carlyle was widely regarded as the best centre half in Ireland, and was a fixture at the Brandywell. It was not only his ability which made Hughie a household name, but his whole approach to the game. He played his heart out game after game, and his determination not to be beaten had an exhilarating effect on his teammates.

Two of his sons, Hilary and Paul, were to develop the football talent they inherited from their father. Hilary signed for Finn Harps when he was 20. By the time he was 21 in 1976, he had impressed Glasgow Celtic enough for them to invite him over for a closer look. He played a few games for the reserves, but it was his performance in a friendly match against Birmingham that really impressed the club. It seemed like a new career with a top club was opening up for him. However, the stringent medical examination uncovered traces of a long-forgotten foot operation which, although it did not affect his game, had fused a toe joint. Apparently this minor flaw was too much for the club's insurers so the transfer was called off. Although tempted by offers of negotiations with West Bromwich Albion, a very dejected young man returned home. However, new vistas opened up when offers came in from America and he went on loan to play for San Diego Jaws. He was to be visited again by injury when, of all things, he had his jaw broken. As a result he missed out on half a season. Even so, his tally of 13 goals made him leading goal scorer for the club that year.

Other teams were impressed. Las Vegas Quicksilvers came in and negotiated his transfer from Finn Harps and Hilary found himself playing in the company of Portuguese internationals Eusebio and Toni. One incident in a match against New York Cosmos was caught on camera. He does not remember much about it, other than it was brief, of little consequence, that he intervened and that Pele and Eusebio were involved. As a result, he has a souvenir which depicts him as arbitrator in a minor altercation between two of the all-time greats of football. He also played against San Jose in the match where George Best scored the spectacular goal which is still shown on TV as an example of the Irish maestro at his most skilful. In a match against Hawaii, he scored the winning goal in a penalty shoot-out and impressed the management there. That was enough to guarantee him a move to Hawaii where he stayed until the club went out of business.

So it was back to Ireland again where he was quickly signed up by Jim McLaughlin for Dundalk. A dispute with Finn Harps over his signing arose but was quickly settled by the FAI in favour of Dundalk. He stayed four seasons with them during the great

Hilary Carlyle mediates between young upstarts Pele and Eusebio in the
Las Vegas Quicksilvers v New York Cosmos match in Las Vegas, 1977. (courtesy Hilary Carlyle)

days when Dundalk put League of Ireland football on the map and where he was idolised by supporters. At the reception after winning the league and cup double, Jim McLaughlin took the unprecedented course of publicly declaring that the club's success was in large measure due to Hilary Carlyle. Injury and neglect, however, were to blight the rest of his career.

He received a serious knee injury playing for the League of Ireland against New Zealand just a week before Dundalk were to play Glasgow Celtic in the European Cup. Knowledgeable observers were of the opinion that his absence cost Dundalk the tie. As he says:

> I limped through another two years before the knee went again while playing against Spurs at White Hart Lane in the European Cup.

Looking back, he reckons that after the first serious injury to his knee, the failure to have the recommended operation in Dublin resulted in further damage and a premature end to his football career.

Hilary Carlyle, after the disappointment of Glasgow Celtic's rejection, showed that he had the ability to perform at the highest level. Other top-class teams, however, would probably have made the same decision, given the medical evidence, which meant he never would have gotten the chance to prove it. Ironically, the flaw, identified by the original medical examination, never inhibited his performances.

When Malcolm Brodie wrote a tribute to Hughie Carlyle in 1959, his final sentence was:

> Hugh has five sons in a family of eight, and in the future, perhaps, the Carlyle name may again figure on the Derry teamsheet.

It would be quarter of a century before this suggestion would be realised. The youngest, Paul, born in 1966, was to follow in his father's footsteps and on the way suffer reverses that bore an uncanny resemblance to those of his older brother.

Hughie died in 1983 and never pushed his sons into the game. Paul's earliest introduction to organised football was playing for Trojans under the guidance of Raymond Carton and Ronnie Ballard. At 15, he was playing for Derry City in the North West League. He then went to Coleraine and in his season there had a few senior games and was included in the team panel for a European Cup match.

Next season, 1985-86, Tony O'Doherty, by that time manager of Derry City Reserves, brought him to the Brandywell. In his first season, Derry City won the first division championship and promotion to the Premier League with Noel King as manager.

Negotiations for his transfer to a Spanish team were opened up where details, to say the least, were clouded. Paul was an amateur and could not be transferred until he signed professional forms. An offer was made to sign a contract for a wage of £25 per week, even though six-figure transfer fees were being discussed. A condition of the transfer was that he accept the weekly wage offered. He refused, at which stage Derry manager Jim McLaughlin offered three other choices; Glasgow Celtic, Liverpool, or Shamrock Rovers. He went for Shamrock Rovers who were flying high at the time and were making a habit of winning the FAI League championship. He did not stay a full season and was soon brought back to Derry City by Jim McLaughlin.

The Derry glory days were just around the corner. In the 1987-88 season, Derry were beaten in the Cup Final by Dundalk. Next year they became the first team to win the treble. Qualification for the European Cup provided Paul with a couple of memorable occasions. One was being the player to score Derry City's first goal in European competitive football while competing in the League of Ireland. This was against Benfica. His second was playing in the return match before 67,000 in the Stadium of Light, Lisbon. At the end of the season, Liverpool declared an interest in him and he duly signed after playing in a couple of reserve matches in the company of Jan Molby, Jim Beglin, Jim Magilton and Ray Houghton.

Paul and Liverpool impressed each other. On finding that a part-time player was fitter than some of his own full-timers, coach Phil Thompson smashed a cup against a wall to emphasise his disapproval of his own players' shortcomings while at the same time acknowledging Paul's superior condition. His welcome to the club where he was treated as an equal was extremely warm. During his time there, he stayed with his aunt and was picked up in the mornings for training by Liverpool legend Alan Hansen as if he had been an old friend. During training, he had suffered some abdominal pain

Paul Carlyle in action for Derry City. (courtesy Paul Carlyle)

which he and the club put down to a hernia. A contract was promised pending a solution to the medical problem which just seemed a formality. Before he left for home to have the medical investigation, he had another occasion to benefit from the players' goodwill when, to his amazement, household names Jim Beglin, Gary Gillespie, John Barnes and Barry Venison turned up to see him off.

When he got home, he made an appointment with a consultant to ascertain the cause of the niggling pain, only to receive crushing news. It seemed like the Carlyle hoodoo had struck again. The consultant diagnosed arthritis and advised him to find another sport or quit football immediately. His reaction was to keep quiet and continue playing for Derry City.

The following season, Steve Bruce, playing alongside him in a Brandywell friendly, was impressed and recommended him to Manchester United. After watching him play, manager Alex Ferguson took him aside and told him that, apart from his inability to head a ball, he was good enough to play for the club. He was to return in three weeks to look around and complete all the signing arrangements, but Paul knew he would never pass the required medical and so never returned to Manchester.

He came back to Derry and the 'post treble' era to a club whose supporters had unrealistically high expectations of continuing success. Manager Jim McLaughlin departed and was replaced by Roy Coyle. Relations were not the best between the new manager and Paul and both parties were probably relieved when Coleraine manager Felix Healy made an offer for him.

Paul tells with some delight of the day when he settled an old score. The game was his debut for Coleraine against Ards, just a week after Coyle had left Derry to manage Ards. Paul had signed for Coleraine on 21 October 1993, married on 22 October, and made his debut the following day. Nothing could go wrong for him. He scored a goal and set up the other three in a 4-1 victory for Coleraine. He describes his goal as the best he ever scored, having received a throw-in in his own half and 'nutmegged' three- or four Ards defenders on the way. He has it on good authority that all the Ards team were transfer-listed the following week.

A stay of a season and a half was followed by a return to Derry when they won the cup and narrowly lost the league. Another move took him to Portadown where, in his first year, his new club won the Irish League and the Ulster Cup. In his second year with Portadown, 1996-97, his arthritis problem started catching up with a vengeance and he found it difficult to play and train. He left on a free transfer to be reunited with Jim McLaughlin again at Dundalk. On reflection, he realises he should have retired earlier as by then he needed two days to recover after matches. He then tried missing alternate matches before he called it a day at the age of 32. He now awaits a double hip-replacement operation.

Paul Carlyle has no regrets, knowing he had the ability to play at the top level, a judgement supported by no less than Kenny Dalglish and Alex Ferguson. After that, he was glad just to have played.

Jim O'Hea and the Athletic Academy
by Michael McGuinness

The story of football in Creggan cannot be told without chronicling the history of the club, since its inception in 1955, that was known variously as Foyle Athletic, Derry Athletic, the Athletic Academy and simply as Athletic FC. Jim O'Hea would be quick to point out that, like at any successful club, success depends on the development of an efficient management team. Few of his friends, acquaintances or admirers, however, would dispute the declaration that the inspiration, direction and success of the club was largely due to Jim O'Hea's leadership. Jim's introduction to football management came at the age of 14 when he and lifelong friends Joe Devine and Barney Callan became founder members of Foyleview FC. When he was 16, the family moved to Creggan. He spent two unhappy years in England working for the Civil Service after which homesickness brought him back to a job in the BSR factory; he was then 19 years of age.

At the factory, he met up with Brendan Fleming and George White who were similarly interested in football. The decision to form a team was an easy one. Finding a name that contained the word Foyle along with a name that had not been used before was more difficult; other teams had followed the prefix Foyle with *Harps, Rovers, Swifts, Rangers*, etc. Eventually they plumped for Foyle Athletic, secure in the knowledge that the name had not been used before. This was soon to be replaced by Derry Athletic, although the local penchant for shortening official names would ensure that Derry Athletic would soon become widely known simply as Athletic. Originally set up by the founders so that they could play themselves, the club added to its playing numbers and went on to compete successfully in the North West and Derry and District football competitions.

However, the club was soon put under pressure to cater for younger players, the pressure coming mainly from Don O'Doherty and Aidan Boyle. Jim also detected a need to provide sport and recreation for upper Creggan, having determined that lower Creggan was well catered for by the Boys' Club.

The dearth of playing fields saw the budding Athletic trespass in the Nuns' Field, the Gaelic pitch attached to the boys' home in Termonbacca, to play their practice games. Fitness and speed were regularly tested by their being frequently chased from the grounds.

The construction of the all-weather pitch at Oakland Park on the site of the old basin was to provide a spur and direction for the club. The park was to be their headquarters, where security of tenure would allow them to develop a long-term strategy. The all-weather surface was to be a determining factor in allowing Athletic to pursue the passing game so dear to the hearts of its management.

From the start, the club was run on non-sectarian lines; Jim O'Hea remembers that every street in Creggan had Protestants, a number of whom played for the club.

A list of some of the youths who came from Creggan, passed through the club and went on to greater things is impressive. Their names and addresses roll easily of Jim's tongue without the aid of any address book. It includes: Brendan Bradley (Malin Gardens); Jim 'Chang' Smith (Dawros Gardens); Eugene McNutt (Balbane Pass); Seánny McLaughlin (Circular Road); Paddy Doherty (Rinmore); Eddie McCallion (Leenan Gardens); Damien Curran (Circular Road); and Cormac 'Curly' O'Donnell (Circular Road). Alongside these prestigious names, Jim also remembers that at one time 29 boys from the Termonbacca Boys' Home were members, perhaps allowing him to make amends for his previous trespassing offences.

When one considers that Athletic was not affiliated to any official football federation, their organisation was remarkable. Nobody received fees for services. When in later years the club was to concentrate on youth, some assistance was given by the WELB for strips and travel arrangements; all other expenses were met through sponsorship and fundraising events. Local businessmen who were former players were consistently generous. At its peak, the club ran seven teams, each with its own manager, and delegation was the name of the game. Prominent among the managers in talent and commitment were: Murray Gormley; John 'Spasy' McGilloway; Barney Callan and Eddie McCallion.

Athletic teams were always great competitors, which is not surprising given the example set by former players Brendan Fleming, the Cassidy brothers and often O'Hea himself. The club motto *To Improve* is apt for an organisation that sets high standards. The respect for the competitive spirit is evident in the extract chosen for the cover of the *25th Anniversary Programme.* It reads:

> The credit belongs to the man who is actually in the arena – whose face is marred by the dust and sweat! A leader who knows the great enthusiasm, the great devotions – and spends himself in a worthy cause. Who at best, if he wins, knows the thrills of high achievement – and if he fails, at least, fails while daring greatly – so that his place shall never be with those cold and timid souls who know neither victory nor defeat.
>
> Theodore Roosevelt

The same programme, published in 1980, reiterated the aims of the club:

- to provide disciplined recreation for the youth of the city
- to promote good sportsmanship
- to improve opportunities for youth development
- to encourage top standards of coaching and counselling
- to expand and foster a more advanced level of competition for youth

There follows a summary of the club's first 25 years:

> Jim O'Hea, Brendan Fleming and George White were the men who decided on the name Derry Athletic – way back in 1955 – and their first side, under-17 years, captured St Eugene's Parish League Championship, with Jimbo Crossan and John McDaid prominent. It was Don

O'Doherty who was the driving force that made Barney Callan and Jim O'Hea adopt an under-13 team then and Athletic soon won the St Mary's FA Cup 6-0. Leo Hickey scored all six goals and also starring in the team were: Billy McNaught, Tony O'Doherty, Paddy Doherty and Charlie Canning. Athletic's coaching quickly brought young starlets to the fore and Brendan Bradley, Don Moore, Jim 'Chang' Smith and Eugene McNutt were among some of the youngsters who reached senior standard.

Athletic won their first D&D trophy, the McKinney Cup, and shortly afterwards branched out into youth and social activities; quizzes, club camps, hikes, tennis and putting all helped to establish the club's reputation.

Athletic cleaned up in D&D youth competitions, and the Long Tower FA was a great soccer source.

The club pioneered cross-channel trips and came back from Nottingham as winners of the Avalon cup, an International Soccer Tournament success.

Annual camps at Portstewart, Buncrana, Galway, Tollymore Forest, Gortin, the Sperrins and Kiltegan were always memorable events.

Sports days, concerts, club notes in the newspapers, all these were exciting new avenues for the imaginative Athletic club.

The North-South cup was another pioneering effort undertaken by Athletic, starring Eddie Mahon, Phil Donaghy, Charlie Fisher, Seamus McDevitt, Noel Hegarty, the Cassidy brothers (Robert, Thomas and Paddy), James McDaid, Fabian Daly, George White, Brendan Fleming, Jim O'Hea, Barney Callan, Joe Kyle, Colm Holmes, Colm Norris and Brian Friel – what a team!

Athletic went undefeated in North West soccer circles for a full season and reached the semifinals of the Irish Junior cup – only to go out on a protest. Paddy Doherty and Murray Gormley were added to the panel. There was one terrific game against the RAF – Jim O'Hea only slightly exaggerates when he says everyone was sent off except Paddy Cassidy. Actually, five RAF players and four Athletic players received their marching orders on this occasion.

The club kept producing 'international' stars, and on a tour in Germany Jim O'Hea guided his team to an 'undefeated' record once again.

Ten-year-old Marie Ramsey became the first girl to play for the club and in fact created new records in many youth competitions.

Athletic players had trials with Arsenal, Aston Villa, Charlton Athletic, Luton, Coventry, Hibernians, Celtic and, of course, Leicester City where in 1980/81 the club had three players signed as full-time professionals: John O'Neill; Paul Ramsey and Gavin Drummond.

The final detail of the Leicester connection reminded me of my own small part in the Athletic story. I had played for Athletic in its early days and, when the fruits of the youth policy began to show, I realised I was in a position to introduce two people whom I respected greatly and who would each benefit from the introduction. The first of these, of course, was Jim. The second was Frank O'Farrell, Republic of Ireland international, who was then manager of Leicester City. I had met Frank when he played for West Ham United and I had gone there on trial. I was not there very long when I detected the respect everyone at the club held for him, both as a player and a person. Above all, I remembered his generosity. Realising I felt a stranger in a strange world, Frank quietly took me aside and said: 'I know what it's like to be away from home, but if you decide to stay, my home is always open to you.' From that incident, and all that I observed during my stay, I knew that he was a sensitive man of talent and integrity. I had no doubt that he and Jim would find common cause in what I was to propose.

Having observed Athletic's commitment to the development of a youth policy, I wrote to Frank informing him of all their valuable work. At the same time, a young Eugene McNutt had caught my eye and it was easy to recommend him as a fine prospect. A short time later, Jim asked me to play in a friendly match in Buncrana, where one of his youth teams was pitted against a team of seasoned players, in the expectation that the younger players might learn a few lessons. One young player stood out that day, the young 14-year-old Seánny McLaughlin who played with a skill, poise and maturity beyond his years. I suggested to Jim that he call Frank right away and include Seánny in his plans. The beginnings of a valuable and lasting relationship had been set up between Leicester City and Athletic.

This cross-channel link, which was to be maintained with various clubs, enabled the club to add ideas and techniques, developed at professional level, to their own, well thought-out strategies.

All in all, the summary in the *25th Anniversary Programme* (above) indicates a resounding success for the aspirations of the club for its first quarter-century. The '80s and '90s were also to bring further successes.

By the early '80s, the club had changed its name and emphasis. It had become the Derry Athletic Football Academy and was to cater exclusively for youth. There were teams for the under-12s, -13s, -15s and -18s. Coaching was intensive, and debate and the exchange of ideas became as important as training in skills and fitness. The change to catering exclusively for youth was taken, as the management perceived a marked increase in aggression in the wider community as the *Troubles* intensified, and that this aggression was beginning to manifest itself on the football field.

The response was to remove competition from the local to the international arena where a number of benefits would accrue. In a club whose policy was non-sectarian, playing at neutral venues allowed participation in events free from sectarian pressures. Players would also gain in experience and confidence as they competed against teams from a wide range of traditions and abilities. Perhaps of even more value were the opportunities for personal development that all these new experiences were to present.

A Churchill Fellowship allowed Jim O'Hea to travel to Germany and arrange a tour of Frankfurt. A very successful trip followed when the Academy won all seven matches.

Over the years they competed in international tournaments in England and Scotland. A high point was reached when the Academy won the Portsmouth International Youth Cup in 1990, with Nigel Melly named as player of the tournament. The opposition had come from England, USA, Canada, Ireland, Sweden, Spain, Italy and Germany.

As a means of preparing for important tournaments, challenge matches were organised against top quality opposition. Variety was essential and preparations could also involve teams in residentials away from the city. Often senior players, who were former members, turned up to lend assistance as did Ciaran Toorish and Rory O'Boyle at one such event at Moville. An interesting departure which demonstrated a willingness to innovate was the participation in a seminar – Speed, Strength and Skill – where the leading tutor was Malcolm McCausland of Stratford AC. Here the aim was to coach local footballers in sprinting techniques and stamina exercises.

The Academy can claim success in achieving its primary goals. One measure of the success was the emergence of 'graduates' John O'Neill, Paul Ramsey, Gary Fleming, David Campbell and Shay Givens as full internationals. The contribution to the personal development of the hundreds who passed through can be guessed at by referring to the guidelines adhered to by the club:

Preparing Mentally for Achievement in Sport

- Look good. Feel good – develop the image of a good player
- Be positive about yourself. You cannot be what you think you are not
- Set yourself (discuss with your coach) a number of small, achievable targets on the route to excellence
- Build a positive support group – family and friends who reinforce your belief
- Become a continual learner – listen to the coach and show him that you can put his advice into action
- Love practice – it's the key to success on Saturdays
- Work on mental toughness – can I concentrate on the whole game? When does my mind go lazy?
- Beware of negative self-talk; after a mistake, learn the discipline of letting go and recovering
- Be strong enough to take responsibility for your mistakes – don't blame others
- Listen and learn from criticism – it's part of developing excellence
- Concentrate on personal excellence and let results take care of themselves
- Accept team responsibility – how can I help the players around me?
- Develop composure – deal with incidents calmly – don't react emotionally – don't lose control
- Develop as a whole person – excellent players are excellent people
- Get football into perspective – an enjoyable life experience – possibly a career – definitely not life or death

Athletic team from 1969 with four schoolboy internationals (with asterisk). Back row, from left: Brian Kearney, Tommy Kyle, Eugene McNutt, Martin Lyttle*, Denis O'Kane, Don Brown, Frank Henry*, Benny Power*, Jim O'Hea (manager). Front row: Seamus McDowell, Charlie Deeny, Noel Fitzpatrick, Shaunnie McLaughlin, Sean McLaughlin, Maurice Russell, Adrian O'Connell*, Eddie Grant (courtesy Jim O'Hea).

It would be hard to imagine that anyone, no matter how moderate their abilities, would not have been enriched by attempting to follow such guidelines.

Although Jim O'Hea would point to the satisfaction of enriching the lives of many as being reward enough, his demeanour, when he tells one story, suggests that one episode was unsurpassed.

At the Academy's award ceremony in May 1986, friends of the Academy and some local businessmen, organised by Don Mullan, sprang a surprise on Jim which led one local newspaper to call it the 'Mexico Farewell'. In the middle of his winding-up speech, Jim was presented with a dream package, which contained tickets and travel arrangements for the World Cup in Mexico. The gesture illustrated the high regard in which he was held and also presented him with the opportunity of observing the 'beautiful game' which he had always advocated at close hand.

He found all the Northern Ireland matches he attended memorable, but one stood out. That was the game between Northern Ireland and Brazil, where John O'Neill gave an accomplished performance against the world's best and David Campbell came on as a substitute. With Paul Ramsey on the panel and two other Athletic players appearing in the arena, Jim O'Hea could rightly reflect with satisfaction on a lifetime dedicated to the service of youth and soccer in Derry.

Jim O'Hea with star pupil, John O'Neill, 1980. (courtesy Jim O'Hea)

FROM 'LONG SHOOTIES' TO LENIN STADIUM: TERRY HARKIN

Terry Harkin was born in Stanley's Walk in September 1941. When the Harkin family moved to Creggan in 1951, Terry was already hooked on football. He puts this down to the influence of his uncle, Justin Morrow, who regularly challenged a six-year-old Terry to 'long shooties' at the back of the house. Whether he knew it then, Justin was instilling a competitive spirit in his young nephew which was to stand him in good stead in his chosen career. His tactic in the regular 'first to ten' competitions was to allow Terry to go nine goals up and then slowly whittle down his lead until he emerged the 10-9 winner. The effect was twofold: the young nephew was, at an early age, honing his striking skills and was beginning to hunger for victories which seemed so close as he regularly forged into what seemed unassailable leads in these titanic struggles; the inevitable defeats rather than demoralising him, only made him more determined to inflict defeat on his torturer. A top-class striker was in the making.

At 11, Terry was holding his place in the Don Bosco's under-14 team, which included Joe Murphy, John Dunne, Tony Toland and Jim McLaughlin. Terry remembers the day that fate intervened to alter the course of Jim's career. Jim, then a goalkeeper, suffered an arm injury and was moved to outside right. He never played between the posts again. Their paths were to cross again, but always as outfield players.

In the season 1951-52, Don Bosco's beat Rosemount 7-2 in an under-14 cup final when the 11-year-old Harkin scored three goals from the outside-left position. Justin Morrow's informal coaching methods were starting to pay dividends. There followed games for St Eugene's Boys' Club under Tony O'Donnell, and a spell for Park Rangers, where two of the management team were Peter Gallagher and Raymond Healy. One wonders what authority was brought to the club by Peter, later head of the North West College of Further and Higher Education, or what economic stability brought by Raymond, who was to become treasurer of the City Council in his more mature years.

At 15, Harkin signed for Derry City Thirds, which was managed by Jackie Coyle, and competed in the North West League, which was affiliated to the IFA. As Coyle also managed the AOH team in the Derry and District League, it was no surprise that he also played for them; he was still only 15. By the age of 17, he had played two games for Derry's first team. After a trial with Wolverhampton Wanderers, he returned to Derry and was signed for Coleraine FC by Billy Nelis. Given the nature of the massive deals arrived at in modern football, Harkin's rewards were modest in the extreme. Jack Doherty, a well-known building contractor, was chairman of Coleraine Football Club and, as a consequence, was able to offer apprenticeships in the building trade to aspiring footballers who signed for the club. Harkin was no exception and, as part of the signing-on arrangement, duly commenced his apprenticeship; the fee was a hammer and saw. These instruments, which he used during his three years as an apprentice joiner, are still prized possessions in the Harkin household.

In 1962, he signed for Port Vale where he was joined by Brian Wright, a colleague from Don Bosco days. Fellow Derrymen Colm Holmes and Paddy McGrory also spent a short while with the club. After two years there, he moved to Crewe where he had a strange mixture of fortunes. Two months had gone by during which he experienced the striker's worst nightmare; he failed to score over that period. An offer came in from Willie Ross, then manager of Derry City, and suddenly the idea of going home seemed very attractive. The Crewe manager suggested he postpone any decision for a weekend. On the following Saturday, Harkin scored one of his most spectacular goals ever. To this day, he is not sure if the competitive urge surfaced with a vengeance or he if took his frustrations out on the ball when he smashed home a memorable goal. From that match on, his season turned right around. He scored 35 league goals that season, which still stands as a record for the club. It is still a puzzle to many that this feat did not earn him an international place at that stage.

His next move was to Cardiff City where, despite playing well, he found himself out of favour with manager Scoular; a further move was inevitable. Jim McKinley, a manager who had a high regard for his abilities, next signed Harkin for Notts County. Within two months, McKinley left and, not for the first time, Harkin found himself out of favour at a club where a change of manager meant a change in playing staff.

After one season, a change of fortune saw Southport manager Billy Bingham bid for Harkin's services. There followed two satisfying years of club football with Harkin describing Bingham as the best manager for whom he ever played. During his spell there, he also, at the age of 28, gained his first international cap. He was to play in five international games – twice against Wales and three other games against Turkey, Russia and Spain. He scored two goals in the 3-1 Northern Ireland defeat of Turkey, but his most memorable experience was the world cup game against Russia. The game in the Lenin Stadium was played before 100,000 people and the occasion, rather than being intimidating, served to stimulate the Irish striker. Never an arrogant man, Harkin remembers the moment before kick-off when, with the ball at his feet, he thought he was the best centre forward in Ireland. The confidence and maturity he'd acquired over the years were obviously at a peak. The Russian press agreed on the quality of his performance, adjudging Harkin and Dougan to be the best of the Irish players.

At club level, Harkin was soon on the move again when, after two years with Southport, a bid came in from Harry Gregg and Shrewsbury, where Jim McLaughlin was on the coaching staff. He had many differences of opinion with Gregg, but is quick to point out that he considers him a generous and honest man. On reflection he would put the differences down to clashes between two similarly strong-willed and stubborn men.

The final move in Harkin's football career was to Finn Harps. His eight years there he regards as his most enjoyable in football even if, after the first three months, he concluded that he had made a mistake. He speaks enthusiastically of the many warm and generous people he met inside and outside football in Donegal. His one big regret was missing the victorious cup final through injury. A high point was scoring Finn Harps' first goal in a European competition against Aberdeen in the 1973-74 UEFA Cup. Although he later played a few games at Dundalk to help out manager and old friend Jim McLaughlin, injury had virtually ended Harkin's senior football career at Finn Park.

Terry Harkin (front row, third from right) in Irish international team, which includes George Best, against Spain, November 1970. (courtesy Terry Harkin)

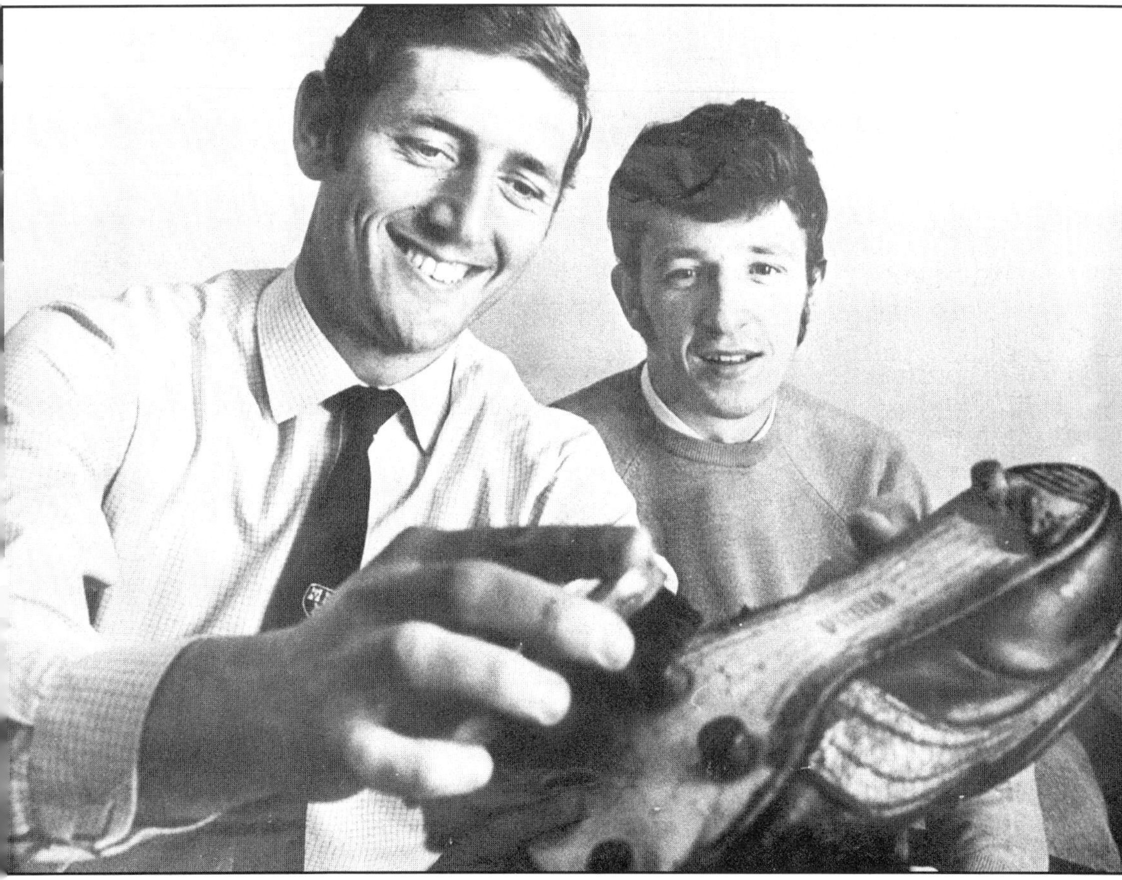

Terry Harkin and Tony O'Doherty photographed in a Moscow hotel preparing for the Northern Ireland World Cup game against the USSR on 22 October 1969. (courtesy Terry Harkin)

He had a relatively long career in football, a career that allowed him to play the game he loved with distinction. He holds no grudges against personalities in the game, even if he could be forgiven for bearing some resentment towards those who might have awarded him representative honours earlier in his career. His skill and enthusiasm for the game could still be witnessed up until a few years ago when, although hindered by the effects of previous injuries, he competed against his peers in the weekly five-a-side matches in the Templemore Sports Complex. His touch, combative spirit and dislike of losing were still evident, even if the pace was a trifle perambulatory compared to the great days.

His opinion of the modern game is that there is too much emphasis on adhering too rigidly to involved tactical plans. Perhaps all good strikers share his opinion of his own role when he says of his own strengths and instincts:

> I didn't need to be told where I should be if I was expected to score goals and no amount of coaching would have changed that.

No doubt Uncle Justin would have agreed.

TEAM-BUILDING THE TONY O'DOHERTY WAY

Tony O'Doherty is remarkably pragmatic about how his footballing career was cut short by the events in Derry in the early '70s. An international footballer attracting considerable interest from clubs in Britain, he was forced to take the road less travelled, because, as he says himself, events overtook him.

> While I understand Bill Shankly's comments about football being more important than life or death, in reality, it's not. I wasn't conscious of ever taking a decision. What was going on was so all-embracing. You had people dying and a total breakdown of law and order. With all that happening, there was no way I could just leave it behind and go off and play football.

O'Doherty was playing at Coleraine when the *Troubles* began to impact on Derry. He'd signed up as a boy in the mid-'60s and quickly made a name for himself. Previously, he'd enjoyed what he describes as 'a broad education', courtesy of a scholarship to St Columb's College – a rare privilege for a son of Creggan. And his travels throughout Ireland as a footballer had left him with a wider perspective on what was happening both socially and politically.

> I was very lucky to be given opportunities my contemporaries weren't and my father Dan was a great organiser. So the genes meant that I was always likely to be an organiser too.

In 1971, O'Doherty put his career on hold to 'organise' his home community. His object was to give young people whose lives were fenced in by the barricades that surrounded their estates a focus in life. And so, out he went and appropriated two sets of nets and set up a football club. *Londonderry Sentinel* reporter Mickey O'Donnell remembered it thus:

> Don't let O'Doherty try to tell you he got them on a loan. Make no bones about it, he stole them – I was with him. There was a crowd of us eight- or nine-year-olds playing football at Bishop's Field when he came up and said it was about time we had our own nets. So he recruited four of us to go up to Piggery Ridge where he dug up the goalposts and got us to carry them home again. And just to make sure nobody stole them back, he took them into his back yard every night until he eventually got some cement and jammed them in the ground good and proper.

O'Doherty got the Bishop's Field pitch lined out and, before long, around 600 boys were playing in different competitions organised by the Creggan Football Association (CFA) at the ground. Tony recalled:

> We weren't trying to keep them in line, we just wanted to offer the boys the same chances we'd had as children.

The influence O'Doherty and colleagues like Charles 'Nucker' Tierney gained through the CFA was to come in useful in steering young people away from anti-social behaviour.

> You'd a situation where maybe 11,000 people were living in a very small area with no amenities and no accepted state authority. Not surprisingly, there was a temptation among some young people to behave in an anti-social manner – not realising that they were being anti-social. We'd no physical authority; we were just recognised as a little group people could talk to. An oul' fella might come up to you and say 'Are you the boy who runs the pitch – I'm having a bit of bother at night.' I'd ask him was it his bowels. But then you'd see what you could do. You might appoint some of the boys to cut gardens or perform community clean-ups. And occasionally you'd put one or two of the bad eggs in charge – to give them a sense of responsibility.

O'Doherty was to become Creggan's unofficial chief of police.

> They called me Bilko, and 'Nucker' was Doberman. To this day, we're known in some parts as the Keystone Cops. I reckon we're due some of these big pay-offs the RUC boys are getting.

Rioting was a common feature in Creggan in the '70s, though not one the CFA felt equipped to deal with.

> If we had a view, it was never a collective one. I think if we had taken a stance either way we would have lost the moral authority we held. We couldn't possibly have stopped it.

While football undoubtedly provided a release for young people, there are events that are completely beyond escapism. Bloody Sunday was one.

> I don't think anyone ever saw a community so devastated. No-one knew what to do. You're brought up with this celluloid notion of 'British fair play', then all of a sudden all your lingering 'certainties' are destroyed. For a period after Bloody Sunday, no-one wanted to talk about community events. I could no more have run football matches than I could have played in one. No doubt it was a major catalyst for the IRA. The queues to join included young people, the middle-aged and the elderly. Everyone was caught up in an all-encompassing community grief.

O'Doherty was eventually to resume his footballing career in 1973 with Finn Harps – becoming the subject of Ireland's most expensive-ever transfer in the process. The deal was completed at the Broomhill Hotel in the Waterside as Creggan was still out of bounds. He went on to pick up a FAI cup winner's medal with Harps in 1974. His second FAI cup medal came while playing for Dundalk, managed by Derryman Jim McLaughlin, when they beat Sligo in 1981. And just for the record books, O'Doherty's brother Donal got a loser's medal after the same match.

A spell at Ballymena was to follow during which O'Doherty got to play in Europe against Roma and the legendary Brazilian, Falcao. Then Derry City's return to the League of Ireland in the mid-'80s saw O'Doherty take up the reins as coach, and indeed player, for a while. After his playing career ended, he managed his home town club for a season in the '90s, picking up the League Cup in the process.

Football wasn't always kind to O'Doherty. He had made the Northern Ireland squad 15 times, gaining caps on three occasions and with more on the cards, when an injury forced him from Billy Bingham's panel. Yet his successes in the Irish League and League of Ireland led him to compete in Europe around 20 times. O'Doherty is still heavily involved in community work in Creggan in projects such as the Creggan Neighbourhood Partnership (CNP) and the Drop-in Centre on Central Drive; he's also a leading light in the Restorative Justice Group.

> In Nationalist areas, it's quite clear that the RUC isn't acceptable. Obviously, everything depends on the political situation, but you can't talk about a police service in isolation; it must be see in the context of the [Good Friday] Agreement. People intrinsically want good order. In Nationalist areas, people have tended to look to Republicans to administer punishment – but Republicans themselves recognise this isn't the answer. I'd like to believe that this is an Irish problem and that we can come up with an Irish solution. Rural Gardaí can service a large area with a small-base group. And this shows that where people have confidence in their police, you don't need numbers and you don't need force.

While O'Doherty doesn't agree with Shankly's thoughts on football being more important than life or death, he does concur that the game can provide many social lessons for young people.

> Being part of a team teaches you that everyone has a role to play, and football also leaves room for solo talent. Modern day gurus use soccer as their model to show how the individual and community can progress together in harmony. And indeed, I think they've got a point.

Distance Swimmer and Deep-Sea Diver: Ray Cossum

Although born in England and describing himself as a 'blow in', Ray Cossum is proud to call himself a Derryman. It would probably be true to say that he and Derry have adopted each other, with Creggan having a particular claim on his 'citizenship'. Born in Folkestone on 17 September 1931, Cossum had his first glimpse of Derry when, as a young sailor in the Royal Navy, he disembarked from his ship along the Quayside. It was the day before his 18th birthday. Harbouring romantic notions about Donegal, the young matelot paid his first visit there shortly after he arrived. He was to develop a great affection for the place, which is as strong today as it was on his first acquaintance.

Donegal, Derry and Creggan were not to be his only love affairs, however. He met Bridie Loughrey of Sloan's Terrace at the 'Mem' and, before he was 20, they married, 'the best decision of my life', he declares. He remembers that the circumstances of the period and his youth required his parents' permission before he could be married. The wedding was in St Eugene's Cathedral and was presided over by Fr Des Mullan, who extracted a promise that their first son would be called Des. When their first son was born, the promise was duly fulfilled.

After they married, Ray and Bridie lived at Sloan's Terrace for a few years. Sometime in the mid-'50s, they swapped houses in an arrangement which took them to Dunmore Gardens. In 1969 another swap took them to Malin Gardens, where Cossum still lives. He never regretted his move to Creggan and is content to remain there for the rest of his days.

During his time in Creggan, Cossum became involved in many activities for which he had little formal training. Coming from Folkestone he had, from his earliest days, loved the sea, so swimming came easy. Jack McClelland, a wrestler and promoter, was also a long-distance swimmer who had been persuaded by Eddie Davis to attempt a swim from Rathmullan to Buncrana for charity; Cossum was also asked to partake.

He was already interested in the challenge presented by the stretch of water from Rathmullan to Buncrana and had prepared mentally and physically, although he was to say of this and other swims:

> My skill of long-distance swimming came by trial and error and dare I say, an abundance of error.

Nevertheless, the untutored swimmer was to successfully complete the five-mile crossing in two hours and 15 minutes. He thus became established as a long-distance swimmer. Not one to sit back and rest on his laurels, Cossum, in 1966, conquered the same distance both ways, non-stop, in a time of four hours and 41 minutes.

On 1 June 1970, he completed the gruelling 17-mile swim from Buncrana to Portsalon in seven hours. To date no one else has attempted either this crossing or the Buncrana to Rathmullan double. The Portsalon venture was to prove excellent preparation for what was to follow shortly. In the following month, he returned to his home town, Folkestone, where he made the final arrangements for his attempt on the big challenge for long-distance swimmers, namely the English Channel crossing.

At 5.15pm on 31 July 1970, Raymond Cossum bade au revoir to bystanders on the beach at Cap Gris Nez and entered the water to begin his attempt to swim the English Channel. As in any long-distance attempt, attention to detail and organisation are of crucial importance. An extract from his account from *STA Newslink* gives an indication:

> You have pre-planned with your pilot, in my case Bert Read of the *Accord*, just where you would like to be stationed during your swim, so that at every glance, you are in constant vision with your boat and, more importantly, no exhaust fumes are blowing in your face.
>
> I had agreed with the pilot and crew to chalk on a blackboard every hour, my stroke rate, the state of tide and how long to refreshments – in my case a plastic cup of beef tea handed down on a net-ended stick, a few gulps to refresh me (no four-course meal!) and no touching the pilot boat; this would mean instant disqualification. Then I had to swim through the night, so a boom with a lamp was swung out over the side of the boat; torches were the order of the day for the pilot and crew, just to confirm I was still in contact with my boat. Then, at long last, beautiful daylight and the encouragement from the boat crew, 'Ray, you're nearly there.'

Training, planning and organisation paid off. At 6.56am on the first day of August 1970, Cossum, on his third attempt at the crossing, reached the English shore within sight of Folkestone, his birthplace; he had achieved one of his great ambitions.

Similar organisation had gone into other long-distance swims, and it is worth listing his major achievements on the way to the cross-channel success:

- Lough Swilly, Co Donegal (10 times) – 2hrs 15mins
- Double Lough Swilly – 4hrs 41mins
- Buncrana to Portsalon (17 miles) – 7hrs
- Portrush to Greencastle (19 miles) – 8hrs
- Across Lough Neagh – 6hrs
- Derry to Moville (20 miles) – 6hrs 51mins
- Rathlin to Ballycastle – 3hrs
- Fair Head to Ballycastle – 2hrs 30mins
- Belfast Lough (twice) – 4hrs
- Lake Windermere – 7hrs 35mins

Cossum's last swim but one was the Channel swim; the last one was Lake Windermere. Brother Eric had sponsored the Channel attempt on the understanding that Ray would spend more time on his other great interest, namely diving. The Lake Windermere swim was to be the last hurrah before he finally gave up serious long-distance swimming, having achieved many highs on the way. He had been interested in diving for a number of years and managed to keep both interests going together. Forsaking serious swimming meant he could spend more time diving. Previously, diving had been interspersed with spells working as a postman and in the BSR and at the Water Service.

The demand for his services as a diver were to take him all over the world, but perhaps the project for which he is best known locally, as a diver, is his long-term salvage operation on the *Laurentic*, for which he has bought the rights. The *Laurentic* was carrying gold bullion to Canada to pay for armaments during the First World War when she hit a mine while leaving Lough Swilly. The gold was worth £5 million in 1917 and all but 22 of the 3,211 gold ingots had been recovered when a seven-year search was called off. The chances of finding gold after such exhaustive attempts must be pretty slim. However the recent find of a *Laurentic* safe raises interesting possibilities.

Cossum's expertise in diving which, like his swimming, was mainly learned through trial and error, was an asset brought to the Derry Sub Aqua Club, of which he was a founder member, and it was to have its own successes. The discovery of the *La Trinidad Valencera* wreck site was one of its most important finds and has provided valuable evidence for the study of the Spanish Armada period.

His expertise as a long-distance swimmer was called upon in 1977 when he was asked to help prepare a group of young Northern Ireland swimmers for an attempt to beat the record for a relay swim of the English Channel. Six young people from both communities were chosen from an initial list of 24. To his great delight, they set a new record, one that still stands today.

No matter how immersed he became in his maritime interests, the reality of the *Troubles* for someone living in Creggan was never far away. With some irony, he tells how he, an Englishman, was accused of harbouring terrorists, was beaten and arrested, only to be released without being charged. He also relates how, during a particularly violent period of the *Troubles*, a voice issued forth from the shadows one evening enquiring: 'Hi, Ray, are there any Brits about?' He never discovered the owner of the voice, but was left to conclude that he was considered a Creggan man first and a Brit somewhere down the line, an assumption with which he would not quarrel.

The most traumatic tasks, ones he never shirks, are those involving the search for victims of drowning accidents; in all, he was involved in the search for 23 bodies. Two incidents he remembers starkly. The first was the loss of young Catherine Teresa McGavigan and Pauline Stella Mooney in the reservoir, and the second the loss of Hugh Anthony Toyer in 1976. All three had disappeared on the same day, but it was only the following day that the boy's disappearance was confirmed as a drowning fatality. When he found the little girls, they were still holding hands. Cossum recovered all three bodies and was to have an 'out of body experience' a short time later, one for which he has no explanation. He describes observing himself lying down as the figures of the three young children hovered near, moved near his prone self and then move slowly away. It would seem he paid a high emotional price for his close involvement in such harrowing experiences. Despite the personal trauma, he is also aware of the

Ray Cossum, professional diver and Channel-swimmer, holding artefacts from the *Laurentic*, 2000. (Larry Doherty)

positive effects of the return of loved ones to the bereaved. Consequently, no request has ever been refused.

Raymond Cossum is now a very fit man of 69 and still diving regularly. He is modest about his achievements and speaks of his good fortune in having been able to fulfil many of his ambitions without seeming to consider how much of his success was determined by his talent and commitment. He is appreciative of all the assistance he received over the years in all his endeavours and the freedom and support of his wife to pursue all his dreams. He has no wish to leave Malin Gardens and the record books all register him as Ray Cossum – from Ireland.

The Judo Master: Terry Watt

Terry Watt was born on 20 December 1946 and spent the first 11 years of his life in 9 Leenan Gardens. A Protestant in a predominantly Catholic estate, the young Terry's earliest indication of difference was that the nuns, while calling on his neighbours, never visited the Watt house (some neighbours may have wished that they had been similarly ignored and saved themselves the contributions expected of them). Despite attending a different school to the majority of his boyhood acquaintances, he remembers his Creggan childhood fondly as a time when religious difference was of little consequence.

Like many of his peers, he watched the Ken Walton wrestling programmes on UTV with interest. Many school-playground wrestling bouts followed as he and his companions tried to emulate their TV heroes. In his enthusiasm, Watt began to explore different forms of self-defence. A neighbour, who shall remain anonymous, was responsible for the next stage of his development. Obviously economical with the truth, this neighbour informed him that the reason for an impending visit to Germany was to take up judo. In preparation for the expected jousting on his friend's return, Watt began to read up on the sport. The expected match on the return of the continental traveller did not materialise, but by that time the future international had already developed an intense interest in the sport of judo.

Family connections were to play an important part in the next phase of his sporting career. Watt was related to Marcus Harrison on his mother's side. Many will remember the sign above his garage business in William Street, which seemed to promise customers the personal attention of the proprietor; it read 'Marcus Harrison (himself)'. On the staff of the thriving business worked Bobby Brady, a Creggan man from Malin Gardens, who was coach to the Kosaka Judo Club. After a short introduction, Watt was soon a committed member.

He made rapid progress under Brady and the late Hugh McCann and, by the age of 20, had become the first judo international in Derry and the first in the city to hold a Black Belt in the sport. Watt was to spend 20 years with the Kosaka club, after which he joined the Long Tower club, where he remains a member.

Over his 38 years involvement in the sport, he has competed at the highest level and demonstrated remarkable consistency over that time. Now a Sixth-Degree Black Belt, Terry has won 190 titles in judo and that includes 15 British titles. He collected a World University bronze medal in Portugal where he competed for Britain in 1969. He represented Ireland in the Munich Olympics in 1972 and Northern Ireland in the Commonwealth Games in 1992. The Munich Olympics was particularly memorable as the Olympiad where Mary Peters won her Gold and where terrorism blighted the Games.

When asked to choose his most memorable moment, Watt will tell you he got his greatest thrill from winning the World Masters' Championship in Canada in 1999. In the same year, the District Sports Council awarded him the Sportsman of the Year Veteran's award.

A keen rugby player and cyclist, he also competed at international level in wrestling and petanque (French boules). One can only speculate on the number of other sports that he might have tried with success had he chosen a speciality other than judo.

A big moment which he shared with the people of Creggan was his participation in the cavalcade around the estate which was organised to pay tribute to the Creggan Olympians who had competed in the 1972 Games. Also sharing the float were St Mary's boxers Charlie Nash and Neil McLaughlin and swimmer Liam Ball. In a wry observation, which reflects the unusual circumstances of the period, he commented: 'They burned a bus to celebrate.' Nevertheless, the participation of its sons in such prestigious events as the Olympics gave great cause for celebration and permitted Creggan residents to look beyond the immediate and difficult circumstances of the '70s.

Despite the unfortunate growth in religious animosity among some, Watt has not allowed religious difference to affect his decisions in sport and life generally and has managed, by his conduct inside and outside sport, to gain respect from sportsmen of all disciplines and persuasions and to retain the affection of the people of Creggan.

The completion of the circle for Watt, as far as his Creggan connections go, seems to have begun with his return in the Millennium year to teach self-defence to St Mary's, St Peter's, St Joseph's and St Cecilia's secondary schools.

These schools can be assured of coaching of the highest order from a man who has achieved success at the highest level and who is still at the top in his chosen sport. Watt travels to Phoenix next year to compete in The World Masters' Championship and looks forward to playing a part in the World Masters' in the year 2002 when it will be held in Derry. The prospect of a return to Derry as champion yet again for this exemplary sportsman would gladden the hearts of his many admirers and not least the people of Creggan.

Judo Master Terry Watt beside appropriate sculpture at Foyle Arts Centre, 2000. (Larry Doherty)

The Modest Olympian: Liam Ball

> His style is all wrong and he defies every law of motion in the water. His turns are a complete mess. In fact, he does everything wrong except swim slow. He has tremendous potential. – Don Easterling, coach at University of Texas, Arlington.

Liam Ball (courtesy the Ball family)

Don Easterling wasn't a man who was easily impressed, but he saw the raw potential in Creggan man Liam Ball, and helped make him one of the top ten swimmers in the world. Not that Liam wasn't world class anyway by the time he reached the US. He'd started his glorious ascent at St Columb's College at the age of 12, returning home from a gala one day to his surprised parents with five winner's medals in his hands. By the age of 14, he held numerous Irish titles and junior records. No-one in the country, north or south, could touch him. A year later, he was competing in the Commonwealth Games in Jamaica, and became the first Irishman to get through to the final of the 200m breaststroke. Later that same summer, he was selected for the European Games in Utrecht – all the while still at school.

In 1968, he was picked for the Irish squad for the Mexico Olympics. And he was chosen again for Munich in 1972, setting two Irish records that stood for 17 years. In between, he won a scholarship to Texas, took two silvers at the ASA Finals in 1969, where he beat all the top British contenders, and competed in the Commonwealth Finals in 1970. Today, however, for most people under the age of 25, Liam Ball is best known as the name of the international triathlon run in his memory in Derry every year. For Liam, who was the best swimmer the city ever produced, died tragically in 1984 at the age of only 33. Interviewed in 1997, his late father Len recalled:

> Liam was born in Epworth Street in Rosemount in 1951, a year before we moved to Lislane Drive in Creggan. As a youngfella, he loved playing in the field outside the house. He was a left-footer so he always played outside left. I think he even won a medal for it at the Long Tower. He probably inherited his love of swimming through me, although I never trained him. That was down to Frank Bradley at the City Baths, who coached for the Young Swimming Alliance of Ulster.

Len himself had learned to swim in a filthy mining stream in his native Wales, which would regularly be strewn with dead dogs and other assorted carcasses.

> We'd come home and my father would inspect your hairline, and if he spotted coal dust there, you were for it.

And while Len modestly refused to take credit for his son's success, it is interesting to note that in the *Journal* article to announce his retirement from competition in March 1975, the first person Liam thanked was his father. Ball Junior told the paper:

> He taught me how to swim, gave me every encouragement and saw me out the door at 6.30 each morning to train.

After passing the 11-plus, Liam went to St Columb's College where Hughie McGeown and Fr Keavney were to nurture the fledgling talent. He began winning medals and started competing in national galas. And for three years running, Liam was to win the College's prestigious Victor Aquarum Best Swimmer Award. Meanwhile, he became the Ulster Grammar Schools' Champion and the fastest youth in Ireland at the breaststroke. In 1964, he broke the under-16 record for 100 yards. In 1965, it was little surprise when he was touted as a contender for the following year's Empire and Commonwealth Games. In early 1966, the *Journal* reported that the swimmer had been selected for the Six Counties panel.

Young Ball's first big international games almost ended in disaster when the organisers brought his heat forward by half-an-hour and forgot to tell him. Liam was actually sitting watching the race start on television when he realised he was supposed to be in it. He dashed to the pool and eventually swam a heat by himself; his performance secured a place in the final. He finished eighth in Jamaica, yet recorded his best-ever time. Encouraged, he devoted the next two years of his life entirely to swimming. No parties, no late nights, he was obsessed with going to Mexico. And there was little surprise when he won his place. Len Ball:

> He was out playing football when we heard the news. And while the rest of us were all excited – he was the first-ever Derry swimmer to go to the Olympics – he was totally calm about it all. When the word got out, a local shop sent up a pint of milk and half-a-dozen eggs as a good luck token. We were so worried about the 'amateur status' rule, that I contacted the Olympic Council in Dublin to check whether it was all right to take them. But it was okay.

While in Mexico, where he fared well, but didn't do enough to make the finals, Liam was offered a scholarship to the University of Texas. He wasn't to take up the place until January 1970, by which time he had two ASA silver medals under his belt, and was officially the fastest breaststroke swimmer in Ireland or Britain.

His arrival in the US was greeted with the headline *Newest UTA Star Swam from Ghetto* and first reports revealed that the young Ball didn't take kindly to 'cold tea', preferring it the traditional Irish way, warmed over a stove, rather than chilled with ice. It was a timely move from the then strife-torn Derry, given that there were days the young Creggan man couldn't even get into William Street Baths because of rioting or curfews. Not that such things bothered Liam. The January before his departure for America, Liam had been at Burntollet when Loyalist rioters stoned a student march.

And the courageous young swimmer had to dive into the freezing river to pull out a girl who had slipped. Len Ball:

> He came into the house wearing his cousin's clothes that day because his own had got torn. He stopped off at his granny's to change on the way so as not to worry us. We didn't even know he'd been at Burntollet. We thought he had gone to the pool.

Later, home on holiday from the States, Liam was hit by a rubber bullet while watching a riot in the Bogside. He quickly pocketed the bullet and brought it back to friends in Dallas – who still have it!

Liam came back from Texas to Europe for the Commonwealth Games in 1970 where he finished seventh in the final. And he returned again for the Munich Olympics in 1972 where he set new Irish records for the 100 and 200 metres breaststroke. Meanwhile, his career at Arlington was flourishing and, in 1973, in recognition of his academic and sporting achievements, Liam was awarded the Outstanding College Athletes of America Certificate which was given to his parents for their mantelpiece. Back in Derry, meanwhile, there were men who were more than happy to pass themselves off as Liam Ball. At the height of the *Troubles*, the Balls, who had only a small gate at the back of the house, would occasionally discover they had unexpected guests letting themselves in the back door. Liam's mother Mary:

> One fella came in and said to me: 'I'm here all day'. He told me not to move and went upstairs and changed into Liam's clothes. He then went out the front, where the army were looking for him, walked over to a wee child and led him by the hand back into the house, as if he was the father.

Liam graduated from UTA in 1974 with a BA in History and got a job managing a new swimming pool in Limerick. He wasn't there long before he was offered a job at the newly opened Templemore Sports Complex in Derry and he decided to come home. In June 1976, he married Dublin swimmer Anne O'Connor, who'd also competed for Ireland at Mexico and Munich and who'd won an ASA gold medal in 1969. The pair had known each other since they met at the European Swimming Championships at Utrecht in 1966. Liam retired from competitive swimming but was still active as a coach, founding the Foyle Amateur Swimming Team. He led the first Christmas Day swim at Lough Swilly in 1976.

He occasionally dabbled in other sports, and even tried his hand at the city's multi-sport Superstars competition, and his record for running up and down Lawrence Hill apparently still stands. His friend and fellow sports enthusiast, Gerry Lynch of Derry City Council, recalled:

> He was an all-round sportsman with a genuine interest in all sports and the people who played and supported them. The triple-discipline sport of triathlon would have appealed to him and, in our opinion, is ideal to be

> associated with his memory. His first love, swimming, is, of course, a major factor in triathlon, but the other two disciplines also evoke powerful images of Liam on foot or on wheels – cruising up and down the Buncrana Road. How appropriate that the event bearing his name uses the very pool and the very roads with which he was most familiar.

Liam later became Sports Officer with Derry City Council before moving to Castlebar to run the swimming pool there. His informality and easy-going nature were legion. Len Ball:

> He never allowed you to run anyone down in his company, and because of that, not a person had a bad word for him. He never dressed up. I only ever once saw him in a suit going to a conference, but when I looked down at his feet he was wearing a pair of flip-flops.

When Liam fell ill with a brain tumour, he did his best to hide it from his family. It was his wife, Anne, who eventually told his parents his condition was terminal. His many friends and neighbours in Mayo offered to pay for emergency private treatment in the US for Liam, but it was too late. Ever a fighter, only months before he died Liam jumped into an ice-cold Castlebar lake in a bid to save a drowning victim.

Liam passed from this life in June 1984. His funeral was, not surprisingly, massive, with shops closing for a half day. Len Ball:

> He was buried in Castlebar, but his spirit is in Derry. Even the local travelling community in Mayo came to his funeral, carrying hand-made wreaths. He was popular with everybody. Liam had struck a deal with the travellers that he would give them free access to the pool's facilities for a time on Saturday, if they kept their site at the back of the centre tidy. The arrangements worked out perfectly.

Scores of tributes were paid to Liam's memory in the local and national press, but the one which the Balls particularly treasure is a poem written by one of his Mayo pals, and which shares the mantelpiece with his Outstanding College Athlete award. It reads:

> We shall miss the rattle of your black
> High Nelly, its saddle bags dung-brown,
> Potholing the mile across the town
> The woollen hat, the face that knew no guile,
> The long wave, the slow smile.

Boxing Clever: Charlie Nash

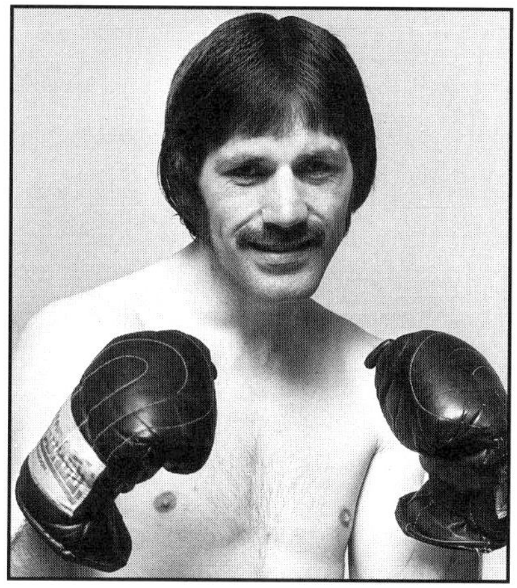
Charlie Nash, European Champion June 1979. (Larry Doherty)

Only a head-butt stopped Creggan man Charlie Nash becoming the lightweight champion of the world. The title-holder, Jim Watt, had just crashed to the floor beneath a flurry of Nash's punches in the first round of their fight. But as the champ struggled to regain his balance, he grabbed the challenger around the waist and cracked his forehead hard into Nash's eyebrow.

Unfortunately, the fight was being held in Watt's home town of Glasgow, so there would be no disqualification. Nash was clattered in blood and by the end of the round, the referee told him he would eventually be forced to stop the fight. Three rounds later he did. Watt got the victory and Derry's most celebrated boxing son never got another shot at the sport's most glittering prize.

Nonetheless, the scale of Nash's achievement is remarkable. From humble beginnings at the Boys' Club at the top of Beechwood Avenue, he rose to become the best boxer in Ireland, then Britain and then Europe. Couple this with a controversial disqualification at the Munich Olympics, which saw Nash lose out to the eventual gold medal winner, and you get some idea of just how powerful a force he was in world sport.

It was no surprise that Nash took up boxing. His grandfather, 'Stiff', had been a renowned fighter, as had several other family members. So at the tender age of ten-and-a-bit, he climbed the stairs to the gym at the back of the Boys' Club and asked the 'man' could he and his pal join up. The 'man' was trainer Tommy Donnelly, and the meeting was the beginning of a beautiful sporting friendship.

> I always had quick hands. There were 13 youngsters in our house, so you had to be fast or your dinner would be gone!

Tommy Donnelly quickly realised his protégé had a special talent and was soon putting him into spar with more experienced boys. Despite his gift, however, Nash lost his first fight. It was against a Belfast lad who was soon to become Ulster Champion – and was probably a bit of a mismatch. But by the time he was 12, the boy from Dunree Gardens had battled through to the final of the 'Ulsters'.

The following year, Nash got through to the Ulster final for a second time, but again found the Belfast judges favoured a Belfast boxer. Perseverance is the mother of success, however. Nash continued to train twice during the week and again at weekends, and by the time he was 15, he was Ulster Juvenile Champion. The victory meant the Derryman qualified for the 1966 All-Ireland Championships to fight in the 15-17 age bracket. He took that title as well at his first attempt.

He moved up a division and by 1968 had added the Ulster Junior crown to his tally. Another trip to Dublin followed and sure enough, he qualified for the Irish Junior final. Unfortunately, Nash and Donnelly nearly missed the decider after getting lost on their road back to the stadium from a snooker hall. The trainer ended up hiring a taxi to lead them home and the boxer ended up doing up his laces on the way into the ring. The omens were bad – as indeed was the result.

Two years later, however, Nash was back in Dublin as Ulster Senior Champion, having beaten the international Jim Montague in the final. (Montague later became British Light-Welterweight Champion.) This time, there were no mistakes and in March 1970, Nash returned to Derry as the All-Ireland Senior Lightweight Champion. He was the first boxer from the city ever to win the title, and his homecoming reception was memorable.

> They took me out of the car at Drumahoe, and got me up on the back of a lorry. They drove me through the city and crowds of people came out to see me – particularly in Creggan. It was fabulous. It was a great time for Creggan. Only a few days later, Dana – who was a near neighbour of ours – won the Eurovision. There were great celebrations in the estate.

The boxer was to repeat his excellent form the following year in Dublin and after he retained his crown, he was invited to join the Irish team for the European Amateur Championships in Madrid. Nash battled well in Spain, beating a handy Bulgarian in his first fight, but lost on a majority decision to the reigning champion in the quarterfinals. All-Ireland success was to follow again in 1972. But the year began with a double tragedy for the 21-year-old boxer.

On January 10, his best friend, Martin 'Mousey' Harkin, suffered a broken jaw at the semifinals of the 'Ulsters' in Ballymena. Nash and Tommy Donnelly took him to hospital, and he was transferred on to Belfast for an operation.

> On Monday morning I was at work when Tommy called into see me. He told me Mousey had died. It was a terrible shock. I had to box in the All-Irelands only a few weeks later. And it was very difficult to go on. But I felt Mousey would have wanted me to.

Ironically, it was on his return from the All-Irelands in Dublin that Nash was to suffer even further heartache. As he and Tommy Donnelly reached Derry, they met hordes of people on the bridge who told them there had been shooting in the town during a Civil Rights demonstration. They made their way to Dunree Gardens, where there were large crowds outside the Nash household.

> People were saying that members of my family had been shot, but no-one knew anything for certain. We made calls to the police station and the

> hospital but couldn't establish very much. So I went over to the morgue. The bodies were lying on the ground covered in sheets. I think it was the fifth or sixth sheet I lifted that I saw my brother, Willie, lying there on the ground.

Willie Nash, who was 19, had been shot dead at the rubble barricade on Bloody Sunday. Nicknamed 'Stiff' after his grandfather, he had been a very useful boxer and was great friends with Jackie Duddy, the other talented young pugilist who died that day. Alex Nash, Charlie's father, was shot and wounded in the arm as he rushed to his dying son.

> It was a very bad time. I used to take out my frustration on the punching bag and on my sparring partners. Boxing and training helped me keep things together. Sometimes if you have a problem and sit about moping, it gets worse. But if you put on a tracksuit and go out for a run, it can really help. Sport is great for discipline. Willie was really into sport. He was the type who wore a shirt and tie when he was marching. He wasn't into rioting – he wasn't political.

Charlie Nash's decision to immerse himself in boxing was to pay off. In early 1972, he and Neil McLaughlin from St Eugene's Club in Derry were picked to join the Irish boxing squad for the Munich Olympics. Two other Creggan men, Terry Watt and Liam Ball, were also picked to compete in judo and swimming respectively.

> It was an absolutely fantastic experience. Fr Joe Carolan drove a carload over for the games. And we would sneak them into the Olympic village by getting other athletes to loan us their passes. Then, of course, you had the trouble there as well. And for a day, it was like being back in Derry, with all these German soldiers wandering about with Bren guns, though they were a lot more friendly than the ones at home.

Nash's first bout, against a Dane, left him with damaged knuckles. So in his next fight, he decided to save his hands by knocking his opponent out in 40 seconds. The quarterfinal beckoned next and a match with the reigning European champion, Jan Sispanski. The Derryman started, all guns blazing, winning the first round and most of the second. But he was given a public warning for hitting the back of his opponent's head.

> It's hardly my fault if the guy keeps turning his head away from my punches, now, is it? I got another public warning in the third round for dropping my head. Then I remember looking up at the lights above, which show you how many seconds are left. And with just 20 seconds left, I went in to throw some punches and was disqualified for ducking too low. The manager of the Irish Olympic team went immediately to the

> jury overseeing the Games. And the ref was eventually dismissed. But they couldn't change his decision and I was out. It was very disappointing. My opponent went on to take the gold.

Nash continued as an amateur, taking the All-Ireland title again in 1973 and 1975. On both occasions, he went on to fight for his country in the European Championships, but lost out both times to the eventual winner, Simon Cutov from Romania.

But while the boxer's lifestyle might have seemed glamourous to some, the reality was very different. A young married man working for the Commercial Paper Company, Nash's financial situation was in no way enhanced by his sport. Expenses for a Home International were a mere 50-pence-a-day, while the overseas allowance was just three dollars.

> By 1975, I had a young child and decided I couldn't afford to box any more. I had to concentrate on making money so I said I'd retire. A few people heard about it and asked me to turn pro. One man came to see me and made me an offer. I raised him a bit – thinking in terms of a colour TV or a washing machine for the house – and we had a deal.

The gap between professional and amateur is a big one – ten rounds rather than three. Strength and stamina are the order of the day, rather than skill alone. But on 6 October 1975, Nash proved he could make the transition with ease, outpointing Ray Ross at the Rialto in Derry, to take the Irish lightweight title. Five consecutive victories followed and the Derry man rose rapidly in the rankings. Then in his seventh outing as a pro, Nash knocked out Liverpudlian Joey Singleton – a former Lonsdale belt holder at light-welterweight – in a British lightweight title eliminator.

A change of management followed, and under the stewardship of Jack Solomon, Nash demanded his crack at the British champion Jim Watt. The fight was arranged for the Sports Complex in Derry, but Watt didn't like fighting outside Glasgow and refused to travel. The Scot eventually relinquished his British crown, and on 25 February 1978, Nash beat Johnny Claydon at the Complex to take the vacant title. The bout was actually stopped in the 12th round on a technicality, after Nash went so many points ahead that it was impossible for Claydon to catch him – even with a knockout. The rules of boxing, indeed, had to be changed subsequently to allow victory by KO at any stage in a contest.

Around this time, Nash agreed to help an amateur featherweight from Monaghan with a bit of sparring. But when young Barry McGuigan landed in Derry, he had little idea what he had let himself in for. Indeed, the visitor later admitted that his Derry host had 'nailed him to the floor'. But the lessons were to pay off for McGuigan, who a few months later took Commonwealth gold, before going on to win the world title at his weight.

Nash's rise in the world rankings continued, and he became number one contender for the European title. Jim Watt was by this stage the holder, but again he relinquished the title rather than fight in Derry. Frenchman Andre Hoylk was instead nominated to fight Nash for the vacant title. And on 27 June 1979, the Creggan boxer became the first man from the city to win a European title, outpointing his opponent over 12 rounds. His home town, which had hosted the contest, was jubilant.

A successful defence followed in Denmark on 6 December against Ken Buchanan, a former world champion. But tragedy struck a few days later when Nash's manager Jack Solomon died. He had been too ill to travel to the fight.

A short time later, Nash signed up with the promoter Mickey Duff who was offering the Derryman a crack at the world title, now held by Jim Watt. The fight was staged on 14 March 1980 at the Calvin Hall in Glasgow, Watt's home turf. And despite flooring the champ in the first round, the Derryman's dreams of glory were shattered when Watt's 'Glasgow Kiss' tore open his eyebrow only seconds later.

Preparations for the title bid, combined with unexplained delays from the European Boxing Board in getting Nash suitable opponents, meant that he'd been forced to give up his European title. But on 14 December 1980 he regained his crown, comfortably defeating Francisco Leon of Spain over 12 rounds. Hopes of a rematch with Jim Watt, however, were in vain. And denied regular fights, Nash was to lose his European title to Joe Gibilisco in May 1981.

Management disputes and problems with cut eyebrows continued to dog the Derry fighter, and in March 1983 he retired from competition, just two months shy of his 32nd birthday. Disillusionment over his inability to get a rematch with Watt also played a part in the decision.

Nevertheless, the Nash legacy is still very apparent in Derry 17 years on. The boxer is a trainer with the Ring Club, his 22-year-old son Charles has been Ulster Senior Champion, while his younger son Conor, who is 14, is currently the Ulster Juvenile Champion.

Unlike many former boxers, Nash has managed to prosper outside the sport. He was always careful to avoid the vices traditionally associated with boxing, such as drinking and gambling, and since his retirement, he has prospered as a businessman. A very modest man, in spite of his great achievements, Nash is anxious to point out that his success was helped in no uncertain terms by the support he got from his wife Betty, children, Julie, Charles, Colleen and Conor, and friends.

> Betty was a constant help and encouragement, and my employers at the Commercial Paper Company – Ernest, and later Alan, McClure – were terrific about giving me time off to fight. And of course, all through the years, I got huge backing from Tommy Donnelly and John Daly, and all my clubmates and sparring partners. I owe them an awful lot. I could never have done it on my own.

John O'Neill: A True Professional

John O'Neill was born in Wellington Street and imbibed football from an early age. His father and uncles were involved with prominent junior team Wellington Rovers whose manager was the famous Peach Campbell, also a relation. His family moved to Creggan when he was just a baby of 18 months. When he was ten, John joined Derry Athletic. The interview published in the programme for his testimonial game describes his progress from there to Leicester City FC:

> I played for that side [Derry Athletic] until I was 14 or 15. Then Jim O'Hea, who was Leicester's Irish scout, sent me over for a trial. They wanted me to sign an apprenticeship, but I wanted to keep studying for my 'A' levels, so I spent the holidays with them. Then, when my grades were good enough to go to university, I signed as a non-contract player and studied at Loughborough University at the same time where I took a three-year degree course in economics. It was in the last year of my course that I broke into the first team, and I made my debut in a 2-2 draw at Burnley in the 1978-79 season. I had to mark Steve Kindon and it was one of the hardest matches I ever had.

The following season Leicester, with John established in the side and managed by Jock Wallace, lifted the second division championship, winning eight of their final ten league games. Said John:

> Jock was a tremendous motivator, with a real 'get up and get 'em approach', and the fans at Leicester worshipped him. I've never known anyone strike up that kind of rapport with supporters anywhere.

So began a topsy-turvy spell in the club's history. Leicester were relegated a year later and narrowly missed out on promotion in 1982 when a 4-1 home defeat by Norwich brought a fine season's work to nought. They picked up just three points out of 12 in the last six games. The same year brought heartbreak in the FA for John and his colleagues. In the third round, they beat a Southampton side, which included Keegan, Channon and Ball, 3-1, won 1-0 at Hereford, then 2-0 at home to Watford, and 5-2 in a remarkable quarterfinal at home to Shrewsbury. Leicester used three 'keepers at different stages of the match – Jim Melrose coming off the bench to replace the injured Mark Wallington between the posts – then getting a knock himself and moving upfield to score twice!

> That was the craziest game I ever played in, but the semifinal was a letdown. Tottenham were comfortable throughout and won 2-0, Ian Wilson scoring an own goal and Tommy Williams breaking his leg.

Leicester were back again, though, in 1983, promoted under the guidance of Gordon Milne.

> I think we played our most attractive football under Gordon. He played for England and Liverpool and wanted us to play the way Liverpool did when he was there. We had a lot of good young players such as Gary Lineker, Alan Smyth and Steve Lynex, and we played some very entertaining football.

In all, John played under five managers at Leicester. Jimmy Bloomfield and Frank McClintock were in charge before he made the first team, Bryan Hamilton completing the list.

The most memorable of John's 39 international appearances for Northern Ireland was, for him, that which proved to be his last. The year was 1986, the country Mexico, the competition the World Cup. The Jalisco Stadium, Guadalajara, with more than 42,000 watching, saw Billy Bingham's men take on mighty Brazil. Despite a vintage performance by veteran 'keeper Pat Jennings they were beaten 3-0 by goals from Careca (2) and Josimar.

> But I'll never forget that day. The atmosphere in the stadium was amazing – the way football should be watched, with musicians in the crowd and people ball-juggling who really should have been out on the pitch!

Playing in the Mexico World Cup proved the greatest experience in John's six-year international career and atoned for the disappointment of Spain in 1982, when he was a regular in the qualifying games, but played only once in the finals, in the 4-1 defeat by France which knocked Bingham's men out of the tournament. But representing his country around the world has brought John some very satisfying moments. He played just once for Northern Ireland under-21s in a 1-1 draw against the Republic in Dublin in 1978. In the same line-up that day were other youngsters who went on to become household names and regular internationals in the years to come; among them Mal Donaghy (then with Larne), Jimmy Nicholl, David McCreery and Billy Hamilton. John's international debut came in a world cup qualifying match against Israel in Tel Aviv in March 1980.

> I think I came through it pretty well and Billy Bingham seemed well pleased. Being a Spurs supporter as a kid, it was wonderful to play in front of Pat Jennings and in the same team as people like Martin O'Neill and Sammy McIlroy. That was a very special year, because we went on to win the British Championship for the first time in half-a-century. We beat Scotland at Windsor Park, then went to Wembley to play England. They went ahead with an own goal by Noel Brotherston, but Terry Cochrane came on as a substitute and scored the equaliser.

A goal from Brotherston gave Bingham's men a 1-0 win over Wales at Ninian Park, Cardiff, and that was enough to clinch the championship. That triumph sparked a very successful spell for Northern Ireland who qualified for Spain in 1982 in dramatic fashion.

> I best remember the game against Scotland at Hampden Park. We went ahead with about 15 minutes left through Billy Hamilton, and even though John Wark equalised more or less immediately, a 1-1 draw was a great result for us. We thought we may have missed out when we only drew 0-0 in the return at Windsor Park, but then Israel beat Portugal 4-1, so we needed a draw with Israel at home in our last match to go through. Gerry Armstrong scored and we won 1-0 in front of a full house.

John played just once in Spain, as a substitute for David McCreery in Madrid in the final match in France, and admitted it was a great disappointment. A goalless draw at another of John's favourite grounds, Wembley, against England clinched the Irish a place in Mexico four years later, and this time he played in all three games – against Algeria, Spain and Brazil.

> In terms of success, Billy Bingham must rate as the best manager I played under. Some of the results he achieved with the small pool of players at his disposal were remarkable. We won the British Championship, we beat Germany, Spain and Romania, drew with France in France – they were remarkable results really.

After a short spell with Queen's Park Rangers, John's distinguished career in football was brought to a premature end. On his very first match with new club Norwich in December 1987, he was the victim of a ferocious tackle by John Fashanu. A nerve on his right knee was severed, as were all the ligaments. Two operations failed to repair the damage sufficiently to allow a return to football and, to this day, feeling has not fully returned to his right foot. He is still held in high regard in the game as a person and a footballer. Gary Lineker, a friend since their early days together at Leicester, demonstrated this by travelling from Barcelona for John's testimonial game at Norwich.

Former managers have registered their opinions. Jock Wallace has gone on record as saying:

> From the outset, I recognised him as a quality person and a quality footballer . . . John has never been a flash guy. He's someone I regard highly for his integrity and honesty . . . I had his respect at Leicester and he will always have mine.

Billy Bingham, the former Northern Ireland team manager, expressed a similar opinion when he said:

> As a defender, he was as solid as a rock with a fierce tackle and a strong will to win. A quiet, thoughtful personality, he was a great team player. Never showy, he epitomised the true professional.

When presented with a questionnaire for publication in his testimonial programme, John, always appreciative of the guidance he received in his early days in Creggan, listed Jim O'Hea as the biggest influence on his career.

Even in Leicester he was to be reminded of his Creggan identity and of the *Troubles*. The occasion was his testimonial reception when a young man approached and declared: 'Many's the time I lay in your mother's back garden.' As it turned out he had indeed, when he served with the British Army on the estate.

John O'Neill marking England's Kevin Keegan in the British Championship, 1980. (Neville Chadwick)

Captain Courageous: Paul Ramsey

Paul, son of Sammy Ramsey, a talented junior footballer, followed a path already trodden by fellow Creggan man John O'Neill. Like O'Neill, references to Ramsey's previous clubs in football programmes list only one, Derry Athletic. Ramsey caught the eye of Athletic manager and Leicester scout Jim O'Hea in a street kickaround when he was just ten years old. Jim describes the circumstances:

> The first thing I noticed about him was his striking Fairisle sweater and his infectious grin. He was a barrel-chested ten-year-old and he just seemed to fill the entire sweater. Anyway, once I had started to watch him, I realised that he had more than just dress sense. Even in a street game, his skills shone through. And his tackling was amazing; he would have tackled a brick wall. So I asked Paul to join my club, Derry Athletic, and, within a few years, he became one of the youngest players ever to turn out for our first team.

March 1979 saw him sign his first forms for Leicester City, followed by an apprentice contract two months later. After his first match as a schoolboy international, for Northern Ireland, Ramsey was made captain for the next match against England, when he led Northern Ireland to a 3-2 victory at Deansgate. As a youth of 17½, he was deemed good enough to turn out for Leicester City against Red Star Belgrade, but inexplicably failed to get a place in the Northern Ireland Youth team.

In March 1981, he made his league debut against Arsenal, as a substitute, in a match that Leicester won 1-0, and fellow Athletic 'old boy' John O'Neill played a starring role. By the time he reached his testimonial game, in November 1989, he had played almost 300 league and cup games for the club.

His favourite position was midfield, but he regularly filled the right-back position with equal competence. At one stage, Paul and Gary McAllister were hailed as the ideal midfield partnership, manager David Pleat identifying it as one of the reasons for the team's upsurge in fortunes. He continued:

> Ramsey is McAllister's minder in midfield and they complement each other nicely. McAllister has the invention, while Ramsey is the industrious one, and it works very well.

In one match, it took the successful combination of their midfield talents to secure a victory over the notorious Wimbledon. The game was played at Filbert Street in February 1987. As expected, it was a bruising encounter that left John O'Neill 'floored and spitting blood' and the two teams reduced to ten men each. When manager Bryan Hamilton was asked, after this bad tempered encounter, if the Dons had perfected the art of the late tackle, he replied: 'No, I would say they have not yet perfected the art of disguising it.' John O'Neill was to later to suffer the consequences of this Wimbledon 'art form', which finished his career. However, it was a game that Ramsey relished and where all his talents shone through. Leicester City won 3-1 after he scored two goals, one from a chipped pass from McAllister, and the second after a skilful move started by the same player. Ramsey was voted man of the match. His all-round contribution and leadership qualities in this and other matches were recognised when he was awarded the captaincy. He continued to score goals regularly, many of them from the right-back position. He stayed 12 years with Leicester and it was during his spell with the club that he won his 14 full international caps.

His international debut could not have been more satisfying: the date was September 1983, the venue was Windsor Park, and the opponents were Austria in a European Championship tie. Ramsey was chosen to play right back and was in good company. The team read: Jennings (Arsenal), Ramsey (Leicester City), Chris Nicholl (Grimsby Town), McClelland (Glasgow Rangers), Donaghy (Luton Town), McIlroy (Stoke City), Martin O'Neill (Notts County), captain, Armstrong (Real Mallorca), Hamilton (Burnley), Whiteside (Manchester United), Stewart (Queen's Park Rangers).

A number of milestones were reached that day, as Pat Jennings celebrated his 100th cap, Chris Nicholl his 50th, and Norman Whiteside scored his first international goal in a 3-1 victory for Northern Ireland. Sports columnist for the *Belfast Telegraph*, Malcolm Brodie, picked Martin O'Neill as man of the match, and of Ramsey's contribution declared:

> It's a long time since anyone has been so impressive in a debut. He is a real find, a gem.

Billy Bingham was similarly enthusiastic when he invited the press to agree with his own assessment:

> Wasn't Ramsey marvellous? To think there was 99 caps difference between him and Pat [Jennings]. You wouldn't have believed it, for he never put a foot wrong.

His next international appearance was in the famous 1-0 victory against West Germany, where Jennings gave a brilliant display of goalkeeping and the *Daily Telegraph* reported:

> In midfield, Ramsey and O'Neill were creative, yet always willing to fall back to help stem the second-half onslaught.

The Creggan man had consolidated his claim as a player of international standing and went on to claim 14 caps in all. The mystery is that there were not more.

After spending 12 years with Leicester, he moved to Cardiff at the instigation of someone who knew him well. When former Leicester reserve team manager Eddie May was appointed manager of Cardiff City, his first requirement was a player with leadership qualities. His first choice was Ramsey, who was duly transferred to the Welsh team and given the captaincy. The move worked out for both parties. That he had lost none of the qualities for which he was chosen is evident in a report by the *South Wales Echo* in April 1993. The match was against Wrexham and the report read:

> Skipper Paul Ramsey led by example, appearing to believe he was single-handedly responsible to ensure progress.

It could have described any match in which he played. Under the Derryman's captaincy Cardiff were promoted to the second division in 1992, although he missed some matches through injury.

He had spent three years at Cardiff when he answered a call from former international colleague John McClelland, who was then manager of Scottish team St Johnstone. McClelland needed a strong character to help turn things around at the club and knew Ramsey would fit the bill. McClelland left the club within a few months of Ramsey's arrival, but the Derryman stayed for two seasons before embarking on his next move, this time to the continent.

Again he was to be brought in for his experience and leadership to play an influential part in the progress of Finnish team KPV from Kokkola. After a season and a half there, he returned to Leicester where he is now involved in coaching youths.

Because most of Ramsey's development and success as a footballer was achieved at a distance from his native city, and therefore difficult to savour, his considerable success has not received the acclaim it might have in his home town. He was a player of international standard who also had a special quality which saw him captain every club he played for. The youth of Leicester are fortunate to have the benefit of his special combination of talents or, to put it another way, Derry's loss is Leicester's gain.

Paul Ramsey with team-mate and English international Gary Lineker. (courtesy Ramsey family)

Northern Ireland team, British Champions in 1984, with Paul Ramsey and John O'Neill, back row, third and fourth from right. (courtesy Ramsey family)

Seán Dolan's and Creggan's GAA Revival

Derry's long love affair with soccer has meant that other sports in the city have perhaps been neglected over the years. Gaelic football, however, did have a very strong following in the early part of the 20th century; at one stage, there were 17 teams in the city. But the growth of the 'garrison game', and the decades-long GAA ban on soccer players, led to the number of Gaelic teams dropping to only two by the 1980s.

Happily, the tide began to turn in the '90s, and nowhere has this been more evident than in Creggan which will shortly boast a 19-acre Centre of Excellence, encompassing three pitches, a handball court, Derry's first GAA club hall, an Irish Language school and community housing.

The achievement of Seán Dolan's GAA Club is all the more remarkable when you consider that when they first came to Creggan, the players regularly had to shift burnt-out cars and lorries off the pitch before they could get their game. The field, unfortunately, lay directly in front of a British Army camp at Piggery Ridge and was the favoured venue for pitched battles of the less sporting kind.

Seán Dolan, a Waterside man, was jailed for IRA activities during the Second World War. He had clearly been a popular character in the North West. A hurler on the County Derry team, he was also a very capable Gaelic football player. Outside sport, he was an accomplished musician, specialising in the cello; he was also a talented linguist. Indeed, his knowledge of Spanish meant that girls were tripping over themselves to get at him; not to go out with him, as he would have liked, but to get him to do their bidding with the contingents of Spanish sailors who would have visited Derry in those times.

Dolan is also remembered as having been very religious; despite the Church's ostracism of IRA members, he attended Mass daily and was a regular communicant.

The Waterside man was eventually arrested with a group of IRA friends in Rosemount in early 1940, after the girl sent to alert them to an impending police raid took a short cut through Brooke Park and missed them.

He was to die of TB on the *Alrawda* Prison Ship on 25 October 1941, aged only 28. A memorial at the Creggan clubhouse states that his death was ' . . . as a result of ill-treatment received while an untried prisoner in a Belfast jail.' Shortly after his death, one of the Waterside's leading GAA clubs, St Patrick's, changed their name to Seán Dolan's in his honour. And in the mid-'70s, the club shifted lock, stock and barrel to its current site above Creggan Heights. The club brought with it a strong reputation in sporting circles. Mickey McNaught captained Derry in the '50s. Indeed five players from the club were to play on the County side during that era. Initially, Dolan's leased its pitch at Creggan from Derry City Council and for 20 years the amenity was pretty basic. There was neither clubhouse nor changing rooms, and teams had to kit out in cars. Anne Sands, the club's Development Officer, commented:

> The club nearly folded a number of times. You had the weekly ritual of removing burnt-out lorries, debris and bottles from the pitch after the

> riots, and support in general for the GAA in the city was at a low. But in the early '90s, there was a turnaround. A good committee was established which included the likes of Danny McGowan, Eamonn McGlinchey, John McChrystal, Noel McChrystal, Theo Duffy, Patsy McChrystal and Paddy McNaught. They put in place development plans and were instrumental in raising funds that allowed us to build and expand.

The first major fundraising drive was a sponsored cycle in 1995, which collected £3,500. Since then, hundreds of thousands of pounds have been accessed in the form of grants and voluntary contributions. Changing rooms were constructed and a new clubhouse, offering a bar, snooker, pool and darts to the members, was opened in June 1998. There is a community-education facility in the building and the new hall, when complete, will cater for dances and concerts. A purpose-built school is included in the development plans.

Anne Sands was appointed in 1999, and the continued growth of the amenity as a social centre means it now employs a total of 12 staff – a number certain to rise as the facilities expand. Membership too is burgeoning. Dolan's now has 400 juveniles and around 300 adults on its books, though not all of these are players.

The footballers currently compete in Division Three of the County League, but Anne Sands would argue that they are good enough for the next section up. The underage teams are meanwhile producing a good crop of young players which would suggest the future is at least secure – if not rosy.

Hurling is, however, less popular with the intake, a clear disappointment to the committee, given that it's not in direct competition with soccer, as could be said about Gaelic football. And Camogie is, as yet, only an aspiration. Anne Sands:

> The main problem is that we've still only one pitch. And that isn't enough.

The benefits to the youngsters who become involved with the club are immediately apparent. It provides them with an alternative to running the streets, and promotes good discipline and team interaction. It is also beneficial from a social point of view. Dolan's under-16s are involved in a cross-community initiative with juniors from Brigade Cricket Club and City of Derry Rugby Club. This allows the children to try other sports and meet others from different backgrounds. Anne Sands:

> The club is a very important facility for Creggan. We want to provide a social outlet – not just for those who enjoy sport, but for the community as a whole. That's what the GAA is about. Basically, it's a way of life.

Seán Dolan's GAA team in 1975. The photo was taken before a game at Claudy. When one of those pictured was asked if they had won the match, he commented: 'No, though we gave a good account of ourselves in the scrap . . .' The editors stress, however, that the bearded chap in the back row had no part in anything untoward. Back (from left): John McChrystal, Mitchel McLaughlin, Eddie Logue, Hugh Wilkinson, Peter Bowe, Donal Ferry, Paddy Ross, Raymond Logue, Danny Moore, Sean Ferry, Willie Ferry, Frankie Clifford. Front (from left): Kevin Doherty, Joe Doherty, Seán O'Kane, Seamus Ferry, Liam Ferry (with young Declan Ferry), Tommy McGlinchey, Eugene Ferry, George Caldwell.

County Derry hurler and IRA man Seán Dolan pictured in the late 1920s. St Patrick's GAA club in the Waterside renamed itself in his honour after he died on a prison ship in 1941. The club then moved to Creggan in the 1970s. (courtesy Dolan's GAA Club).

CHAPTER 6

Making Money . . . and Making None

Unemployment and poverty have always plagued Creggan. Time and again, statistics have shown that it is one of the most socially deprived areas in Northern Ireland and Britain. At stages during the '70s and '80s, more than 90% of the male population was officially jobless.

A large part of the problem has been political. Until recent years, international investors got little encouragement to come to Nationalist areas, and backing for indigenous industries was scant. More pertinently perhaps, discrimination against Catholics in the workplace was widespread. The decline in the manufacturing sector in Western Europe, as multinationals headed to the Far East, compounded the situation.

The death knell for large-scale 'traditional' industry in Creggan was perhaps sounded in 1997 when United Technologies Automotive (UTA), which made parts for Citroen, shut up shop. Previously, the Bligh's Lane plant had encompassed the Essex factory, which supplied Ford. And before that it had housed the BSR factory, which manufactured components for record players and tape recorders.

But the end of multinational involvement at Bligh's Lane has afforded opportunities for newer economic initiatives. The UTA site, it is envisaged, will flourish as a business park for local entrepreneurs. And significantly perhaps, many of the workers who were employed at UTA are retraining in the IT sector which is presently burgeoning in the city.

Much of the turnaround in Creggan's economic fortunes is due to Creggan Enterprises Limited and the growth in the 'social economy'. But it's with the area's most renowned employer ever, BSR, that we begin our look at how Creggan men and women put bread upon their tables.

The BSR Story

The BSR plant at Bligh's Lane was always more than just a factory. Some have labelled it a small town; the journalist Lawrence Moore describes it here as one of the largest social clubs in Ireland. But, however the BSR is defined, its importance to Derry and to Creggan cannot go unrecorded. In this extended piece, first published in the newspaper Streetlife *in 1990, Lawrence takes a nostalgic and often humorous look at the huge contribution – both financial and social – which the plant was to make during its two decades as Derry's largest employer.*

The gates clanged close, the uniformed security man wrapped a chain around the bars and secured the operation with a heavy padlock. Something in the region of 150 workers watched the ritual at the Bligh's Lane gate, some in stony silence, others hurling abuse in the impassive face of the official. Most thought that this was yet another sequel in the never-ending series of disputes, strikes, walkouts and lockouts that seemed to be an integral part of life at the Derry subsidiary of Birmingham Sound Reproducers – to all in the city, the BSR.

Yet, among that crowd in January 1967, some of the more astute workers felt a deep sense of foreboding. Yes, closedown notices had been posted on the gates before, but this time an extra ingredient had been present. The previous three weeks at the factory had been depressingly unreal: a funereal atmosphere had hung over the plant and it was like presiding over the obsequies of a long-suffering friend.

For almost two decades, the BSR was the focal point for the vast majority of male workers in the Derry area. At full production, 2,050 workers were on the company's payroll in three separate factories in the city. A staggering 35,000 record changers and 12,000 tape decks were produced each week when the assembly lines were flat out; 10,000 motors were also produced for the parent factory at Old Hill in Birmingham. Quality, quantity and costs were infinitely superior to those at Old Hill and the new manufacturing unit at East Kilbride, just outside Glasgow in Scotland. Given these statistical gems, why did the company call an abrupt halt to its Derry operations? What was the economic sense in turning its back on such a lucrative manufacturing capacity? After a silence of 25 years, we now know the full facts behind the BSR decision to close the Derry factories and some popular misconceptions are laid to rest.

Derryware Engineering, a local company occupying a section of what was the old Derry shipyard, was engaged in the manufacturing of printing machines in the city. Andrew McOwen, a former Naval Officer, who had been appointed to this, his first civilian job after 25 years in the Royal Navy, managed the company. Among other skilled local personnel at the factory were Hammie Anderson, John Doherty and Tommy McGill. In 1951, a rather dignified, bespectacled visitor was being shown around the factory (known locally as Swains) and he was introduced to McOwen and Tommy McGill. Dr Daniel McDonald was the owner of a small engineering facility in Old Hill in Birmingham. The factory employed 100 people, who were mainly engaged in the production of small electric motors and other electrical equipment. During the war, McDonald had been prominent in the production of communications equipment for ships and tanks, but with the cessation of hostilities found himself needing new challenges. He was in Northern Ireland to investigate the possibility of setting up a factory to expand his Birmingham-based operation and talked the project over with McGill and McOwen.

They told him of the ready-made workforce, and a further attraction was the availability of a vacant factory at Bligh's Lane in the city. McDonald told both men he had almost certainly decided on Derry for his factory and he invited Tommy McGill, Andrew McOwen, John Doherty and Hammie Anderson over to Birmingham for a week to look over his operation in Old Hill.

When they arrived in Birmingham, the Derry group was decidedly less than impressed with what it saw. Three rows of terraced houses formed a triangle and inside the triangle was the much-talked-about McDonald factory, all 5,000 sq ft of it. During their tour of the factory, they found the Dickensian exterior maintained on the shop floor as workers laboured in antiquated and primitive operations that amazed the Derry contingent. McGill commented to McOwen about being able to improve on what he had seen in Birmingham. McOwen met McDonald in a corridor and during their conversation let the doctor know of McGill's sentiments.

McGill thought Derry could do all that was being done in England and do it a lot better and quicker,. When asked to elaborate, McGill named four operations that were being carried out manually that could be automated quite easily. McDonald said nothing for a few minutes and at the end of an awkward silence, he picked up the telephone and said: 'Send Larry Guest in, and ask him to bring the new drawings with him.' Larry Guest was the chief designer at the Birmingham factory, a quiet man, but one who was held in high esteem by McDonald. The Derry group soon found that McDonald's confidence in his chief designer was not misplaced and that he was also a very likeable person. Guest handed the drawings to his boss, who in turn handed them to McGill. 'Could you produce that in Derry?' he asked McGill. On inspection, McGill saw that the sheets were various drawings of a small electric motor consisting of two coils, stator pack, rotor and end shields. The Derry men studied the drawings for some time then said to McDonald:

> How many do you want to make, per day, per week? Do you want them produced in batch or continuous process? Special tooling would be required; would you supply it or would you want Derry to make it?

For the second time McDonald went quiet. Eventually he told McGill to leave things for now – they would talk again the following morning.

Next morning, the doctor had all his answers ready. He wanted 5,000 motors per week, 1,000 per day, Monday to Friday. No tooling was available for the new product, it would need to be manufactured in Derry and would this be a problem? McGill told him it would be no problem at all, provided they could get the machines they needed. McDonald told McGill to go out to the warehouse where machinery was stored and to take anything he needed for the new Derry Toolroom. McGill went round as directed and with a piece of chalk, he marked 'Derry' on a variety of machines including lathes, milling machines, grinders and anything he thought necessary for stocking a Toolroom.

At the end of the week, the Derry group returned home and the following Monday, 3 February 1951, Tommy McGill went to the empty factory at Bligh's Lane to take stock. The premises were completely empty and the offices didn't even have light bulbs. Two lorries and two trailers were despatched from Old Hill with the machinery McGill had selected in Birmingham, but until they arrived, other things were an immediate priority. He bought a sheet of plywood in town, found two packing boxes in the old canteen and made an impromptu table on which he proceeded to design the tools needed for producing the motors. Two weeks later, the lorries arrived with the machinery from Birmingham and McGill started to recruit for the BSR in Derry. John Doherty and Hammie Anderson were both turners with Swains, and both came to the BSR. Jimmy Whoriskey, Eddie Long and Hughie Murray soon followed; Victor Peoples was approached by McGill, but he was in steady employment and declined the offer. He would eventually join the staff two months later, however, and another Swain employee, a red-haired local, would also make the move to Bligh's Lane; his name was Paddy Henderson.

The tooling-up for the new assembly line went ahead at a great pace and McDonald came to Derry every third week to check on progress. He was impressed at the skills and enthusiasm displayed by the small staff at Bligh's Lane and talked eagerly about future progress in Derry. Within months, the first assembly line took shape as production started in the Motor Department, situated just beside the Toolroom at one end of the factory. Two general handymen-cum-security staff, Tommy Seaton and Paddy McBride, were employed to check-in lorries bringing machinery and equipment from Old Hill. As production of motors increased, a production supervisor was required, and the man appointed was Joe Millar from the nearby Creggan estate. Joe brought his own unique brand of leadership to the motors and used the less attractive jobs like the solder pot to motivate the less-than-enthusiastic members of his workforce.

During those early days, all motor production was exclusively for the English factory at Birmingham, which was engaged in the production of the TU 8, a single-deck record player that was proving to be very popular. Motors were also produced in Derry for the Post Office in England and, as a consequence, the assembly line in Derry expanded quickly.

McDonald and his chief designer Larry Guest were so impressed with the quality and quantity of the Derry work that drawings were produced for a completely automatic record changer that was initially scheduled for construction at Birmingham.

The BSR chief brought the drawings to the city and informed McGill and the Derry staff that Bligh's Lane would also produce the new changer. This was a striking testimony to the skill and adaptability of the Derry workforce and was all the more startling when one considers that it was less than one year from an empty factory to producing a sophisticated and innovative piece of equipment that would revolutionise music reproduction.

The wheels had started to move, the main protagonists were in position, and the momentum would build to an amazing crescendo that would, in the process, fashion a workplace that would produce record players, tape decks, national headlines, entertainers, sportsmen and unforgettable characters at a phenomenal rate.

The faltering steps were now becoming a confident stride; the embryo that was the McDonald plan now heaved to healthy birth and the economic barometer in Derry looked set to rise. Chief designer in Birmingham, Larry Guest, became a frequent visitor to Derry and the interpretation of the visits by the Bligh's Lane management was that Derry's potential was being carefully monitored with a view to rapid expansion. The breakthrough came when the drawings for the new record changer were given to the Bligh's Lane plant with instructions to begin tooling immediately. New equipment began arriving on a weekly basis and recruitment moved into overdrive.

Toolroom personnel were given top priority; Victor Peoples joined the company and was Toolroom foreman in a short time. The department expanded quickly and soon justified the confidence of the Old Hill parent factory in allowing the Derry group to manufacture all the tooling for the new changer and many other subsequent projects. Men like Paddy McKay, Jack Godfrey, Jimmy Myles, Brian Heap, Denis McKinney, Mickey McGuinness, Brendan Doherty, Leo Smith, Joe Grimes and others would consistently produce work of an exceptionally high standard and would introduce many new and innovative devices that would make life a lot easier for their production colleagues.

The Toolroom became something of an elitist group within the factory, although the reputation was inflicted rather than sought. They certainly liked their own company and every year they organised their own Christmas party, usually in Donegal. Barry McLaughlin took charge of this event and during the proceedings every member of the group had to contribute something to the evening's festivities – either song, story or verse. The entire ritual was recorded on audiotape and, as most of the gathering had fought a losing battle with Arthur Guinness and Johnny Walker in the course of the evening, the completed tape was absolutely hilarious. A sequel to the December party was a New-Year get-together to listen to the Christmas tape.

On the production front, the Motor Department and main assembly lines had begun to generate their own momentum. Joe Millar headed the motors and Harry McCauley was his chargehand; 5,000 motors were produced weekly, half of which were transported back to Old Hill, some destined for the GPO in England. The main assembly line in the Motor Department in 1955 contained within its ranks the McCarron brothers (James and Paddy), Patsy McIntyre, James McCloskey, Monty Montgomery, John and Willie Cooley, Billy Heaney, Raymond McGlinchey, Mickey Ball, Matt Nixon, George Callaghan and many others.

An example of the lunacy that passed as normality within the factory was always evident when someone was getting married. On one occasion in the motors, Billy Taylor was stripped to his underwear, painted in green Spectra colour, hoisted by a rope to the roof rafter and as he dangled precariously was sketched by Vincent McMonagle sitting below. Works of lesser ability adorn the walls of the Louvre in Paris. Jimmy 'Red' Loughrey was a worker in the sub-assembly of the motors. Jimmy was a professional boxer of moderate ability who hardly caused Willie Pep or Sandy Saddler sleepless nights. A favourite ploy of his 'mates' was to send him to the store for some item or other, and, as he made his way up the factory floor, the entire department would, in unison, count from 1 to 10 as a referee would do to an unfortunate boxer. The banter apart, work was of the highest standard and production targets were met with continuous regularity.

By early 1952, the tooling was ready for the new record changer and management thoughts were firmly set on early production. Derry informed McDonald that all would be ready to set up the first production run by the end of March or early April. Other departments began to flex their production muscles, and component parts were starting to filter through from the Machine Shop, Press Shop and Automatics. These departments were in their infancy, but had enough experience and equipment to supply the necessary components for the proposed start-up. Paddy Henderson was given the responsibility of supervising the first assembly line to produce record changers at Bligh's Lane in Derry. The first schedule ever issued to the Derry factory was for over 100 record changers per week, and this from a workforce with absolutely no background or previous experience in light engineering or assembly procedures.

Derry's potential was given full rein and all departments grew in tandem. Three final assembly lines, under the control of Tommy Young, saw production rise steadily from those modest days in April, and Eddie O'Donnell was appointed chargehand to take some of the increasing load off Young. As numbers grew, other supervisors included George Meehan and Charlie McGuinness. Among the workers was a young lad who worked at fixing transit screws on the main plate, and who in later years would make quite a name for himself in Irish and European soccer, John 'Jobby' Crossan. Pat McDevitt and Ed Stewart were also among the early recruits to the final assembly line.

The completed changers were packed, in those early days, at the end of the production lines. Barry Hampsey was in charge of the packing and Willie White, Barry's brother Gerry and Pius Gallagher made up the packing team. A most important function in the final assembly lines was the testing of changers with records for both playing and 'dropping', and this test bay was under the control of Brendan McGrillis. Jackie Keys and Willie Brown listened to music all day in a job that was envied by many in other departments. The final test department was staffed by Teddy Dooley, Owen Rafferty and Neil Doran. The foreman was Jim 'Tiger' Robb. This section took random changers that were already passed and gave them a thorough and complete re-check to ensure that the quality of the finished product was of the highest standard.

The phenomenal growth of the Derry operation can be gauged by an incident that happened in 1951. On a visit to the Derry factory at Bligh's Lane, Dr McDonald was being driven into the premises by his personal driver, Frank Hone. McDonald told Frank, who incidentally was one of the first employees of BSR in Derry, to drive the car into the almost empty factory. Frank stopped the car where the Press Shop would eventually be situated and McDonald got out and was met by two members of management. As they walked leisurely through the near-deserted plant, McDonald turned to both and said: 'I can see the day very soon when this factory will be filled with workers and 4,000 record changers will be produced every week.' Little did he know that his projection was far short of what would ultimately be achieved and the eventual consequences escaped the trio as they strolled through the silent factory.

The factory was now expanding at a furious pace. Hand presses were brought in from Old Hill and orders were placed for new power presses to augment the manual presses as components began to be supplied from source in Derry. This was in effect the stirrings of the Press Shop, and one of the original group, who went to Birmingham to look the place over prior to BSR coming to Derry, was John Doherty from Creggan. John was given responsibility for the Press Shop, a mammoth task, as practically every pressed part in the changer would begin life in this department. Bligh's Lane was fast becoming self-sufficient, and with the advent of new equipment, courtesy of the generous grant scheme the NI Government offered to induce potential employers to invest in the province, the Press Shop grew rapidly.

Huge power presses were purchased, and it was fascinating to watch as the gigantic Hordern-Mason-Edwards (HMEs) were winched into position. These 100-ton presses had to have special vibration pads fitted, so intense was the pressure exerted during operations. Johnny Whoriskey and Mickey Coleman had many anxious moments as these giants were manoeuvred into position. The HME was primarily used for pressing out turntables; other heavy-duty power presses included the 15-ton Sweeney & Blocksidge used for main plate pressing. Allied to the Press Shop, but situated for convenience close to the Motor Department, was the Lamination Department. Here, the massive Schuler power presses, roll-fed from huge rolls of steel, produced laminations for stator packs and rotors for the production of motors. George McDaid was in charge of this department.

The Press Shop abounded with characters, all unique in their own right. On the guillotine were Ned McCafferty and James McCauley. This pair cropped the steel into rectangles ready for various pressing jobs. Seamus Deeney, a councillor in the old Derry Corporation, was chargehand, as was Eddie Molly from the Waterside, and Johnny McIntyre. Sammy Campbell, Ray McCallion and Sammy Curry were setters, and Dan O'Donnell and Willie O'Donnell were the department fitters. Paddy 'Hard-Wrought' Doherty collected and tied up the scrap steel, and press operators included Larry 'Bright Eyes' Richmond, George Millar, Harry Holmes, 'Tando' Doherty, Tommy Gibson, Paddy McIntyre, John Reddin, Richard Coyle, Noel Reddin, Ronnie Kennedy, Danny Moran and a host of others whose pranks would have made a sick cat laugh. Another member of the Press Shop staff was Eddie Long. Eddie is fondly remembered for coming out of the front office the night Derry City were engaged in a replay with Linfield in the semi-final of the Irish Cup at Solitude in the 1950s. I can still see him holding up two fingers of his left hand and one on his right – the smile on his face told the overtime workers who had won. Eddie had a sudden and premature death; he collapsed while leaving the factory and died a short time later.

The Press Shop was one of the biggest departments in the factory and was an intimidating sight to behold, a sea of noise and swinging metal that churned out components of every size and shape from the very bowels of the plant.

As the payroll grew, other departments sprang up to put finishing touches to component parts. A Blacking Shop was located beside the Press Shop to chemically put a black coating on some pressed parts including motor end shields. Hand-dipped baths were introduced to put a bronze-like finish on other pressed parts and a spray booth was set up to spray turntables and main plates. With the passage of time, these departments would employ more sophisticated and automatic techniques, but now a new, if antiquated, process meant more jobs.

Another system introduced with some urgency was the stores. With rocketing production and increased schedules, the priority was for a centralised point to store, distribute and co-ordinate all bought-in items required for production. The man with this responsibility was Monsey Morrow. In the early 1950s, American writer Nat Hiken created a TV character called Sergeant Bilko who became a smash hit on Stateside television. Monsey Morrow was the personification of Sergeant Bilko. Stories about his exploits are legendary and everybody who approached his store felt his wit at one time or another. He used to 'run a book' at the local greyhound track and his blatant stunt was to be seen with a wad of notes conducting his business. In reality, what he had was a bundle of stage money with a single pound note wrapped around the bundle. A particularly brazen exploit occurred in 1958; at that time, an American heartthrob called Troy Donahue had an enormously successful song in the hit parade called *Send Me The Pillow That You Dream On*. Monsey appeared at work with this huge pillow, wrapped in the finest paper, and announced that he had been sent the pillow by the American singer. He would raffle the pillow the following Friday, and notices to this effect appeared all over the factory. The tickets went like hot cakes and a gigantic profit was made from a Littlewoods pillow.

Stories about his 'illegal trading' in cross-border cigarettes aroused interest in many quarters, some of them beyond the confines of the factory, and hurried removal of stocks prevented many calamities. His wit was razor-sharp. On one occasion a certain chargehand went to the stores for a packet of drills. He was quite liberal in the use of these drills, and Monsey said to him:

> Mr McOwen [the factory manager] thinks you are doing a fantastic job.
>
> Is that right? replied the chargehand.
>
> Aye, replied Monsey, he said that anybody going through that amount of drills must be here 24-hours-a-day.

The swift, exaggerated, business walk was as characteristic of the man as his many notorious deals and outlandish projects. He was as difficult to handle as a spoonful of mercury, but he was loved, as all impish rogues are. In the company of BSR characters, Monsey Morrow was head and shoulders above the rest.

The vacant factory, occupied by Tommy McGill in 1951, now assumed the status of a vibrant, pulsating manufacturing unit, employing over 700 men. Production of record changers had risen to unimagined numbers in a ridiculously short time, and plans were drawn up for a new extension to be built beside the existing factory at Bligh's Lane. The 44,000 sq ft factory was ready for occupation in June 1959 and the news broke that a big development, capable of employing up to 2,000 additional workers, was destined for the 'new factory', as it became known.

The news generated great interest in the local community and was greeted with enthusiasm by the trade unions, church leaders and local politicians. The scourge of male unemployment in Derry looked set to end after generations of shameful neglect by successive regimes, which believed that country areas started at Mallusk. Derry had come out of the darkness and into the sunlight – or had it? It's often in the midst of euphoria that disappointment is thinly camouflaged, and so it was to prove. For the immediate future though, the city basked in the warm glow of industrial growth.

Activity was intense, the whole focus of the factory was on the final assembly lines as the men worked feverishly; nobody spoke, and an air of expectancy filled the plant. Suddenly, the work stopped, an interminable pause and then one of the operatives lifted a piece of chalk and walked towards the huge blackboard at the end of the line. Workers from other departments strained to watch developments – the man put the chalk to his mouth and then wrote in large numbers 10/- (50p). The roar that greeted this bonus figure reverberated around the factory, and rumour has it that windows shook in Stanley's Walk. An incredible 35,000 record changers had been produced in one week in the Bligh's Lane factory and the men were justifiably proud.

Things had indeed come a long way in five short years; it was on Monday 26 April 1952 that the first-ever production schedule was issued to Bligh's Lane for 100 record changers per week. The workforce now stood on the pinnacle of the production mountain and spat in the world's eye.

Twelve hundred men were now at the Bligh's Lane plant, and as well as producing record changers, some 12,000 tape decks, 4,000 battery motors and substantial numbers of pressed components were shipped from the factory. McDonald had invested every penny of his money and had borrowed heavily to finance the Derry operation. It was now his proud boast that records all round the world were played on units manufactured in Derry.

However, the enormous potential and productivity of the local workers contained within it the seeds of their own destruction. An inevitable consequence of such high output was the huge stockpiling of changers as trading became sluggish. The market was volatile, rather than consistent, and a sinister new phrase crept into the workers' vocabulary – 'seasonal pay-offs'. By the end of the 1950s and early '60s, pay-offs became a depressing fact of life at the factory. In fairness to the company, almost all those laid off were reinstated when the orders started to pour in again.

In 1959, the local director of the BSR in Derry, Mr JB McNulty, made an announcement that gave the city cause for great optimism and the workers a supreme vote of confidence. A new project, designed to give employment to at least 2,000 extra workers, was destined for the Derry area and was the culmination of many months of hard work behind the scenes by local man Tommy McGill. The project was put to McGill almost nine months previously, and he intimated that Derry was the ideal location for such an operation. McGill himself was now Chief Production Engineer for the BSR group of companies, and his brief extended to factories at Derry, Old Hill, Stourbridge and East Kilbride.

McDonald told McGill of the plans he had for Derry and placed him in charge of a team of designers in Birmingham, who were engaged in the design and building of prototype fridges. These were destined to be produced in Derry and, when the project was completed, McGill was instructed to return home to purchase a suitable site for a new factory for the project.

Accompanying McGill on the search was the company architect who was a nephew of McDonald's wife. He designed and built the new factory in Birmingham and houses for key workers in England and Scotland. The pair travelled extensively around the North West and looked at possible sites in Eglinton, Letterkenny, Ballybofey and Buncrana. They eventually decided on a location in Burt, Co Donegal, as the site for the new factory to produce the range of products McDonald had in mind.

Fifty acres were purchased and, when word filtered out, it caused no end of amusement among the locals who thought the buyers were mad. The land was constantly under water, and the joke was that it was bought by the gallon, not by the acre. This was to have underestimated the astuteness of the two buyers and future events would prove that the purchase was one of the most lucrative ever undertaken on behalf of the BSR

McGill and the company architect were charged with getting the project off the ground as quickly as possible. The factory was designed and McGill laid out the specific areas within the plant for systematic production techniques. He then catalogued a complete inventory for plant equipment and placed orders for the most urgent items. This is the complete communiqué sent to senior design engineers in Birmingham and top-level staff at Bligh's Lane in Derry by Dr McDonald on 23 September 1966.

> I have decided to put a crash programme in Derry to design and produce washing machines in the new factory in Drumahoe. Beyond this I have in mind the possibility that we will establish a much larger unit in the Londonderry area for producing an extended range of white goods including gas and electric cookers, various types of washing machines and refrigerators etc. Our aim is to be in production by the end of 1967 at Drumahoe with an inexpensive twin-tub washing machine and at the same time, have designs prepared during 1967 for an inexpensive automatic washing machine. The design and organisation of the production of these machines will be entirely the responsibility of the Londonderry factory, although guidance and help can be sought from Old Hill when required.
>
> This project has a bearing on the question on where to manufacture the bulk of our record changers. Since it is uncertain that we can obtain sufficient labour at Stourbridge to take over the Derry record changers production, you must decide now that the bulk of changer production remains in Derry, including the new UA50, which is at present being designed.
>
> Mr T McGill has been put in charge, for the time being, of the domestic appliance development in Londonderry. It must be appreciated by everyone that a very large team indeed will be required eventually to cope with the various units we have in mind for production.

The memo was greeted by the Derry management with euphoria, and the development at Burt was cancelled in favour of the existing factory at Drumahoe, so keen was McDonald to get things moving in Derry. Some senior staff at Birmingham received the news with considerably less enthusiasm than their Derry counterparts, but the gathering storm clouds had not yet appeared on the Derry horizon.

The Bligh's Lane workforce had by now become a finely honed, highly experienced productive unit, capable of turning out units of the highest quality. Men and boys worked hard and they played hard. As in all large families, tensions sometimes spilled over, and it's no exaggeration to say that more fights took place outside the factories than ever took place inside Madison Square Garden. Many a heated argument ended up with the immortal words 'see you outside at six', to the accompanying 'gee up' from expectant mates on either side. The hostilities seldom lasted more than minutes and both combatants usually walked home together.

In the late '50s, the company, always aware of the intense interest in sport among the men, donated trophies and a cup to inaugurate an interdepartmental soccer league and KO Cup competition. The rivalry was white-hot among the teams, and some of the crowds at the games would have made today's senior clubs blush.

Some stirring battles took place, and the dominant teams were the Inspection, managed by Paddy Hutton, and the Motors, guided by Pascal McCallion. In the 1964 season, the Inspection won all three trophies: the Monarch Cup, Shield and League; the cup final was played at Meenan Park before a packed house. Soccer, while dominant, was not the only sport, and the BSR fielded a cricket team in the very popular Derry Trades' League. In 1960, the team reached the final of the Trades' Cup, only to lose narrowly to Burns, Laird & Martus in the decider. The BSR team that contested that final were: Frank Rafferty, John Elliott, Billy Elliott, Owen Rafferty, Jackie McIntyre, Lawrence Moore, Jimmy Kelso, Norman Christie, Barney McElhinney (Capt), John McGill and Hugh McQuilkin.

The undiscovered reservoir of talent that existed within the walls of the Bligh's Lane factory would have made London impresario Lew Grade green with envy.

This talent was given full and free reign at a special and unforgettable evening in Derry's Guildhall. The workers had, for some years, contributed weekly to a building fund project that was designed to alleviate the huge cost of a proposed new church being built close to the factory in the Creggan estate. It is interesting to note that the Protestant workers gave willingly to the fund and the gesture was generously acknowledged by their Catholic workmates. When the sum reached substantial proportions, some workers hit on the novel idea of presenting the then Bishop of Derry, Dr Neil Farren, a cheque at a special concert given by the workers of the factory. Admission would be free and auditions were held in the canteen of the 'new factory' to establish a suitable programme for the evening. The Press Shop's Johnny McIntyre took charge of the proceedings. A cast was eventually decided upon, a date set, the dignitaries invited and all was ready for the big 'curtain up'.

The historic Guildhall was packed to the rafters as the first BSR concert party got under way. Johnny McIntyre compered the show and set the proceedings in motion by introducing George 'Mr Piano' Millar, who was a brilliant pianist, singer and comedy man. George left the big audience clamouring for more as he moved through his act with a silky professionalism. Later in the show, he teamed up with the diminutive Gerry Gallagher in a double act that was nothing short of superb.

An act followed that is still talked of today with admiration. A number of workers formed a skiffle group called The Hayseeds, and their music brought the house down. They opened their programme with *Don't You Rock Me, Daddy O*, and the reception was unbelievable at the finish. The group later performed throughout the North West, and some went on to become professional musicians. Just for the record, The Hayseeds were Bosco Hegarty, Sean Coyle, Jim Toland, Victor Hagan, Jim McMonagle, Gerry Hegarty, Jerry Doherty, Charlie McGuigan and Sean Villa.

Comedy was an undoubted strong point, given the background of the performers. Tommy Kelly, once a regular on radio with Gerry Anderson, had the audience in the palm of his hand as he strolled through a cracking routine that would have made a cat laugh. His adaptation of 'The Absent-Minded Professor' had even his co-players in stitches. A harmonica band, consisting of Danny Doherty, the McCarron brothers, John McCamphill, Charlie McDowell and Jimmy Ramsey produced some rousing numbers. Other acts on this memorable night were Harry Clarke with the Howard Keel voice, Willie McLaughlin singing in the velvety Nat King Cole style, Frankie Mooney, Noel Martin who was a majestic accordionist, Jimmy 'Oakie' Ramsey on guitar and Sean Carr on the magic piccolo.

An incident of real hilarity occurred during the second half of the concert. Eugene Brennan, an excellent bass-baritone, was due to go on stage early on. Eugene had very poor eyesight, but did not want to wear his glasses while performing. Sean Carr preceded him on the programme and he asked Sean to count the number of steps from the microphone to the wings on the way off. Carr finished and told Eugene there were 12 steps to the microphone. What the pair did not allow for was Eugene's steps being longer than Carr's; Brennan ended up six feet past the mike and only the first two rows heard his song. The number he sang was the lovely ballad *Trees*. Towards the end of the number, a high note on the word 'trees' was called for, and somebody from the third row yelled 'timber!' The whole house erupted into howls of laughter. It is a measure of the success of the night that even now, 30 years on, the evening is still talked about by those fortunate enough to have been in the audience. Never before or since has the Guildhall housed such a crowd, and people even watched from the wings. As for the artistes, they had to go to work the next day and face the same audience in Bligh's Lane; that was more daunting by far than their stage nerves.

The phenomenal success of the Guildhall presentation concert spread quickly around the North West. Requests came in for the show to appear at venues in Derry and Donegal, and the BSR concert partly 'took to the road'. Performances were given to packed houses all over Derry and Donegal and in the Town Hall in Coleraine. The object of the tours was to raise funds for different parishes, and at some venues the behind-the-scenes activities were nothing less than organised confusion. At one concert in Donegal, the performers kept arriving at different times during the evening. Compere Johnny McIntyre had a nightmare experience as he introduced some specific act only to be told from the wings that they had not yet arrived. Jimmy Tarbuck earned a fortune for less daunting tasks than those of the heroic McIntyre.

In all, from various forms of fundraising in the BSR, substantial sums were presented for the new church building fund. One ingenious idea by the Toolroom workers was to run a boat from Derry Quay to the Blackpool Illuminations. A delegation went to Belfast to discuss the venture with the shipping line and they were very much in favour of the idea. The only snag was that the boat would not go from Derry – the intending travellers would have to make the journey to Belfast. The delegation, quite correctly, declined the offer, as they felt the novelty of the whole idea would be lost if the trip did not start and finish in Derry.

Another great BSR character was Jim 'Rocky' McGrory, a fervent worker in all fund-raising activities. Jimmy was a fitter/chargehand in the Machine Shop, and behind a gruff exterior was a bespectacled marshmallow. His constant companion was a 3lb hand mallet which he had christened 'Tiny'. 'Tiny' was produced, in displays of mock indignation, to revive flagging spirits and to 'repair' machines that had broken down. Many an operator had come to 'Rocky' to complain about his machine being out of commission. Jimmy immediately reached for 'Tiny' and it was amazing how many times a strategic blow put the machine back into production.

A subordinate of Rocky's in the Machine Shop felt the full fury of the workers' favourite pastime, 'slagging'. Charlie from Hogg's Folly worked on the centre spindles and was prone to producing the odd reject component. He was the proud owner of an old Ford and was something of a careful driver. Whenever he came to a road junction, he would get out of the car, walk to the junction and look both ways before getting back into the car to continue. Charlie was going with a girl from Strabane and on his way to see her one night, some of his mates happened to be behind him on their way to a dance in Sion Mills. Every few hundred yards, the driver's window of the Ford would be wound down and a handful of centre spindles would bounce along the road. On another occasion, in the old Palace Cinema in Shipquay Street, Charlie was spotted with the girlfriend in the front row of the balcony. They were making quite a noise and a few of his mates slipped up to see what was going on. Imagine their expressions when they saw the pair sharing a packet of Cornflakes between them. Charlie reported for work as usual the following morning – the George Cross has been awarded for less.

The year 1960 was one of transition and no little turmoil in the history of the BSR in Derry. It had hardly been ushered in when, with indecent haste, the company closed both its Derry factories, ceased trading in the city as BSR and re-opened some weeks later as Monarch Electric, a subsidiary of Birmingham Sound Reproducers. The brass plate on the front of the main building never displayed anything other than BSR

The sinister element in this new equation was, as far as the deposed workforce was concerned, the employment of a new and much younger labour force. Many of the original workers felt that they had been discarded for teenagers whose earning potential was considerably less than their own. That point could still be debated to this day, but what is not in question is that quite a few of those paid off in 1960 would never work for the company again. Most, however, would be re-employed, although it would be almost a year before some of them would see the inside of the factory again. The whole episode had been a disastrous example of industrial relations and a weighty atmosphere hung over the factory for a long time.

One of the management casualties in the big shake up was factory manager Andrew McOwen. The former Naval Officer was pensioned off, although subsequent events would allow him to rejoin the company in a new and exciting capacity.

McOwen's successor, Clive Burcher, was a 6'3" member of staff from Old Hill whose credentials were never the subject of discussion. Burcher was neutral rather than pragmatic and was probably best summed up by a senior management member as 'the best reason yet for having a works committee'. On the production front, things moved slowly forward and the ambitious plans announced by McDonald seemed unaffected by the traumatic events at the start of 1960. Factory space at Drumahoe increased from 50,000 to 400,000 sq ft in anticipation of the proposed new 'white' range of products destined for the complex.

The summer of 1961 saw the unveiling of a unique and innovative system for training apprentices; this was Dr Daniel McDonald's brainchild. He took over a vacant factory at Pennyburn, formerly occupied by Aspin Ltd, and announced the setting up of a new £¼ million 'Super Tech'. The idea was to establish a technical college attached to the company with company-employed tutors. These would instruct the apprentices in toolmaking, production engineering, engineering drawing, and design and time study, and Andrew McOwen was re-employed as vice-principal of the college. The first students were enrolled in September 1961, needing a minimum educational standard of Junior Certificate. The project was watched with great interest by firms not only in Northern Ireland but in Great Britain. Discussions took place between the company, the Ministry of Commerce, the Ministry of Education and the Local Education Authority to prepare a programme that would combine the efforts of the new college and the existing Municipal Technical Colleges. Around £100,000 worth of the most up-to-date machine tools were immediately installed and the successful trainees had the added advantage of practical training in production units already established at Bligh's Lane and Drumahoe. In conjunction with the practical training they would receive, apprentices would also be able to sit examinations in engineering.

The 'Super Tech' project brought many compliments to McDonald from eminent industrialists and educationalists. The venture was symptomatic of McDonald's strength of purpose and resolve. Born at Fort William in Scotland, he was the fourth son of a Huguenot mother and a father who ran a grocery business in the town. He went to Glasgow University and took a degree in electrical engineering; at 25 he joined an electrical firm in Rugby and stayed three years doing research in the laboratory. In 1937, McDonald toyed with the idea of going into production of medical and surgical equipment, but his knowledge of such items was rather limited. He felt there was a market for the products so he entered University for the second time at Birmingham. McDonald qualified as a Doctor of Medicine but never practised a single hour in his life. He forsook the idea of manufacturing medical equipment and, with £300, set up the foundations of BSR, manufacturing amplifiers in a Birmingham shed.

The communiqué sent by McDonald to senior staff in both Derry and Old Hill in respect of future developments at Derry caused great consternation at the parent plant in Birmingham. Towards the latter part of 1966, McDonald had his mind fully made up about all future plans for the Derry and Birmingham factories. He called a meeting of his senior design and supervisory staff together with the full board of directors in the boardroom at Old Hill. McDonald started the meeting by outlining the phenomenal progress made by the Derry plant, both in production figures attained and the adaptability of the local workforce. He went on to repeat what he had earlier informed them by memorandum, namely that a new and extensive range of products would be produced at Drumahoe in Londonderry. The assembled group was told that a ready-made workforce existed in Derry and that further recruitment would present no problems, unlike the situation in Birmingham, where labour was at a premium. Some restlessness among the group went unnoticed as the chairman continued his address.

He further explained that other plans for the Derry area were at an advanced stage and he would reveal these towards the end of the meeting. The next lines hit the meeting like a bombshell:

> . . . consequently, I have decided to cease all production at Old Hill and Stourbridge and move all the relevant production to Bligh's Lane and Drumahoe in Londonderry. The factories at Old Hill will become warehouses, to stock surplus units produced at the Londonderry factories. I have purchased 40 acres of land at Kilfennan, a short distance from the Drumahoe factories, to build houses for you, my key workers in this new and exciting time in the company's history. Planning permission has already been granted, the drawings completed. Gentlemen, we are ready to go.

He continued to speak but his audience has ceased to listen; most were stunned and some were angry. McDonald sensed the change in the atmosphere and asked for questions. Some expressed reservations about the whole scheme and others remained silent. The chairman answered all their questions and, in his logical way, presented Derry as the only realistic future for the continued growth of the company. Those present asked for time to consider the proposals among themselves and would give their answer the following morning.

They met later that evening in a hotel in Birmingham and, after a long meeting, decided to reject the planned move to Derry. The main argument was that if they did not like Derry, or Derry did not like them, they would have cut themselves off from the society where they had lived for years. Family considerations also came up as important elements in the move to Ireland. No, the decision was to remain in Birmingham.

The following morning McDonald was told of the key workers' decision and he asked again for the men to meet in the boardroom at noon. This time McDonald offered all those prepared to go to Derry free accommodation, huge pay increases, some up to 40%, and a company car for all.

The group met again in the hotel and after a long meeting once again declined the offer. Two directors who attended the meeting were anti-Derry all down the years and no doubt had a great say on the eventual outcome. They informed McDonald of their decision the next morning and added that many were very angry that Derry was held in greater esteem than the parent factory in England. The chairman had played his last card; he had failed to carry his board and his key workers with him and he capitulated. The entire plan was reversed. All plans originally in place for Derry would now be transferred to Birmingham. Derry would, by virtue of the decision of fifty men, cease production at the earliest convenient time; the tail had finally wagged the dog.

As if by cue, a dispute occurred in Derry over the recruitment of non-union personnel at the Bligh's Lane factory on Tuesday 17 January 1967. The company quoted an agreement made in 1962 that none of its factories would be closed shops; any workers would be free to join a trade union, but no worker would be forced into so doing. The dispute deepened during the course of the day and the workers at Bligh's Lane went on unofficial strike, a most fortuitous move for the company in the light of recent events. The BSR board moved quickly and ordered the closure of Drumahoe, a factory not involved in the Bligh's Lane dispute. They issued the final memorandum to the Derry management.

> The board of BSR Ltd has given careful consideration to the situation at its factories at Bligh's Lane and Drumahoe, not only to the present dispute but primarily to the return of the capital investment there. Despite the fact that since the company opened the factory in 1951, it would be difficult to make out an economic case for the project due to the remoteness of the area and the heavy transport expenses running at up to £100,000 every year, the company nevertheless spent considerable money on plant, factories and a training college, all of benefit to the people of Londonderry. It should be remembered that when the company first went to Londonderry it was privately owned, now that it is a public company the board is answerable to the shareholders. Economic considerations must become paramount.
>
> Although in this context the present dispute is largely irrelevant, we feel that the public should be fully aware of the facts. Over the last 15 years, disputes have not been uncommon, but the company was prepared to negotiate settlements with the unions on demands which were fair and reasonable. Early on Tuesday morning 17 January, union members approached management with the demand that either the company accept a closed shop or its members would stop work at 10.30am, which they subsequently did. Regretfully, the company had no alternative but to refuse this demand, which was a direct contravention of the agreement between company and union in 1962. We must also state that management in Londonderry was informed by the Branch Secretary of the union concerned that this demand was unofficial.
>
> Recently, in an effort to make the Derry factories more economic, pending an investigation into the possibility of diversifying into new products, it was decided to take certain lines of production from the

BSR workers on their way to Requiem Mass for Pope Pius XII, 1958. *(Derry Journal)*

> companies on the mainland and produce these in Derry. It is ironical that the increased labour force required for this new production should have been the source of the present dispute, in as much that the union members in the factory demanded that all those taken on should be union members. Unfortunately, the results of our investigation into producing new products in Derry have proved most disappointing. As we cannot make out an economic case, and as returns from these would not foresee an overall economic return from the capital invested in Londonderry, we have regretfully decided that the factories at Bligh's Lane and Drumahoe will not re-open.

Countless words have been written and many theories propounded as to why BSR pulled out of Derry. This is the first time that the real reason has been revealed. I don't intend to comment in depth on what I have presented, suffice to say that it was a savage blow to a city and a workforce, which lifted a Scottish academic with an instinct for business from relative obscurity to become a leading industrialist in the UK and beyond. Daniel McDonald retired to Bermuda a virtual recluse. What he established in Derry was, for him, manufacturing units at Bligh's Lane and Drumahoe. Someone more eloquent than I once described them as the biggest social clubs in Ireland, such was the affinity within their walls. I have, on occasion, passed by the complex at Bligh's Lane, and stopped at the perimeter fence and looked down. Memories have come flooding back of great times and fabulous people, and I swear, that if you listen very hard, the sound of 1,200 male voices raised in song to welcome the weekend can be distinctly heard.

Tape deck assembly section, BSR, early '60s. (PJ Hegarty)

Above: Denis Crumlish operating an automatic lathe, BSR, late '50s. (Dan O'Donnell)

George McGowan pressing mainplates, BSR, late '50s. (Dan O'Donnell)

Press Shop night shift meal break in the BSR. In the centre, George Millar's impression of Groucho Marx, late '50s. (courtesy Dan O'Donnell)

The Spirit of Self-Help

God is said to help those who help themselves. And if there was ever an area forced to rely on itself for help, that area was Creggan. The tradition stems from the 'sales of work' in the '50s to raise money for the new St Mary's Church and is apparent to this day in the development of new home-spun industry by Creggan Enterprises Limited (CEL). One name which has become almost synonymous with self-help in Creggan is Conal McFeely's. And here, he tells how the efforts of the unsung community leaders of the early Creggan estate inspired this latter-day drive for a vibrant local economy.

This is a rare opportunity for me – as someone born, bred, educated and still resident in the Creggan district – to recall the significance of the self-help ethos within our community, and to pay tribute to those individuals and groups who have fostered and nurtured the sense of neighbourliness in our midst over the last half century.

Undoubtedly, Creggan has experienced difficult times since the estate was first established in 1946 (particularly over the past 30 years of the *Troubles*), but its story is a valuable lesson in how local residents and groups can counter the indifference, if not the hostility, of society's power brokers – those who hold the political reins and control the purse strings.

Despite its position of disadvantage, Creggan was always a proud and resourceful place, contributing much to the wider community. As a child, I hero-worshipped Terry Harkin, the professional footballer and Terry Watt, the international judo champion from across the street in Leenan Gardens. We all basked in the sporting achievements of swimmer Liam Ball, and our boxing Olympian Charlie Nash (a world championship contender as a pro-fighter). Creggan punched its weight in the world of entertainment too, from Dana, to Roma Downey, to Bronagh Gallagher, not forgetting The Undertones

Yet, when the wider community hears the name 'Creggan', it tends not to think of these achievers. It recalls, instead, the darkness of the *Troubles*, and no wonder. In those three decades, the area suffered disproportionately. Many of those killed and wounded on Bloody Sunday came from Creggan. Conflict with the British Army and the RUC was the order of the day, and it was hardly coincidental that people from this community were to the fore in the campaign for social justice – on so many levels.

I, personally, was influenced by individuals in the community who went about their business almost anonymously – people like Bridget Bond, Paddy McKeever, Tommy McManus, Mary Nelis, Tom Doherty, Eamonn Melaugh and John McChrystal. I remember the 'sale of work' organised and run by local women in every street; and I remember the accomplishments of Creggan Tenants' Association and the Foyle Hill Tenants' Association, the forerunners to the many similar groups and organisations now in being.

I recall my father, who was the Site Foreman with Farrens – one of the contractors who built the estate in 1946 – telling of the excitement people in the town felt when they secured a new home in Creggan; indeed of his own joy in getting a house in

Leenan Gardens. But they were hard times in which to raise a family of ten.

Creggan, like other areas, experienced the fickle nature of multinational investment, thanks to Monarch Electric, Essex International, Coates Viyella and United Technologies Automotive. But none of these is remembered with the same mixture of fondness and resentment as Birmingham Sound Reproducers, the BSR.

The impact of the BSR's closure on the city and its economy was devastating – despite the sweatshop conditions and the inadequacy of the wages. And interestingly, since 1967, Derry has been struggling to get its unemployment figure down to the Northern Ireland average. It was during this period – my formative years – that I was introduced to the politics of self-help, community action and social justice by my parents and people like Bert Gallagher, Willie White, Bridget Bond, Kathy Harkin and my brother Donncha.

Generations of political neglect and lack of economic opportunity clearly heightened their sense of social and economic exclusion, and steeled the community to fight for what was theirs. Creggan residents were the backbone of the success of Derry Credit Union and, in 1968, they were again to the fore in demanding civil rights and social justice.

Many local people were killed or seriously injured in the course of the conflict, and hundreds more imprisoned as a direct result of the *Troubles*. Yet, in so many ways, the residents of Creggan have spearheaded the local campaigns for equality, social justice and economic rights that are now enshrined in the Good Friday Agreement. It would be negligent of any publication recording the history of the area to omit the contribution of men and women such as Minnie O'Hagan, Fr Martin Rooney, Danny Cassidy, Molly Fleming, Séamas Heaney, Deirdre McCluskey, Anne Molloy, Teresa McKeever, Martin McCafferty, Kathleen McLaughlin, Kevin O'Carroll, Harry O'Hagan, Tony O'Doherty, Joan Murray, Margaret McGlinchey, Don Mullan, Martin White, Charles Tierney, Mary Crumley, Fr Stephen McLaughlin, John Bradley, Gerry Quinn, John Kelly, Eileen Johnston and Gerry Gallagher, all of whom helped build the ethos of self-help, and I am sure readers are aware of many others who made similarly enormous contributions. Their long years of campaigning have persuaded government agencies and others to address the social and economic needs of the area.

The many Protestant families who lived in the area during the 1950s and '60s contributed, in my view, to the sense of community that best describes Creggan. My own experience was the good neighbourliness and spirit of civic responsibility that emanated from the eleven Protestant families who lived in lower Leenan Gardens. The Duncan family, for example, played a major role in preparing St Mary's Church for its official opening in 1959 by making bunting and flags.

Creggan Enterprises Limited (CEL) draws inspiration from the efforts of all of the above, and its pride and joy, the Ráth Mór Centre, is a symbol of the decades of struggle of the community – past and present – and a monument to the self-help ethos. CEL has succeeded, where conventional economic approaches have failed the community, and it has, I believe, convinced sceptics – particularly policy makers – that a community ownership approach, if properly resourced, can be a catalyst for renewal and revival.

CEL, for example, has helped a wide range of local groups through the disbursement of profits; it has created a locally-owned infrastructure which provides in the region of 120 jobs; it has led to the retention of skills and earnings estimated at £800,000 per year – money earned, spent and circulated within the locality. Since its formation in November 1994, CEL has been directly responsible for attracting nearly £12m in investment to Creggan.

Nor does it rest on its laurels: after the closure of United Technologies Automotive (UTA) in July 1997 (with the loss of 600 jobs), CEL is now in ownership of part of the site and is in the process of developing a new indigenous enterprise park costing £700,000. In the Creggan of the future, CEL seeks to:

- create equality of opportunity for all residents
- develop an environmentally friendly and vibrant neighbourhood
- create greater community safety for all residents
- enhance Creggan's profile as a centre of learning and an ideal place to locate knowledge-based businesses
- sustain and further develop the area's indigenous base to harmonise support for the social economy sector
- promote Creggan as a welcoming community and a place to bring up a family

Many residents in Creggan remain disadvantaged in terms of unemployment and low income. It happens, not through any fault of their own, but because the current system of economic governance discriminates against the most vulnerable sections of society. I am convinced that Creggan's future sustainability will be secured by the creation of a social economy, using local resources to meet community needs.

The history of self-help in Creggan is a compelling one, intertwined as it is with the socio-economic and political experiences of the area. It is a story borne of despair, but filled with hope – testimony to the commitment, courage and perseverance of remarkable people, living in remarkable times in a remarkable place. I remain proud of my roots, in awe of the many people I've been privileged to know in Creggan and – to those unfortunate enough not to have grown up there – a few words of sympathy:

You'll never know what you missed.

Above: Ráth Mór site before development. (courtesy Conal McFeely)
Below: The Ráth Mór Centre today, 2000. (Larry Doherty)

Tackling 30 Years of Neglect: Creggan Neighbourhood Partnership

The neglect and isolation suffered by Creggan, both before and since the *Troubles*, has left a legacy of endemic poverty and associated social problems in its wake. Official research conducted by Manchester University shows that the estate's main wards – St Peter's, Creggan Central and Creggan South – are the three most deprived of Northern Ireland's 566 electoral areas, when measured for 'extent' of deprivation. The phenomenally high percentage of children entitled to free school meals is another indicator that Creggan families currently suffer some of the highest levels of poverty to be found across the North.

Heading up the organisations trying to tackle the problems at the coalface is the Creggan Neighbourhood Partnership (CNP). Based at the old 'Corned Beef Tin' on Central Drive, the CNP acts as an umbrella body for almost 30 voluntary groups, sports clubs, schools and youth organisations dedicated to improving life in the area. CNP's project manager Martin Gallagher, who was a founder member of the Glenowen Fisheries Co-operative in 1988, says their overriding aim is to improve the quality of life for people in the area:

> We provide a range of services from training in IT, literacy and numeracy, to a drop-in centre, to environmental clean-up schemes. We're currently running the European Computer Driving Licence course which is recognised all over the EU by employers and gives a great grounding in IT. But it's not just training for jobs we offer, it's also very handy for day-to-day use – for parents who want to help their children with homework.

The CNP's offices boast an IT training suite along with recreational facilities for the 100 or so youngsters who use the 'Corned Beef Tin' as a club. Tackling the exclusion suffered by young people in the community is a major concern of the partnership. The CNP also finds itself at the coalface when it comes to dealing with one of the more obvious symptoms of deprivation – the rise in anti-social behaviour. A pilot Community Restorative Justice (CRJ) scheme was set up after the Partnership was inundated with people who were at a loss because of what is perceived as a policing vacuum in the estate. Martin Gallagher says the initiative has proved very successful:

> We deal with a massive number of complaints, the vast majority of which we manage to sort out. For example, we're currently trying to get to grips with car crime. Youngfellas are buying wrecks of cars at £40 or £50 and getting up to all sorts of things in them. We also deal with problems such as noisy neighbours, assaults and damage to property. There has been a huge upsurge during the past few years in vandalism, burglaries and general anti-social behaviour. Trained mediators talk to both sides involved in the dispute and try to get an agreement. We try to make people see the

Volunteers, workers and IT trainees at Creggan Neighbourhood Partnership graduations, May 2000. (courtesy Creggan Neighbourhood Partnership)

> other point of view and explain to those carrying out the offences, or their parents, that their behaviour is causing suffering and is not acceptable in Creggan. You tell them that the community could reject them if they continue to misbehave, that they could be barred from the shops and amenities, or whatever.

In its recent Report into Poverty and Deprivation in the Creggan Area, the CNP lists nine areas which need investment as a matter of priority: pre-school provision; youth provision; education and training; health; employment; counselling and support services; finance management; the physical infrastructure and culture. The partnership has developed an inter-sectoral approach to implement an area-based plan, which is aimed to bring about fundamental change in Creggan.

Day-to-day issues, however, provide the focus for much of CNP's work. Speeding cars in the estate led to a campaign for traffic-calming measures. The Partnership began negotiations with the DoE and in the interim erected large signs at danger spots as a warning to drivers. Since then, the Roads Service has introduced speed cushions, raised junctions and mini-roundabouts.

Hoax 999 calls are another problem. In partnership with BT, the CNP launched an education programme in schools warning of the dangers to life by nuisance call-outs. The project involved recruiting young students from secondary schools and training them to make a presentation to other pupils using BT's 999 video and associated materials.

Illegal dumping, particularly in the Glassagh Road and Bligh's Lane area, sparked an environmental clean-up campaign. Rubbish ranging from TVs to kitchen units to household waste was being discarded there by residents and outsiders. Not only was one of the city's most scenic areas being destroyed, but also a large number of rats were thriving on the site.

After meetings with the CNP, Derry City Council carried out a major clean-up which made a huge difference to the area. Local young people have also participated in a clean-up from Creggan Shops to Creggan Heights.

In January, the CNP moved premises from the Ráth Mór Centre to the 'Corned Beef Tin' on Central Drive. The partnership says it is important to deliver its services in the heart of the estate and that the new location gives it a prime spot. Expansion plans currently centre on the development of youth provisions and the growth of training services. Martin Gallagher explained:

> Training has become very important to the Partnership and it's an area we'd like to develop. We've currently a waiting list of 200 hoping to get onto our courses. And we're trying to link in with other educational institutions to co-ordinate call-centre training. Ideally, as we develop we would like to become more involved with mainstream training and employment schemes.

Rural Creggan Revisited: The Development of the Country Park

It is no surprise that one of Creggan's modern-day success stories draws largely on the area's number one asset, its outstanding natural beauty. The development of a major country park has long been a goal of keen angler Gerry Quinn, and in this section he explains how he and others have come to make the dream a reality.

In 1992, the Glenowen Fisheries Workers' Co-operative, established by local unemployed graduates, Gerry Quinn, Seán Semple, Martin Gallagher and Malachy Coyle, opened the first 'put and take' rainbow trout fishery in the entire North West, using a redundant ten-acre reservoir leased from Derry City Council. This project, which currently employs four full-time permanent staff and has been used by some 30,000 anglers in the intervening period, has become one of the market-leaders and has been hailed as a tremendous success (eg winning Co-op of The Year award 1993).

Glenowen Fisheries has developed a major proposal for a Creggan Country Park, developing a further range of sustainable facilities of a social and recreational nature for all members of all the community, and creating jobs and training in marketable skills. This will act as a vehicle for addressing the serious problems of unemployment/poverty; social exclusion/marginalisation; deprivation; lack of social and recreational facilities; and lack of training and employment opportunities in Creggan.

The underlying philosophy of the Creggan Country Park proposals involves a self-help strategy, building on the existing achievements of Glenowen Fisheries by investing in the local human, social and technical resources, providing sustainable jobs and training in marketable skills within Creggan. Creggan Country Park proposes an integrated and innovative response to the economic, social and environmental needs of this community.

The extent of need in Creggan can be gauged from the fact that a special EU URBAN programme, targeting communities in multiple-deprived areas marked by socio-economic indicators significantly worse than the average values for the city in which they are located, has earmarked Creggan as one of three neighbourhoods in Derry that merit attention.

Creggan Country Park is a proposal very much in keeping with the conclusion of the 'Making A Difference' Community Audit document (Housing Research Centre, Magee College 1995), that in Creggan, URBAN should be used to support existing self-help strategies within the local community and the recognised need for investment in local human, social and technical resources.

In order to achieve these aims and objectives, a new company, Creggan Country Park Enterprises, has been set up, its membership comprising two directors representing Glenowen Fisheries, two representing Derry City Council, and others from the private and community sectors.

The objectives of the Park include: providing tourist facilities and facilities for community-based businesses; training members of the local community for jobs in areas such as Sports and Recreation, and Amenity Horticulture; developing the wooded areas at Creggan Reservoir; and opening up the reservoirs for further leisure, tourism and social use.

It is envisaged that the Park will eventually offer a range of outdoor pursuits, country sports, and water sports, and will house angling and pitch-and-putt facilities. It will also have educational uses, offering local schools use of an outdoor classroom, and it aims to serve as a centre for cross-community initiatives.

The Creggan Reservoir lands are 100 acres in total, running along the northern city boundary between Derry's Creggan Estate and the border. Glenowen Fisheries leases 29.5 acres from Derry City Council (owners of the site) while the rest, a prime location for outdoor recreation, lies unused and undeveloped.

Realising the potential for business expansion, and the creation of self-sustaining employment in environment-related schemes, community-based recreation and tourist facilities, Glenowen Fisheries began to seek support for developing the entire 100-acre site.

In March 1993, following initial discussions with the IFI and the Northern Ireland Tourist Board, approaches were made to Derry City Council concerning a possible community tourism scheme, to be coupled with an extensive programme of environmental improvements.

In the summer of 1993, a landscape architect, John Morrison, was engaged to develop a site plan and drawings for an environmental scheme. The initial proposals were presented to a Derry City Council Working Party in February 1994, where there was an agreement to support further development at Creggan reservoirs. The plans were also presented for possible inclusion in a special EU URBAN programme.

A 'Developers' Brief' was prepared with IFI assistance, and, in May 1995, a Derry City Council Working Party agreed to enter into a working relationship with Glenowen Fisheries on the basis of the Glenowen Fisheries organisation developing and managing the whole 100-acre site.

With funding from the local District Partnership, an economic appraisal was commissioned and completed by Deloitte & Touche in May 1997. Its findings were accepted by the District Partnership and an application made to them in July 1996 resulted in an offer of £200,000.

An application, in December 1996 to the URBAN programme for £652,000, was also approved, while Derry City Council agreed to contribute £100,000 per year for three years for capital works.

In February 1996 the new company, Creggan Country Park Enterprises, was registered with Company House. Throughout the period since early 1993, work with consultants (architect and quantity surveyor) on the scheme has been ongoing, and Outline Planning permission has been sought and approved, as has an application for Full Planning Permission in respect of our proposed Activity Centre.

With funding secured for the initial first phase of the project from the EU URBAN programme (£652,000), Derry City Council (£300,000) and the District

Creggan Country Park, 2000. (Larry Doherty)

Partnership (£200,000), a major programme of capital works has begun, to be completed in Spring 2001.

A major landscape programme is almost complete, with a second now being prepared for tender, while work is proceeding on the building of an Activity Centre which will facilitate the use of the middle reservoir for water sports, and house a restaurant, sports and tackle shop, administration block, showers and changing facilities, and community space.

The building will have an energy-saving turf roof, while a wood-burning boiler, using willow that will be grown on site, will heat it. There will also be a hydroelectric turbine installed on-site to harness the existing flow of water, and this will provide a welcome addition to the overall cash-flow.

CHAPTER 7

Trouble Erupts

The danger of driving justice underground became apparent in Derry in the late 1960s. And just as predicted by Archie Halliday, the Unionist councillor who opposed gerrymandering, the inequity sown in the '30s began to arise and wreak havoc.

Civil Rights marches, inspired perhaps by the revolutions in America and France, provoked the fury of the Stormont Government. Action sparked reaction, and reaction sparked more action. Within the space of a few months, Derry was immersed in the *Troubles.*

Creggan – and its inhabitants – would become intrinsic to the conflict. The area was to pay heavily as it became a symbol of Nationalist resistance. Dozens of Creggan people were killed, hundreds jailed, and thousands forced to endure endless raids, gun battles and riots on their doorstep.

The British security forces would find life no easier as they attempted to establish 'normality' in the estate. Soldiers and RUC men were blown up, shot, stoned and subject to endless vilification – as one of them will recount later in this chapter.

The greatest watershed in the *Troubles,* however, was undoubtedly Bloody Sunday, and nowhere was to feel the effects more than Creggan. Despite the efforts of conscientious pacifists like Eamonn Melaugh, support for the IRA rocketed. And as Donncha MacNiallais recalls, questions about morality were set aside as people in Creggan joined the army – *their* army.

Above: IRA show of strength in Creggan, early '70s. (Eamonn Melaugh)
Below: Rainy day 'checkpoint' on Fanad Drive, early '70s. (Eamonn Melaugh)

The playing fields of Creggan just after Operation Motorman, 1972.
Above: St Peter's School grounds. Below: Bishop's Field football pitch. (Eamonn Melaugh)

Creggan's early warning system, early '70s. (Eamonn Melaugh)

Brought to its Knees

In his second contribution for this book, Gerry Murray recalls the start of the Troubles *and how they affected Creggan Estate.*

The year 1968 remains set in the public mind as that which heralded a new era in the modern Ireland, and unleashed forces still powerful almost 30 years later. In the preceding years, we grew up, in the words of TS Eliot, 'assured of certain certainties'. In the summer of that fateful year, however, we watched on television riots from Paris to Berlin. Russian tanks rolled into Czechoslovakia, and a modern martyr and hero, Jan Palack, torched himself to death in protest at the invasion of his country.

Before the year was over, Derry was destined to appear on television screens across the world. The first marches for civil rights were eagerly grasped by our parents, anxious to see a better future for us in terms of jobs, housing and the ability to control the destiny of our city. The famous words uttered five years earlier by Martin Luther King, 'I have a dream', had a powerful meaning for our parents and symbolised their determination to see wrongs put right. There was a great sense of unity of purpose and a lack of dissent. The politics of non-violence and the songs of the American Civil Rights movement were readily embraced in the spirit of hope and determination.

For the first few years of the *Troubles*, the Bogside was the centre of media attention; marches and riots took place down-the-town; the British Army appeared on the streets in August 1969 and was initially feted. Within two years all was changed, and changed utterly. Football, one of the barometers of my early life took a downturn as Derry City was forced out of senior football. The words of Phil Coulter had a tangible meaning as 'the town had been brought to its knees'. Football had been caught up in the general anarchy. One of the most enjoyable footballing experiences was to watch TV as Poland drew at Wembley and thus qualified for the 1974 World Cup finals at the expense of England.

The accelerated descent into violence seemed to occur in July of 1971, when Seamus Cusack from Melmore Gardens and Dessie Beattie from Rosemount were shot dead by the British Army. There were a number of eyewitnesses who stated that both were unarmed when shot, and forensic tests showed that Dessie Beattie had not handled explosives. All this information was completely contrary to Army statements. For many young people in Creggan, these deaths were a defining moment in their attitudes to the British Army.

The Cusack family was widely known and popular in Creggan. The deaths of these two young men were seen as an attack on a close-knit community. Black flags appeared in Creggan, barricades were erected and severe rioting occurred at the Army base at Bligh's Lane. Live bullets were fired, this time by the IRA which had a swell of new recruits due to the deaths.

The Army response was to launch a massive search operation in Creggan, flooding the estate with CS gas. That summer of 1971 was a landmark in Creggan's history. By the time we went back to St Columb's at the start of September, Internment had been introduced, and two young men of very different backgrounds had died in Creggan. On 10 August, a 23-year-old British soldier, Paul Challoner, was shot dead at Bligh's Lane; he was the first British soldier to die in Derry. Eight days later, Eamon Lafferty, a 19-year-old commander of the IRA, died in a gun battle at Kildrum Gardens.

The following year, 1972, I left St Columb's, as the estate lived through a further period of violence. Although it was a quarter-century ago, the memories of that fateful year are vivid today. The year started with the massacre of Bloody Sunday, a wound that remains very open. Six of those killed were from Creggan, and the funerals of all the victims took place from St Mary's. The row of 13 coffins in front of the high altar was a chilling sight. Creggan was universal in regarding the state and its security forces as alien and hostile – in short, the enemy.

In studying 'A' level English, we were reading Shakespeare's *Henry IV*, the central theme of which was the legitimacy of Henry's rule. On the streets of Derry, the legitimacy and sovereignty of the British state over the North of Ireland were similarly live issues, but were far from being of only academic interest. Operation Motorman in July 1972 initiated the military occupation and surveillance of Creggan.

From 1971, a litany of death was to continue unabated in Creggan for many years to come. Civilians, such as Kathleen Thompson and Daniel Hegarty, were shot dead by the British Army, while civilians, such as John Dunne, died as a result of IRA actions. Eugene McGillan and Colm Keenan were both classmates of mine at the Christian Brothers', and as IRA volunteers they died together, shot by the Army in early 1972. David Wray and Martin Carroll were two of the young British soldiers who lost their lives in Creggan in the '70s. Marcus McCausland from Limavady, an officer in the UDR, was found shot dead at Braehead Road in March 1972. A few months later, a 19-year-old Royal Irish Ranger from Creggan, Willie Best, was abducted by the Official IRA while on leave at home and found shot dead at William Street. These were but a few of the many deaths that occurred on the streets of Creggan in the early years of the *Troubles*. They highlight how the cycle of continuing and spiralling violence was tearing at the very fabric of society, not only in Creggan, but also throughout the entire city and beyond. The shadow of death, violent death, became a very present feature of our lives, as the 'age of innocence' faded. A very large percentage of the population of Creggan had some relative who was either killed or injured, arrested or interned during those years. I did not agree with the Republican analysis of the conflict or the solution based on armed force, but there I was at the end of 1972, carrying the coffin of a cousin, killed on IRA active service.

Slowly but surely, the unity that existed in the early days of the Civil Rights movement began to disappear. There was the main division between those who believed in physical-force Republicanism, and those who adhered to constitutional Nationalism. It is a division that has persisted in the community, and has been a cause of bitter dispute within families and between neighbours. The death of Ranger Willie Best put in sharp focus the divisions that had opened up in Creggan. There were condemnations of the killing, and a sense of outrage that was widely felt. The use of armed force was abhorred by the majority of the people of Creggan, and now it had been visited on one of their own people, by their own people.

There was also the inescapable fact that armed force was the policy of the British Government and carried out ruthlessly by the British Army. The previous six months had seen Bloody Sunday, and a few days before Willie Best's death, a British Army sniper shot dead the unarmed, fifteen-year-old Manus Deery. A few days after the death of Willie Best, the Administrator of Creggan, Fr Martin Rooney, chaired a public meeting in St Mary's Secondary School to protest against the killing and call for an end to armed conflict. The meeting ended in uproar and vociferous support for the IRA. Fr Rooney hardly got a hearing, and was branded as an enemy of the popular struggle. This was the same Fr Rooney who, in the previous September, had sent a telegram to the then British Prime Minister, Ted Heath, calling for the withdrawal of the British Army from Creggan and pointing out that the use of CS gas was making Creggan 'a vast gas chamber'.

In spite of the bitter divisions engendered by the *Troubles*, it was clear that what united the Creggan community was a stronger force than those deep differences of opinion. The priests who served in Creggan throughout those turbulent years were a major factor in holding the community together, in helping their people in times of distress and mourning. This did not happen just by accident, but was a result of the strong sense of bonding between priest and people that preceded the years of mayhem. Fathers Martin Rooney, George McLaughlin and Joe Carolan, in particular, were not only spiritual leaders in name, but men who showed tremendous qualities of leadership, courage and compassion.

Governments in London came and went in the '70s. Nondescript Secretaries of State presided over the continued military occupation of Creggan. The best hope for progress, the power-sharing executive, was brought down by violence. The Hunger Strikes brought the death of another of my generation in Creggan, Mickey Devine, and there appeared no way out of the despair and hopelessness of the continuing cycle of politically related deaths. Another generation grew up and left Creggan and has helped in the reconstruction of Derry. The unacceptably high levels of unemployment remain a challenge to all concerned about the future of Creggan and the entire city. There are hopeful and welcome signs that the war in Ireland is ending and the wounds in Creggan can be bound up in a spirit of tolerance and generosity to all. This is nothing less than Creggan and its succeeding generations deserve.

A Tragic Case: The McCool Fire

John McCool, a 15-year-old student from Dunree Gardens, was looking forward to his holidays as he made his way home from St Columb's College on 25 June 1970. By 7.00pm, he, like many of his contemporaries, was drawn to the riots in the Bogside where attendance for young men was almost obligatory. Staying out late was a luxury not readily afforded to young McCool, so it was with some trepidation that he approached his home around 12.15am. His father's greeting was quiet and restrained; his mother was in the living room; his younger brother Kieran and sister Sinéad lay sleeping on the settee and nine-year-old Bernadette and three-year-old Carol were asleep in the bedroom over the living room. John looked into the kitchen where his father Tommy was in conversation with Joe Coyle from Rathkeele Way, a colleague in the Republican movement. Tommy, a veteran Republican, had been arrested in 1957 and sentenced to 12 years for possession of firearms; he served five, an amnesty having been granted in 1962. As John looked around the kitchen, his eye took in a crate of bottles containing what could only have been petrol. Small pieces of cloth were draped around the kitchen and the cooker was on, making the kitchen very warm. No explanations were given and he was not invited to give assistance. Thinking himself fortunate to escape reprimand for his late return, he retired quietly to the living room.

At approximately 12.45am, Tommy Carlin, another Republican from Creggan Heights, called at the door and joined John's father and Joe Coyle in the kitchen. About ten minutes later there was a tremendous explosion. The survival instinct propelled John out into the front garden where all was confusion. His mother, Kieran and sister Sinéad had also escaped. Thick smoke billowed from the upstairs bedroom. As neighbours tried in vain to gain access, he remembers being restrained as he tried to return, knowing Bernadette and Carol had been almost directly above the blast. Before he was sedated, he was reassured to see Bernadette being taken away in the ambulance, still alive, raising his hopes for her survival.

On recovering consciousness next morning, he was not surprised to hear that his father and Joe Coyle had died in the blast and that Tommy Carlin was seriously ill (he was to die in hospital 11 days later). He was not prepared for the news that Bernadette and Carol had also died.

Lost Lives – a comprehensive reference book which records the deaths of everyone who died as a result of the *Troubles* up to 1999 – describes the coroner's findings:

> At the inquest the coroner said it was one of the greatest tragedies in Derry in living memory. He said during his 47 years as coroner he had never had to deal with such a tragic case, adding that exactly what had happened on the night of the fire would never be known.

The inquest jury returned a verdict of misadventure. Despite the inability to determine exactly what happened that night, it seems clear that the conditions were a recipe for disaster. A fireman at the scene had 'found the remains of a wooden crate containing the bases of bottles' and a police investigation had 'found traces of paraffin or petrol on the broken glass of two milk bottles and five mineral bottles'. The production of this evidence supports John's unequivocal admission that he had witnessed the making of petrol bombs. Open containers of petrol, in a confined space, in a small warm room, would have needed just a spark to create disaster.

The three Republicans, Tommy McCool, Joe Coyle and Tommy Carlin, have been described as being, in the period just before their deaths, 'the core of the Derry Provisional IRA'. The same source, *The Provisional IRA* by Eamonn Mallie, described them as having 'a commitment to defending Catholics' and of being 'poorly equipped'. The popular perception of the nightly rioting as defence of the Bogside and the absence of 'equipment' could explain the choice of the crude petrol bomb as a defensive weapon.

John has confused memories of the funeral preparations. Friends and neighbours could not have been more thoughtful. There were practicalities. All his clothes, except those he stood up in, had been destroyed. He remembers Alex, his father's brother, taking him to Burton's outfitters and giving him his choice of suits. He picked a navy suit and suede boots. He felt compelled to visit the house and experienced feelings of disbelief when damage to Bernadette and Carol's bedroom was less than he expected. He was to discover later that they had died of smoke inhalation.

At the funeral, concerned mourners felt obliged to push him to the front when he drifted back in the crush as the cortege moved to St Mary's Church and on to the City Cemetery. Despite hints of the circumstances surrounding the disaster, the personal tragedy of the family was the uppermost concern of the community, as evidenced in the report of the *Derry Journal*:

> Almost 1,000 people attended the funeral yesterday of Mr Thomas McCool (40) and his two daughters Bernadette (9) and Carol (3), three of the four victims of a fire tragedy in their home at 25 Dunree Gardens, Creggan Estate, on Friday night . . . Requiem Mass was celebrated by Rev M Rooney, Priest-in-Charge, St Mary's and Rev J Carolan officiated at the graveside. Other priests in attendance were Rev J Irwin, CC, St Mary's, Very Rev J Coulter, President of St Columb's College and Rev J Ryder, St Columb's College. Among those attending the funeral were Mr Eddie McAteer, President of the Nationalist Party, Mr John Hume MP, Mr Kevin Agnew, chairman of NICRA and Mr Eamonn McCann.

Membership of the IRA was in little doubt after the funeral; the *Derry Journal* reported:

> Crowds lined the route as the Tricolour-draped coffin of Mr McCool left St Mary's Church after Requiem Mass on its way to the City Cemetery. Eleven members of the IRA formed a guard of honour and, at the graveside, a member of Fianna Éireann, the Republican youth movement, sounded the Last Post.

With the funeral over, Tommy's wife Josie had to cope with the loss of a husband, two children and a home, and face the task of holding the rest of her family together. Relatives were particularly supportive, but no one could accommodate all the family at one address. She was determined to have the family return to Dunree Gardens and, when refurbishment was complete, they duly returned. In spite of a good neighbourhood and good friends, the old home held too many painful memories, which even the stay of seven years could not ease. She left with her family and headed for Westland Street.

Josie did not know that John had joined the IRA until he was arrested and charged with possession of explosives in 1973. In his case, the IRA departed from its usual stance of non-recognition of the courts by advising legal defence. John spent three years in Magilligan Prison, where part of the punishment was being permitted the view of the scenic Inishowen Peninsula, just across the water in Donegal, but denied the luxury of visiting there. When he was released in 1976, he almost immediately fulfilled a dream built up over three years when he cycled the length of the Foyle shoreline of Inishowen.

A lasting impression of his day of release was his mother's tears when he emerged a free man. These were the first she had shed openly since the loss of her husband and two daughters. It was then he realised that she felt free to do so because they were tears of relief and he marvelled at the strength of the woman who had quietly coped in spite of enormous trials.

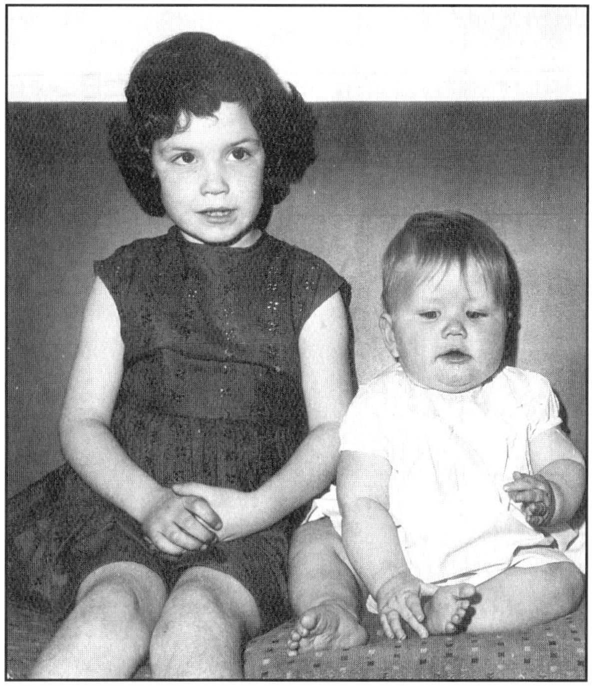

Bernadette and Carol McCool, circa 1967. (courtesy Josie McCool)

Wedding photograph of Tommy and Josie McCool, August 1953. (courtesy Josie McCool)

Growing Up Without a Mother: The Thompson Family

On the evening of Saturday 6 November 1971, British soldiers conducting house raids in Creggan shot dead Kathleen Thompson in the garden of her Kildrum Gardens home. The troops were to claim the mother-of-six was caught in crossfire. But several residents testified that there had been no shooting at the soldiers that night. There were suggestions that someone in the Thompson garden had been banging a binlid to alert people to the searches. The killing went largely unreported in the British press; this was the era when the official version of events was rarely challenged. But the loss to Kathleen's friends and relatives in the Creggan community was heartfelt, as her son David outlines in the following account.

My mother was a generous, fun-loving, strictish woman and a great believer in her faith. She was a small black-haired, blue-eyed woman with glasses, who seemed to be bright. This woman was largely responsible for my values in life today. She would tell me in passing remarks always to be straight and always to pay your debts, no matter what they are. My two younger brothers and myself were lucky enough to be at an age where we could get to know her for the person she was. She always seemed to have the answer to everything we asked; always the old sayings: 'It's a long road that has no turning', or 'burn me for a fool and you will have wise ashes'.

Our mother always seemed to be busy from early morning, usually 6.30am. She always seemed to be on top of things: washing done; my father seen off to work; us dressed for school and then ten o'clock Mass and down the town. Nothing seemed to upset her. I suppose, as teenagers, that's the way it seemed at the time. She was always interested in politics, yet never forced her views on her children. She was always willing to get involved in practical jokes and poked fun at our style at the time. This woman loved the 'pictures'. From a very early age, I can always remember her going to the pictures. Every Tuesday night, without fail, she and my Aunt Mary would set sail. As she would say, she loved a good Western and gangster films with the likes of John Wayne, Robert Mitchum and Alan Ladd. These I remember, because she would sometimes take us to the early show at 6.30pm.

This small woman, whom I still now see bustling about the house, was generous to us and to those she could help. There are always stories after such an event as my mother's shooting. But to neighbours and friends, when needed, she was always there. Whether with good advice, or more practical help, her big heart seemed to touch so many, far and near. This small woman could stop three grown teenagers' arguments, and there were plenty, with ready remarks and gestures. She was not always able to break up these arguments with remarks in our early years, and the good 'sally rod', as she called it, was produced for the well-directed slap or two.

When I look at our family now, I sometimes see it as two different halves. The older three, who were lucky enough to know our mother longer, and most surely set on the right path, were told to be fair, help others when you could, and that family is the most important thing. The other family is my two younger sisters and my brother who were too young to know her as we did, simply because we had more time, not enough, but more than they had. My two sisters dig deep for memories of our mother and are fondly remembered as children of a very young age. The youngest, a boy, was only seven when our mother was killed; he has some memories, but not the same as we older three. We were at an age that we could exchange views, jokes and some argument; he has none, just how we answer his questions. But how do you explain something in your heart and memory? Kathleen Thompson was probably the same as every other mother in Derry, but to us she was very special.

Joining the Army

One of the great unseen casualties of the conflict was innocence. In the very early days, children like Donncha MacNiallais got to take a soldier home to Sunday dinner and hold a 'real live' rifle. But only months later, youngsters were stoning the same troops on the streets, choking on CS gas and dodging rubber bullets. And then, as Donncha recalls here, the rubber bullets gave way to lead ones . . .

My earliest memory of the *Troubles,* as they are called, was my father coming home from a Civil Rights march and laughing about having been batoned by the RUC. The only previous contact I had with police was when my father had taken me to Rosemount Barracks to collect a ten-bob-note (50p) which I had found and which had not been claimed. In those days, you were very worried about burning in hell if you dared tell a lie or cursed.

Anyway, I knew nothing about 'Brits Out', discrimination or gerrymandering. I had never heard of Gerry Fitt, the IRA, or even Seán South. *Brave Father Murphy* was the title of a song I didn't really like and I preferred to read *Biggles* books and the *Beano.* Me and my mates were into football (soccer), walks to the 'Black Hut' and out the 'line' (summer only), and chopping down trees for the 15th which, incidentally, held no religious connotations for any of us. We all lived at one end of Rathkeele Way and were all going to join the army when we grew up.

Even when August '69 happened and fear was the order of the day, our lives didn't change all that much. We were too young to riot, and besides, the Bogside was away down-the-town. Then the phone box at the top of our street started ringing all the time and word spread that some Orangewoman was on the other end saying nasty things about our parentage and general hygiene. We took turns listening; I was very shocked at her language and even more shocked at the language some of the boys responded with. That's when we stared to understand that this was very serious stuff indeed. One of the older boys in the street, Charlie McLaughlin, told us that the B-Specials were 'comin' in'. We understood without being told that these were people to be feared, though I thought they were men with big Bs on their chests like something out of the *Superman* comics. Shortly after that, a B-Special called George, who also worked in a mobile shop, was forced out of our street by a group of women on his weekly call to Rathkeele. I had never found George to be anything other than polite and all right, so I felt very uncomfortable about this.

So many things were happening that you didn't dwell too long on one thing or another. The Brits were here now and we thought this was great. I don't remember anyone objecting to their presence at that time and we had no notion as to the implications for the future. Like a lot of families, we had a soldier in for Christmas dinner and when his mates came to collect him that evening, we got a chance to hold a real live SLR [self-loading rifle], minus the mag, of course. For boys used to a couple of minutes touching Charlie McLaughlin's Johnny-7, this was something else. We faced a new year with no particular worries and pretty bored with our cowboy guns.

Around this time, I started reading newspapers and followed with interest the events unfolding elsewhere, especially in Belfast where tension was rising. We also noticed for the first time the letters 'PIRA' appearing on gable walls or, more precisely, the cemetery wall down by Kildrum Gardens. Most of this was done by a boy slightly older than myself called Kevin. We later became very good friends but at that time, since he lived in Rathlin Drive, and at the very bottom too, I didn't think he was 'very good friend' material. In any case, we had found a new interest – collecting copper. This took up a lot of our time but became something akin to gold fever. We went everywhere to find it, so it was very timely that places started to get bombed or burnt – that made our job a whole lot easier. A pair of pliers was now essential equipment, but our measly little things were a bit pathetic when we saw the men with huge shears that could cut through copper coiling an inch-thick with no effort. They just did it for money; we enjoyed it.

In 1970, Joe Coyle died. He had lived in the middle of Rathkeele, a sort of no-man's-land between our end of the street and the other, which we regarded as a bit snobby. At that time it was said that Joe was a 'Republican' – a description whispered, as if hearing it would do you harm.

Rioting down the Bog was fast becoming a weekly occurrence, but for us it was still down-the-town and far away from us. By this time, British Military Police (MPs), later accompanied by RUC men (never women) were patrolling the streets with the peaks on their caps so far down that they had to raise their heads and peer down their noses to see you. They established a base at Bligh's Lane, where we heard they ran a club for young people. We didn't need anyone to organise activities for us so we didn't go, but there were no political objections from any of us.

We arrived in 1971 with no notion of the momentous events which were going to occur that year. We had a park in Kildrum that included a tarmac pitch. Everyone hung around the park; the older boys and girls would strum their guitars and sing Bob Dylan songs; we played football and handball and avoided girls at all costs. One day we were up at Iniscarn when two MP jeeps drove past. Toots, who lived across the street, let fly with a couple of stones; he missed, but I was puzzled – what was all this about? I was very unsure of whether this was right, not in any political sense, but in terms of morality. I still had visions of burning in hell or at the very least getting a good belting if our Mas found out. Still, for us this was a watershed – our first offensive action.

In the run-up to the summer of '71, we did our usual things like playing football, walks out the 'line', ignored girls and collected copper. The walks out the line were good craic; we always turned them into an adventure as if we were going on some jungle trek, seeing how far we could go along the very edge of the Foyle, taunting the 'coachies' or the 'gypsies' for a chase – no politically correct terminology or thoughts in our vocabulary at that time – even though we were actually scared of our lives of them.

The walks out the line also meant that we got to see the British Army rat jeeps going out to the border and we decided – I don't remember who suggested it – to ambush them. Rat jeeps were open-top jeeps which presented easy targets for anyone with a mind to attacking them. We managed to get three crates of bottles from a conveniently located warehouse on the Letterkenny Road and lined up along the top of Iona Park.

There were about ten of us and we gave it 'lilty', to say the least. The Brits didn't know what hit them and stopped up the road. Their pride was hurt more than anything else as we stood and jeered them.

Afterwards I thought about what we had done. I didn't regard it as particularly brave and still worried about the morality of it, but slowly, and with no prompting from anyone, we were beginning to see the British Army as the enemy. Going down the Bog on Saturdays and Sundays was now slightly more appealing than football. Rubber bullets and gas were no deterrent – we were 13 and invincible and the Brits didn't have a clue how to cope. The only thing we feared was the dye and that was only because we believed the propaganda that it stayed on your clothes and skin for months – our Mas would kill us if we came home purple on Saturday.

But of course this was more than just good fun; people were being killed in Belfast. Derry's turn came in July '71 when Seamus Cusack and Dessie Beattie were killed. We weren't there, but went down the next day to see the trails of blood at Abbey Park and Lecky Road. They were thick and congealed and I will never forget the sight of Dessie Beattie's bloody hand print on the ground after he had crawled or been dragged from the spot where he was shot. This was the reality, not the exhilaration of hitting a Brit with a stone at 20 yards.

Events moved quickly then; Internment was introduced on 9 August 1971. Our Das, in common with many Creggan people, laid siege to Rosemount Barracks. We went to the Brandywell, where rioting was much better fun and people weren't afraid to throw petrol bombs, even if the Brits were going to shoot you. We still took our pliers with us because you never knew when copper would become available.

Nine days after Internment, Eamon Lafferty was killed just above the Kildrum Park. There were many stories about that morning, particularly about dead soldiers in the morgue. One thing is beyond doubt – 19-year-old Lafferty's bravery. For years after, British soldiers when posted to Creggan visited the scene of his death to salute a brave man. In November, Kathleen Thompson, exhibiting a more innocent bravery, died in her back yard, shot by British soldiers trying to do what Eamon Lafferty had prevented – enter Creggan and raid homes. This time there were more than IRA volunteers opposing them – local people in their hundreds were on the darkened streets using what they could to drive the British down the Coach Road back into the Mex Army Camp.

A cold and threatening 1972 dawned; Bloody Sunday was a matter of weeks away. In Rathkeele, the families of Willie Best and Tony Diamond were blissfully unaware of the future. For us 13-year-olds going-on-men, there were no more questions about morality – we fulfilled our childhood ambitions and joined the army, *our* army.

Bloody Sunday

Creggan was to pay a massive toll through the three decades of the *Troubles*. IRA and INLA personnel were to die at the hands of the army; soldiers and RUC men were to die at the hands of the IRA and INLA; and of course, Republicans were to perish at the hands of other Republicans. There were also civilian casualties inflicted by both sides; schoolchildren, women, pensioners, innocent bystanders – every death a horror story in itself. But the one atrocity which became almost synonymous with the estate was Bloody Sunday.

The damage done to Creggan by Bloody Sunday is apparent everywhere in this book. Many of the contributors or those interviewed describe it as a turning point or a watershed, not just in the history of the estate but in the history of Ireland. Six Creggan men and boys were to die in the shootings; 13 coffins were left standing on St Mary's altar; an entire country was left in mourning.

Jack Duddy, a talented young boxer from Central Drive, was shot in the back as he tried to outrun Father Daly, who, it is suggested, may have been the intended target. Duddy was 17.

Willie Nash, a docker from Dunree Gardens, was killed close to a rubble barricade on Rossville Street. The new Inquiry into Bloody Sunday, chaired by Lord Saville, is currently investigating if he may have been shot by an Army sniper from the old City Walls. Nash's father Alex was shot and wounded as he went to help him.

John Young, a draper from Westway, was also shot dead at the rubble barricade; and again it is being suggested he was shot from the Walls. Young's brother was arrested and held overnight after he tried to get another of those shot to hospital.

Eyewitnesses say Barney McGuigan, a foreman from Iniscarn Crescent, was killed as he went to help a man who was lying dying. Many people said he died waving a white handkerchief in the air.

Michael Kelly, an apprentice mechanic from Dunmore Gardens, was shot in the stomach at the rubble barricade. He was dead on admission to Altnagelvin Hospital.

Willie McKinney, a keen amateur cameraman, was from Westway. He was shot at the steps in Glenfada Park. Witness statements say he may have been attempting to tend to another of those shot when he was killed.

Seven other Derry men were to die on Bloody Sunday: Gerald Donaghy, Paddy Doherty, Hugh Gilmour, Michael McDaid, Kevin McElhinney, Gerard McKinney and Jim Wray. John Johnston was to die five months later from his injuries.

The victims – all unarmed – were killed by soldiers from the Parachute Regiment as they took part in a march against Internment. The Northern Ireland Government at Stormont had banned the demonstration, and the initial investigation into the deaths, conducted by the then Lord Chief Justice, Lord Widgery, exonerated the soldiers from all blame.

The Widgery Report was to stand unrepudiated until 1998. Then, after huge international pressure and a challenge in the European Court by Madden & Finucane Solicitors, the British Government announced a new judicial investigation into the deaths. A major catalyst in expediting the Tribunal was undoubtedly the best-selling book *Eyewitness Bloody Sunday*, written by Don Mullan from Leenan Gardens in Creggan.

The new Saville Inquiry, which is chaired by a panel of three Commonwealth judges, is expected to run until 2002 at the earliest. Widgery had wrapped up his investigation by 18 April 1972 – less than three months after the shootings.

Many of those who fought for the new Inquiry are, not surprisingly, from Creggan. The Bloody Sunday Justice Campaign was headed for the past decade or so by two Creggan men, John Kelly and Mickey McKinney. And the solicitor representing the McGuigan family at the Inquiry, Des Doherty, is from Rinmore. This section will look at their recollections of 30 January 1972 and their fight for justice for the Bloody Sunday dead.

John Kelly

Michael Kelly was 17 when he was killed. His mother didn't want him to go on the march – and only gave in after considerable persuasion. Indeed, she even followed her son down along the march route and saw him last only a few minutes before he died. Michael's older brother John was one of the first on the scene after he was shot.

> Michael wasn't political in any way; he'd never been on a march before in his life. He would have been away in Belfast at the Polytech all through the week, training to be a sewing machine mechanic. And at the weekends, he had pigeons he was rearing and he was going out with a girl called Bernie Doherty. He'd never been involved in rioting either. I took him down once to see one at the Essex factory. But after they fired some [CS] gas, I had to take him home.

Michael's political innocence led to him joining the very front line of the march, beside one of the organisers, Ivan Cooper, MP, though the Kelly family doubts very much if Michael would even have known who the MP was.

John Kelly joined the march separately with his friends and proceeded with them down as far as Chamberlain Street, before deciding to go over to Free Derry Corner to hear the speeches.

> We met Barney McGuigan, whom I knew, and chatted for a few minutes. After the Paras moved in, I got separated from the other guys and ran to Joseph Place. I then hid behind one of the 'Threepenny Bits' (old hexagonal concrete structures on Rossville Street) before running across to Lisfannon Park. I met my brother-in-law there, and the two of us decided to head towards Abbey Park where we could see crowds of people. But the first time we dashed out, two bullets bounced right in front of us – they had to have come from the walls. So we dived back in, waited until

> things quietened down and then ran across. At Abbey Park, there was a man on the ground, Gerry McKinney. At the time, we thought he'd had a heart attack. But as we were standing there, another of my brother-in-laws shouted: 'John, John, it's Mickey. He's been shot.'

John and his two brothers-in-law helped carry Michael to an ambulance. The vehicle was to carry 13 people – including four of the dead or injured – the three miles to Altnagelvin Hospital. At one point on the journey, soldiers attempted to stop the ambulance. But by that stage John was having none of it and angrily told them to 'fuck off'.

> We carried Michael into Casualty and laid him down. A doctor checked him and said: 'I'm sorry, he's dead.' I asked him to check him again, which he did. But again, all the doctor said was: 'Sorry, he's dead.'

Phones were still in scarce supply in Creggan in 1972, so John had to ring a house in Malin Gardens to get word through to his parents. His father and sister 'Fia came over to the hospital.

> I distinctly remember the Paras in the foyer of Altnagelvin laughing and joking as if nothing had happened. When my father arrived, he was told Michael was dead. He was grief-stricken and slid down the wall. We tried to comfort him as best we could and then we brought him down to the morgue where he had to formally identify Michael's body. There were three bodies on the floor of the morgue, while others were lying on trolleys or in the freezer compartments. We had to go through a few before we found Michael. On the way out, we were stopped by the RUC who asked if we'd answer a few questions. But we just told them that we'd enough problems and left.

As the Kellys were leaving the hospital, however, they were to suffer further trauma. An Army Saracen drew up, and soldiers dragged out three bodies. They took them into the hospital, got them pronounced dead then dragged them back to the Saracen again. By that stage, the soldiers had been holding the bodies for over an hour-and-a-half.

Back in Creggan, John's mother Kathleen had been told Michael had been shot in the leg and was okay. So when the family returned from the hospital to break the news, the effect was devastating.

> The house was racked with grief. I remember my wife Margaret throwing her arms round me and saying 'I'll never nag you again'. My mother was totally overcome and had to be heavily sedated. But during the night, we heard this noise. She was down at the coffin, crying 'Michael, son – Michael, son' and trying to lift him out of the casket.

Michael Kelly was buried side by side with four of the other victims in the City Cemetery on the Wednesday after he was killed. The loss to his family was to be immeasurable. Kathleen Kelly, in particular, was completely unable to come to terms with the death of her son.

> She suffered desperately. One night when there was snow on the ground, she was stopped going into the cemetery with a blanket she was going to put on Michael's grave. We had to replace the little ceramic picture of Michael that was on the headstone, because my mother wore out the first one by touching it and kissing it. All the mothers were to suffer terribly. All Derry mothers believe the sun shines out of their sons.

Mrs Kelly kept dozens of little mementos of her son such as his aftershave and a bar of chocolate he had been eating shortly before he died. But, fortunately, she also held on to the clothes he was wearing when he was shot. And these are to be presented as evidence at the new Inquiry.

> She really hated the Paras for what they did. But I remember one day a soldier was shot in Westland Street and she went out to help. I asked her why she'd done it and she told me that he was somebody's son and she only hated the Paras.

Mickey McKinney

Willie McKinney, the eldest of ten children, was three days off his 27th birthday when he was killed. He worked as a compositor with the *Derry Journal*, where he was recognised as an 'outstanding craftsman'. However, his chief interest outside work was photography and he had gone to the anti-Internment march to record the events with his cine camera.

Willie's brother Mickey, a former chairman of the Bloody Sunday Justice Campaign, remembers the ominous mood in the household in the days running up to the march.

> The week before Bloody Sunday, Willie had been filming the march at Magilligan, and afterwards I remember him talking about how abusive the soldiers had been. In the run-up to the march, we were very conscious of the news reports and in particular, the strong line coming from Stormont that the march wouldn't be tolerated. I had an eerie feeling about the Sunday. I felt it was going to be different. The morning of the march, I remember Willie coming back after a walk and talking about how the area was sealed off and the large number of soldiers that were around.

Mickey and Willie joined the rally separately, with different groups of friends. Joe, another brother, was to leave Creggan in the company of John Young, who was himself to die.

> I got split up from my friends at William Street. The entire area was jammed packed. There was a riot going on so I stood at Bradley's Bar and tried to see what was going on. I remember at one stage seeing a Lynx helicopter flying very low overhead across the junction of William Street and Rossville Street, and a soldier giving a 'V' sign to the crowd.

A speaker on the lorry preceding the march began calling people to Free Derry Corner for the rally, so Mickey cut into the Bogside where he was to learn of the first shootings.

At Glenfada Park, he ran into his girlfriend (now wife) Goretti, and, realising the situation was dangerous, they made their way to his aunt's house at St Columb's Wells.

> The [CS] gas was very thick. Then we saw the APCs [Armoured Personnel Carriers] and Bedfords coming in, so we decided it wasn't wise to hang about. Just as we got in the door of the house, which was packed, all hell broke loose outside. We could hear the shooting and see hundreds of people running down the street towards the chapel. Someone said: 'There's five or six people dead down at the phone box at Rossville Flats.' But my brother George, who'd also made it to my aunt's house, said he'd been speaking to Willie and that he was okay. But that was before the shooting. We were more concerned about Joe, because he was the young one. Before we left my aunt's, I was standing in the hallway, when I saw a grey Cortina pull up and two men holding up a man who was holding his stomach. I know now that it was Paddy Campbell and that he'd been shot.

After the shooting died down, Mickey and Goretti headed for Creggan Heights, where Goretti lived. After tea, they went to Mass, where Fr Rooney spoke about the tragic events of the day. Mickey – still oblivious to his brother's death – then decided to return to his own home on Westway to let his parents know he was okay. As he approached the house, he noticed Fr McLaughlin's car nearby. Two men from the street had been shot the previous day, and Mickey assumed that one of them must have taken a turn for the worse.

> When I got to the house, I heard my mother crying. Then, as I entered, my father approached me and told me Willie had died. I ran into the hall and broke down crying, Fr McLaughlin trying to console me. The next morning I was wakened by my father crying downstairs. I never heard anyone crying as sore in my life. It was the full realisation that he'd lost

> his son. I remember him saying: 'Why didn't they wound him? Why didn't they wound him?'

Willie had been shot in Glenfada Park – he and one of the injured, Joe Mahon, falling side by side. The current Tribunal will investigate the possibility that the two men may have been hit by the same bullet. The McKinney family still has the film footage Willie was taking that day.

> Willie never took part in riots, but if anything was happening, he wanted to record it. The last time I saw him he was up a tree filming the march as it came down Southway. The film eventually gave out as the march was coming into Rossville Street.

Mickey comments that his mother Annie, though deeply distraught at her son's death, never grieved in front of her family.

> Very deliberately, she kept it private. She was afraid that if any of us saw her in a state, that we'd have joined up. She was very sensitive. My father was bereft. A relative of one of the other victims met him one day in a lift at Du Pont where they worked. My father was crying, and when the man asked him why, he said: 'I just want to see my son.' That was 12 years after Bloody Sunday. All the relatives have similar stories. The effect of Bloody Sunday was devastating. In Creggan, the pain was felt by the whole community. There was always the feeling that the victims could have been anybody. The community gave us immense support and still does, even yet.

The McKinney family, like the other Bloody Sunday relatives, will not rest until everyone wounded or killed on 30 January 1972 is declared totally innocent of every allegation made against them.

> We are determined to pursue the three demands that we've always held. We've come so far, but if the new Tribunal doesn't reach the proper conclusion, I personally won't cease until the truth is revealed.

Des Doherty

The Kelly and McKinney families, like relatives of the other victims, didn't go to the Widgery Tribunal in Coleraine, and the Lord Chief Justice's findings were no surprise to them. For two decades, the only time the families ever met up was for the commemoration ceremony and march. However, on the 20th anniversary, they decided to make a big push for public support. Eamonn McCann had published his book, *Bloody Sunday in Derry*, which included harrowing accounts of the victims' deaths; the work struck a chord with both the Derry community and the public at large. The Bloody Sunday Justice Campaign (BSJC) was formed, and the families began contacting religious leaders and politicians for help. Some of those approached were 'stand-offish' at the beginning, but later came on board. The BSJC set itself three objectives – demands that still stand to this day:

- a full declaration that the dead and injured were innocent
- the complete repudiation of the Widgery Report
- the prosecution of those who planned and participated in Bloody Sunday

The relatives were to try and get the European Court to hear the case. But it was thrown out because of the 20-year delay in bringing the suit. Downing Street, likewise, was to refuse appeals for a new inquiry. But in a letter to the SDLP leader, John Hume, the British Prime Minister, John Major, acknowledged that all those killed or injured were innocent of all allegations of handling firebombs or nail bombs when they were shot.

The campaign gathered momentum: petitions were gathered and delivered to Westminster; meetings were held with the Republic's Tánaiste, Dick Spring; British-Irish Rights Watch uncovered a confidential cabinet document from the day after Bloody Sunday, in which Prime Minister Ted Heath advised Lord Widgery to remember that Britain was fighting '. . . not only a military war but a propaganda war.'

The annual Bloody Sunday lecture was initiated to raise the public's awareness of the issues. And at one such lecture, the Dublin-based Derryman, Don Mullan, suggested that a book should be compiled from civilian statements taken after Bloody Sunday – most of which had been rejected by Lord Widgery as unsuitable for consideration.

The Bloody Sunday Trust was set up and employed a Limerick-based law professor, Dermot Walsh, to analyse Widgery's findings. Walsh's damning report and Don Mullan's book were given to the Irish Government, which used them to make its own submission to Downing Street.

The Irish Government's report was published the same day that a new judicial investigation into the events of Bloody Sunday was announced in the House of Commons by the Prime Minister, Tony Blair. He told MPs that Lord Widgery hadn't considered all the available evidence. And after a series of preliminary hearings, the Saville Inquiry – the biggest tribunal ever to be staged in Ireland or Britain – got underway at Derry's Guildhall in March 2000.

Solicitor Des Doherty – who is originally from Rinmore – represents the interests of the McGuigan family at the Tribunal. He is the only legal representative there from Creggan and his interest in the case has spanned a lifetime. As a seven-year-old boy, he served as altar boy at the Bloody Sunday funerals.

> My main memory of Bloody Sunday is that because my father was going on the march we didn't go for a drive after lunch, as we used to do religiously. I spent the afternoon playing football on my own. The streets

> of Creggan were empty as everyone was at the march. I have a vague recollection of waiting for my father to come back. My mother, though I mightn't have been aware of it, was worried sick. My father had been at the front of the march and helped Lord Brockway onto a lorry when the trouble started. One of my enduring images is the photo, which appeared in one of the papers, of blood on the Civil Rights Banner. We were asked about it in school and were able to say what it was. The banner had been used to cover the body of Barney McGuigan.

The Dohertys lived at the top circle of Rinmore. No-one from the immediate area was killed, though a neighbour, Michael Bradley, was injured. By and large, however the families in the area were spared the traumas experienced elsewhere.

> I was serving the ten o'clock Masses all that week; it was always a bit of a bonus getting out of school to do them. I remember being in the company of priests like Fr Rooney, Fr McLaughlin and Fr McIvor, and them all whispering about the events; I began to pick up what happened. It was the first time violence or death had become reality for me. It was unbelievable.

The night before the funerals, Des Doherty served at the ceremonies as the bodies were moved into St Mary's Chapel. The altar, which had always seemed like such an expanse to the schoolboy, was vastly constricted with the 13 'huge' coffins. The image of the coffins would never leave him.

> My abiding memory is of holding a big candlestick – it seemed like about seven-foot-long – and the wax falling off the candle into my eye. But Michael Kelly's mother saw what happened, took a piece of tissue and wetted it and cleaned out the eye. I knew it was her, as I'd always seen her at Mass. She just got to me in time – she was very sympathetic.

RTÉ was on hand to film the proceedings and young Doherty ran home proudly to tell all to watch him on TV. The family was one of the very few to get RTÉ in Creggan.

> I was totally over-focused on the fact that I was on the TV when it was completely meaningless, given the scale and sense of tragedy that was surrounding us.

In the years after the funerals, Des Doherty went to St Peter's High School before heading to university and qualifying as a solicitor. But his huge interest in the killings of his neighbours never waned.

Then in 1998, when the Saville Inquiry was announced, his practice became heavily involved in compiling witness statements from civilians who had been on the original march.

Anti-Internment march leaving Creggan on Bloody Sunday. (Larry Doherty)

The Creggan man himself was to take over a hundred statements – many of which pertained to the shooting dead of Barney McGuigan. The McGuigan family then appointed Des to represent their interests at the tribunal.

> I was honoured and privileged to be asked. I think it's vitally important to clear the good name of Barney McGuigan, a stalwart of the community, whom I believe was murdered – pure and simple. It could just have easily have been my own father who was killed. As the coroner at the Omagh Inquest said recently about the bomb there, Bloody Sunday was a lottery.

The solicitor reckons it helps that he came from a Creggan background and witnessed Bloody Sunday and Motorman at first hand; it gives him an added passion for what he's doing.

> A case like the Saville Inquiry is the reason why you got into law. You just want to work on it no matter what it entails. I've already devoted two years of my life to it and it will probably take another two or three until it's concluded. But we hope to bring this case to closure. That is what this Inquiry is about. When an injustice is done, it must be undone – and be seen to be undone. It is part of the healing process.

The Derry Journal
Established 1772
FRIDAY, 4th FEBRUARY, 1972
PRICE — 5p (Britain and Overseas — 7p)

The skies wept, too, as Derry laid its dead to rest

Two pictures that need no words to tell their story. Poignantly they illustrate the heartbreak that is Derry's.

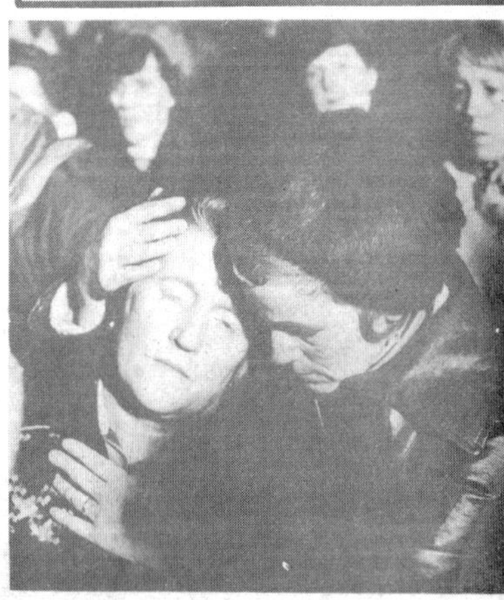

IRELAND WAS UNITED in grief on Wednesday. St. Mary's Church in the Creggan estate was the centre of world attention for a poignant hour as Derry buried its murdered dead.

Church and State, priests and people, joined in a unique ceremony which expressed the emotion of a sorrowing nation.

From north and south, from east and west they came, the mourning thousands, to honour the dead, to comfort the bereaved, to pledge by their living presence a Christian response to horrific tragedy.

There were few dry eyes among the distinguished congregation. Outside the thronging thousands ignored the bitter cold, and even the driving rain seemed Heaven's tears.

There was His Eminence Cardinal Conway, an impressive figure in his traditional garb of a Prince of the Church. Most Rev. Dr. Anthony MacFeely, Bishop of Raphoe, come to underline the identity of feeling of his neighbouring diocese with the people of Derry, with whom he has so many personal ties; there were five Irish Government Ministers, symbols of the nation's homage to suffering Derry; nine brightly-robed Mayors from Twenty-six County cities and towns, representing their people present in spirit if unable to make the journey physically; there were the elected public representatives of all the people from the northernmost end to the southernmost tip of the country, illustrating the indivisibility of the land and the nation.

There were the 200 priests from every corner of the land, most making their first visit to Derry on this sad pilgrimage.

There were the hundreds of stricken relatives, sustained however by the overwhelming manifestation of a national sharing in their individual grief.

There were the thousands of people from all parts of the land, many of whom had made long and arduous journeys to be present.

There were the deeply-affected thousands of local people from every area, every street, of the city, present in mourning accord to share in yet another tragic but historic occasion in the serried story of their city, on ground hallowed centuries ago by the blood of martyrs.

There was the angelically-rendered music from the choir, which blended so wonderfully with the rich liturgy of Church ceremonial, performed beneath the blinding glare of twentieth century communication paraphernalia.

Heart-Rending Ceremony

There were the central figures of His Lordship Most Rev. Dr. Farren, Bishop of Derry, officiating at the most heart-rending ceremony of his long episcopate, and the twelve black-robed priests, who concelebrated the Solemn Requiem Mass with him, which had drawn together such a vast and reverent multitude.

Seven of those priests had, seventy-two hours earlier, shared with their people in the Bogside the terror unleashed on the streets and risked injury and death to bring succour and the Last Rites of the Church to dead and dying.

And, before the high altar, thirteen coffins reposed, the stark reminders of the purpose of the sombre gathering, containing the remains of thirteen young men, struck down ere they could experience a normal life span.

Many of the relatives, overcome by the immensity of the tragedy, broke down and wept. Doctors and Knights of Malta moved swiftly and noiselessly to give medical aid and comfort to those whose emotions became uncontrollable as the true significance of the size of the loss struck with stunning clarity.

Sorrow and Compassion

The crowded church was hushed as His Lordship put in words the thoughts of everyone, in slow and measured tones which illustrated his own deep feeling for his bereaved flock. He spoke in sorrow and with compassion and appealed for Christian forbearance in the face of the terrible events that had made necessary the nation-wide act of homage in the Creggan church.

And then, as the ceremony ended, began the last sad journeys. One by one the coffins were borne out of the church, down the aisle by relatives and friends, the congregation standing in final salutation to the dead.

First there was the funeral procession of Bernard McGuigan, then John Young, then Jackie Duddy, then Jim Wray, then Gerard Donaghy, then Michael McDaid, then William McKinney, whose body was transferred to the chapel mortuary for burial yesterday.

Then together, to be buried side by side, came the remains of William Nash, Kevin McElhinney, Hugh Gilmour, Patrick Doherty and Michael Kelly.

The remains of Gerald McKinney were removed to Iskaheen for burial in Iskaheen graveyard.

Weeping Mourners

As the funerals moved down the short hill to the city cemetery many of the

Continued on Page 3

How the *Derry Journal* reported the Bloody Sunday funerals.

Above: Funeral of Bloody Sunday victim, John Young. (Larry Doherty)
Below: Crowds gathered outside St Mary's Church for Bloody Sunday funerals. (Larry Doherty)

Crowds along route of Bloody Sunday funerals. (Larry Doherty)

The Killing of Ranger Best

One of the most controversial killings witnessed in Creggan during the early Troubles *was that of a young local man who had joined the British Army and was visiting his mother on home leave. William Best, who was 19 and from Rathkeele Way, had been serving with the Royal Irish Rangers in Germany. One of seven children, he was abducted and shot dead by the Official IRA after going to make a phone call on a Saturday night. Best's death on 21 May 1972 led to major protests from the community and clergy in Creggan, as the author Eamonn McCann recounts here in an extract from his book* War and an Irish Town.

In Derry it was not the Provo bombing campaign but the Officials' shooting of a Creggan teenager, home on leave from the British army, which gave Catholic Tories the opportunity to come storming out to oppose the IRA. Nineteen-year-old Ranger Best, stationed in Germany, had foolhardily decided to spend his leave at home. As he wandered about the area renewing contacts with old friends he was twice warned by Official units to get out 'for your own good'. But he did not. So he was picked up by an Official Patrol and taken 'for questioning' to the shop in Meenan Park. Once there, he was doomed. The man who presided over the 'trial' explained afterwards:

> Once we had him there was nothing we could do but execute him. Our military orders after Bloody Sunday were to kill every British soldier we could. They didn't say anything about local soldiers. He was a British soldier and that is all there was to it.

Best was driven with a hood over his head to a piece of waste ground near William Street, told to get out and to walk straight ahead. After he had taken a few steps he was shot in the back of the skull. His body was found early next morning. Had Best been an 'ordinary' soldier there would have followed a ritual, and largely disregarded, condemnation from the clergy and perhaps a statement from Mr Hume to the effect that this was not the proper way to proceed; but the majority of the people of the area would have considered it an act of war, maybe something which they were less passionately in favour of pursuing than they had been a few months previously, but an act of war nonetheless. But Best was not, of course, an ordinary soldier. He was a local lad, the son of solid and inoffensive parents who lived in a council house in Creggan, and his killing outraged that very feeling of communal solidarity which the last three years had created and which was absolutely essential to the maintenance of Free Derry. 'If he had stayed in Germany he would have been safe enough,' complained a local housewife the day after his death. 'He was killed because he came home to see his mother.' It was a line of argument which struck deep chords, not least in the hearts of local mothers.

The day after his death 400 women marched to the Official headquarters in Meenan Square. Two members of the organisation, neither of whom had been present at the 'trial' or execution of Best, were unfortunate enough to be manning the premises at the time. Their encounter with the protesters was bruising. The British media seized on the issue with unconcealed glee. 'Women call on IRA to get out' was smeared across the front pages. The five women who had led the march were accorded the handy reference-title 'the Derry Peace Women' and quickly became the darlings of the Tory Press. The Church, too, quickly showed its talent for seizing the time and called a 'peace meeting' in a school hall in Creggan. Sharing the platform with local priests were a member of the local police committee, Mr John Maultsaid, Mr Frank McCauley ['Onlooker'], Tom Doherty, a former Nationalist councillor, and some others of like ilk. Their message was clear: 'Things have gone too far. It is time to call a halt.' Most of the audience of 2,000 agreed. Johnnie White mounted the platform and asked for the mike to explain the Officials' position. The chairman, the parish priest of Creggan, Father Martin Rooney, refused, telling him that 'You are not wanted. You are an alien influence', after which the meeting broke up in some confusion. What was quite clear was that for the first time in many months the people of the area were, sometimes literally, fighting among themselves, a luxury no embattled community could afford.

The bishop turned out for Ranger Best's funeral, flanked by 25 priests. (Two days previously, 15-year-old Manus Deery had been buried. He had been shot for no particular reason by an Army sniper from the city walls as he was on his way home from a fish-and-chip shop with the family supper. He got the standard two priests.) For the next week, it seemed that no edition of the BBC's *World at One* and no front page of any newspaper was complete without quotes from a local priest or a 'peace woman' explaining that the IRA was no more than a tiny minority within the area and that the majority of peace-loving people were in the process of evicting them. Father Hugh O'Neill, administrator of St Eugene's Cathedral, was particularly prominent. Father O'Neill had once accused me of being the Devil, Satan himself in human form. He was on surer theological ground now, asserting that the IRA had no respect for the law of man or God.

> They are finished – it's the end of the road for the IRA. Those Officials are not the IRA at all. They are communists pretending to be the IRA. The people have rejected them.

Father O'Neill also alleged that there were North Koreans in the area up to no good, a revelation which resulted in a confrontation between a *Daily Express* reporter and a waiter from the Rice Bowl restaurant from which the waiter, quite possibly, has not yet recovered. At Mass the following Sunday, the Church pursued the attack. The pulpits became for the day political platforms from which a co-ordinated series of anti-IRA – anti-Official IRA in particular – speeches were delivered.

The killing of Best and the reaction to it detonated a number of minor political explosions both locally and nationally. The fact that the clergy had openly entered the political lists against them forced the local Officials to define more clearly than they had ever dared before their attitude to the Church and to its role in politics. Hitherto, their attitude had been not so much ill defined as undefined. They were members of an organisation which, at national level, claimed to be Marxist or 'moving towards

Marxism'. The local group, since its absorption of the Labour Party left after Internment, had moved sharply to the left of the leadership's position and was probably the least 'Catholic' Republican group in the country. Since August 1971, however, there had been neither the occasion nor, it appeared, the necessity to express this in action. The 'defence of the area' was the task at hand; the enemy was the British army. The Officials fought alongside the Provos to keep the Army out and the occasional questioning of the means of doing this by the Church and the SDLP was not urgent enough to demand answer. For its part, the Church was unable in the same period to denounce the Officials as forthrightly as it would have liked. But now, as the Church and the middle classes roused Catholic wrath against them, and as Father O'Neill argued that the killing of a local Catholic was a direct product of their 'alien ideology', the Officials had either to cut and run or to fight back. To their credit, they did the latter, producing perhaps the fiercest class-oriented, anti-Church polemic ever to issue from within our community.

> We are not a Catholic organisation. We never said that we were. If there is anyone in this community who has been giving us support in the belief that we are some sort of militant, Catholic, Nationalist organisation, let them withdraw their support now. We are nothing of the sort. We are out to build a revolutionary socialist party of the Irish working class.

It was, in Derry, fairly daring stuff and its authors expected that it would receive a fairly hostile reception when it was distributed in the Starry Plough [Derry's own Republican paper] around the Creggan and the Bogside; but the reaction was more complex. The Church's open entry into politics had deprived it of the total inviolability normally conferred on it by its 'spiritual' role. Those who wished to 'stand by the IRA' had to oppose the clergy on this issue. If the role of the IRA was being openly questioned for the first time in ten months, the role of the Church was under similar scrutiny for the first time in 50 years. That too, in its own contradictory way, helped to loosen the bonds holding the area together. The Provisionals, after some hesitation, realized that the flak aimed at the Officials was certain to damage them as well and asserted their own refusal to accept the Church's dictate. Initially they had tried to use the reaction to the Best killing to divert support away from the Officials and towards themselves. But that was much too delicate a manoeuvre to come off and was quickly abandoned.

The Officials' leadership in Dublin called a cease-fire three weeks after the Best affair on 23 May. They insisted at the time that this had nothing to do with the 'peace women's' still buoyant campaign; few accepted this. What happened was that the elements in the Official leadership which had wanted, anyway, to call a cease-fire found the time ripe in the post-Best atmosphere. They had continued to insist that their organisation was not engaged in any offensive, military operations – this despite the fact that since Bloody Sunday active service units had been doing little other that seeking out ways and means to shoot and blow up soldiers. This, insisted the leadership, was 'defence and retaliation', not to be confused with the offensive and sectarian behaviour of the Provisionals. The common people had continued to have great difficulty discerning the difference between the Officials defensively blowing up two soldiers in Brooke Park on 5 April and the Provisionals offensively shooting one a week later. The stated reason for the cease-fire was that military operations were aggravating the sectarian situation, forcing the Protestants into an even more intransigent position and leading on towards open civil war; the way forward was to concentrate on politics.

A Soldier's Impressions of Creggan

Life was no picnic for the occupying forces, particularly in the wake of Bloody Sunday. Squaddies serving in Creggan in the '70s could expect to be bricked and abused if they were lucky – bombed or shot if they weren't. Mick Corbett, a former Grenadier Guard, did two tours of duty in Derry where he saw two comrades killed and friends maimed. A few years ago, he revisited the estate and was inspired to write the following piece.

The black barrel of my rifle rested on a sandbag and poked out through the observation slit of the sangar across the Bogside towards the city centre. The temperature was well below zero and the minutes had ticked slowly by, as they always did on guard duty. I felt the familiar craving for a mug of tea and the company of my mates; alas, there was more time to kill before being relieved by the next guard. The post was a crude but impressive structure, built by Army Engineers after Motorman. It was strategically placed to give a good view of the surrounding area, raised on stilts, at the top of a hill, tight against a factory wall. As I looked down from my vantage point, the cold, fresh, night air gave the street lights a sparkling, crystalline quality, and the only sound to be heard was a cat meowing below. Earlier, Saturday night revellers from the Stardust had staggered their way uphill to home; occasionally a stone was thrown in my direction but fell way short. To relieve the boredom I would aim my rifle and pretend to shoot them as they passed. A group of high-spirited youths had hung around singing rebel songs, screaming for 'limey bastards' to 'fuck off back home'.

At the beginning of my stag, I heard a shot ring out from below, where the Royal Horse Artillery was barracked for patrolling the Bogside. I imagined a frightened squaddie being frogmarched in front of the Commanding Officer in the morning to face a charge. I later learnt it was far more serious than that, a feud between a NCO and a private had turned nasty, ending in death for the Sergeant. In melancholic mood, I'd watched the lights along a row of terraced houses going out, one by one, as the occupants made their way to bed. I pictured couples making soft, exquisite love, tucked between clean, crisp sheets. Lucky sods. The urge to lie and stretch in a clean bed, as we were allowed every third day, became overwhelming. It beat trying to snatch 40 winks fully dressed beneath the nylon material of a fetid sleeping bag. A dull thud interrupted my thought and brought home the reason for my being in Derry. I looked around for the source of the explosion and within seconds spotted, down in the city below, orange flames snaking high above a building; minutes later, sirens screamed.

This incident happened back in the winter of 1972 during my first tour of the Creggan, and was long forgotten until I sat riveted to the BBC TV series *The Provos.* A well-known Derry Provo appeared on screen talking frankly about his part in the bombing of the city centre. It dawned on me that he could have been the one who planted the bomb all those years ago. It put a human face behind the conflict. He struck me as someone in the building trade, a salt of the earth type. Although you could never accuse him of being a builder, more a destroyer – committed to the destruction of British rule and Protestant domination in the North of Ireland. From the comfort of my armchair, living in a so called 'normal' stable society, where they'd recently banned handguns, it was hard to believe he'd probably been responsible – directly or indirectly – for killing other British soldiers. I resented him. What had he ever done apart from destroying lives and property? Fuck him! Then I double-checked and reprimanded myself for making judgements about a man I'd never met and remembered back to the autumn of 1997 when I returned to Derry, the Creggan, and viewed at first hand the enormous strides made by people living in an abnormal society trying to get back to normality after years of conflict. Who the hell was I to judge? To be honest I felt confused, angry, and sick of the patronising attitudes you got from people over here when you tried to discuss the subject. After a few drinks it was all strident voices and accusations about loyalty to a stupid flag.

A few years back, studying for a degree, I saw the logic of a United Ireland and felt a strong – and possibly crazy – desire to meet former IRA men and record their experiences. It's one of my little fantasies. I believe there are innumerable lessons to be learnt from the conflict over the last 30 years. Self doubts apart, this impulse led me back to Derry where I was fortunate enough to meet two people from the Nationalist community who didn't want my blood. That meeting, and subsequent contact with Mickey McGuinness [joint editor of this book], had a profound impact on me. The first time I spoke to Mickey, I told him I was a student doing an MA on the Creggan; he phoned me and invited me over to the 50th anniversary of the estate. I declined and confessed I was an ex-squaddie, which didn't bother him. He seemed to understand and went out of his way to keep in touch. The first time I met him, I knew that I could trust him. Mickey had been there on Bloody Sunday when the Paras opened fire and Seamus lived a few doors down the road from Mints, who at the time was a 15-year-old gunman pursuing a shoot-to-kill policy on British soldiers. This was real history. Mickey told me later that Seamus had suspicions about me, thought I might be Military Intelligence. He was friendly though, and we had a good exchange of views. It made me realise the pitfalls of judging fellow humans who have views honed from a life experience totally different to yourself. Like the old saying, 'you have to walk a mile in someone's shoes before you can understand them'. Before our meeting, I'd strolled around the Creggan, alone, trying to understand why I was there and searching for enlightenment. As I did so, memories, as if from another life, came flooding back.

Months after Bloody Sunday and the smashed barricades of Motorman, I arrived on the Creggan with the Grenadier Guards. A sombre mood of despondency hung over the estate like a dark cloud. The run-down old factory in Bligh's Lane, where we stayed, seemed to compound the effect. They crammed us like sardines, platoon by platoon into makeshift, partitioned sections under a leaking roof where we were visited by the odd scaly-tailed rodent. I shared a rickety, metal bunk with Nikko, who lusted for his girlfriend back home. In the early hours, thinking I was asleep, soft sighs would rise from below as he gently, but inadvertently, rocked the frame, locked in his own intimate fantasy until a final deep gasp, then silence, as he drifted back to sleep. To the occupants at the top of the hill, Bligh's Lane camp must have been like a collection of festering warts on the face of a friend. It was a hastily constructed fortress of corrugated metal, surrounded by miles of jagged, rusting barbed wire, interspersed with pillbox-type sangars, where young Brits' eyes scanned hungrily for firm buttocks, pert young breasts and tight labial silhouettes in tight blue denim. Even better for them, the sad, forlorn hope of seeing and shooting that elusive sniper. If you had any sense, you kept clear of sangar walls unless you wanted to catch something, as they bore the brunt of frustration from young male loins.

Despite the boredom and frustration, sangar duty did have its moments. Some 18 months later, up on Piggery Ridge, two of our sangars felt the red-hot wrath of Irish Republicanism in the form of RPG7 rockets. Taffy was on guard in sangar four when it was hit. In the aftermath, three lads rushed to his aid expecting a mess of blood, dismembered limbs and gore. Instead they found a mop of lively red hair, sticking out from under a pile of sandbags, he was flat on his back, legs apart with his flies undone. Major 'Manners', as he was nicknamed by the locals, 3 Company Commander, strutted over, peered down the end of his nose at the prostrate figure, ordered 'leave him, he's dead', turned on the ball of his feet and strolled back to the comfort of the officers' mess. Much to our relief, Taff was OK, just concussed and badly shaken. For the rest of the tour, his broad shoulders endured the weight of endless jibes. More disturbing, and contrary to his easy going nature, before going to sleep, he followed a ritual of punching and sticking pins into an Action Man doll adorned with a major's epaulettes.

Near Christmas, a rare event occurred, as the four of us loped out of base, past the jeering faces of Bligh's Lane factory workers. A brown-haired, middle-aged woman strode purposefully towards us impervious to the aerial bombardment that we came under from the kids grouped at the top of the hill. As we passed, she patted each of us on the back, and said in cheery voice 'Merry Christmas and God bless youse, boys'. That small thing amazed me. I later wondered what had made her do such a thing. Was she Willie Best's Mum? Or had she seen past the uniform to see us for what we really were, just snotty-nosed kids with big rifles? Boys like her own sons, perhaps? It was easy to like people of the Creggan who went quietly about their lives, not trying to kill us and endeavouring, against the odds, to raise their families decently. They were truly the salt of the earth.

Creggan resembled the council estates we came from in England, and like everywhere, some homes were kept better than others as the search platoon found to their cost. They had the unenviable task of rooting around the intimate nooks and crannies of homes where families lived out their private lives and kept their worldly possessions. After a raid in Leenan Gardens during the early hours, the search team was whisked back to camp, ordered into the showers, combat kit bundled into bin bags and sent down to Fort George for laundering. Later in the day, as I was having my evening meal, mad Malc sidled over to me and described the morning's events. He told me he was assigned to search the main bedroom. After the occupants' departure, he lifted the bed to find a limp mess of used Gossamers, skiddy pants and soiled Dr Whites. The cats, rabbiting out back in the fields, had introduced fleas to the lethal cocktail and it stunk to high heaven. The mattresses were stained the colour of nicotine. Malc stifled the urge to vomit as he got on with the job. He found nothing of note and went downstairs to find his team leader interviewing the man of the house. Malc told me:

> The old man stood around in manky old Y-fronts, no shirt or trousers, scratching his balls. Then he asked if we wanted a cup of tea. Imagine it, those hands on your cup, needless to say we declined his offer.

I finished my meal, but somehow it had lost its attraction.

The average squaddie, if I was anything to go by, was an immature 19-year-old, selfishly engrossed in the insularity of army life, who paid little attention to news and current affairs. The Regiment represented a microcosm of the big wide world outside. What any of us knew about Ireland could be written on a pinhead. So we parroted the usual platitudes about representing the rule of law and keeping the warring factions apart. Yet it was plain to see that in Derry there was no overt sectarian conflict between Protestants and Catholics; the natural barrier of the River Foyle separated them. Yet, an incident during my first patrol made me realise how deeply ingrained the conflict was. The four of us were moving slowly and self-consciously along Creggan Broadway, resplendent in our shiny new flak vests with rifles held firmly, ready for the first sucker wanting to mess with us, instead we were met by a motley tribe of young, stone-throwing Cregganites. A toddler crawled along the pavement, inches from me, the target. As stones landed around us, a piece of paving slab just missed him. I bent down and asked 'are you all right little fella?' He screwed his face into a grimace, raised his little hand and made a V sign. Then I heard the crash of a door as Mum came charging down the path like a rhino, bust bouncing, her face flame-red and fists tightly clenched, she screamed: 'Fuck off limey, and leave my wee nadger alone.'

Shocked, I turned back to keep an eye on the stone-throwers, just in time to see a big round boulder bounce off the pavement and smash into my shin. Inadvertently, the pain caused me to let out a wimpish yelp. The kids loved it and showed their appreciation by cheering as I limped down the street, pursued by the neighbourhood mongrels barking and snapping at my heels. I felt stupid and soon realised that showing concern was naively misplaced. It was a jungle and I had better wise up. It also dawned on me that a rifle, flak vest and ammo were no answer to the sheer bloody hatred I saw in the eyes of that embryonic little Republican.

Mac, the Corporal in our section, had a strange obsession for rooting around back gardens. After discovering a cache of homemade mortar rounds, explosives and ammunition, he became a man possessed. We spent night after night foraging for arms. Not to be outdone, other teams followed suit; bets were placed on who could find the most. We found loads. Regrettably, there was a downside. Some thoughtful young soul in the local IRA unit sought to teach us a lesson by placing a booby trap, designed especially for a sqauddie's size ten boot, in the back of Leenan Gardens; it killed a little boy.

The next booby trap had the desired effect; one of our sections was on VCP [vehicle checkpoint] duty at Rosemount when a metal detector went missing – a hand-held device that was scanned over people and emitted a shrill sound if metal was detected.

It turned up again a while later and was picked up by a rookie fresh from the training depot and new to the battalion. The blast shredded his hand and damaged his baby face and eyes. We never heard of him again. A few days later, unknowingly, I was posted on the sangar where the blast took place, I looked around trying to find the source of an unpleasant smell. High up on the sandbagged interior were small, shrimp-like pieces of flesh. I mentioned it to the Platoon Commander who turned, raised his head aloofly and sneered 'surely you're not squeamish?' As the first tour progressed, the Company I was in had two other notable casualties. Beck was out on patrol when he heard the crack of a shot and felt his rifle jerk; as he looked down, he saw a neat hole drilled all the way through the butt. Luckily, the shot narrowly missed his stomach. His mate Keg was not so fortunate, but still lucky enough; he felt a sledgehammer-like blow in his leg while riding shotgun in a Land Rover, an Armalite round passed clean through his thigh to end up lodged in the inner thigh of his other leg, just missing his manhood. When we left the Creggan in March 1973, little did we know that we would return a year later.

It was a baking hot day in May when we were called out to support another section down by the shops who'd stopped two teenage girls suspected of carrying arms. I was positioned in an alleyway on Central Drive near the place they kneecapped touts. The jungle telegraph had sent warning to get everyone on the streets. I was soon surrounded by men and women jostling and bustling around me. They shouted and screamed abuse, accusing me of a litany of crimes I was far too young to have committed. Panic hit me as I became aware they were trying to cut me off from the rest of my patrol. All eyes fell on me, my legs began to shake and my top lip quivered, until a woman with lank hair and hate-filled eyes came to my rescue by spitting her phlegm in my face. I lashed out with my rifle butt. That drove them frothing-at-the-mouth mad. My thoughts turned to escape by shooting over their heads; if that didn't work, I felt the raw fear of shooting to kill. Fortunately, neither scenario materialised, as backup arrived and we were driven back to camp at breakneck speed, stones and rocks crashing against the sides of the Land Rover. The girls were later charged with carrying arms.

Life in camp behind the corrugated metal and sandbags grew more tedious as the tour progressed being on a continual cycle of guard duty, standby and patrolling. The pettiest things drove you mad – no privacy, thieving of kit, other men's BO, farts, bad breath, smelly socks, lack of sleep and others' taste in music. Jim played *Band on the Run* by Wings day and night, McCartney whining on loop. I fumed inwardly but did nothing except imagine punching his face into a red pulp. Who needed the IRA when you had the insipid banality of Wings? On guard duty or patrol, it was there in my mind, playing away. To keep my sanity, I listened to the only other tape available, Black Sabbath's *Paranoid*, which reflected my state of mind; it beat Wings though, anything but bloody Wings. The pressure of living in a small portakabin with twenty or so other blokes took its toll; it made me selfish and out for number one. Sod the heroics, just stay sharp and focused to get back home in one piece, that was my sole aim. Most evenings, as the sun turned into a giant orange orb before sinking over the horizon, the young guns of the IRA would loose off a few rounds from Central Drive, as if to emphasise a point. One evening, it triggered a gun battle where we fired two hundred rounds; the only victims were the residents of Creggan Heights, whose houses were riddled like colanders. One family, sitting innocently watching TV, got the fright of their lives as their screen disintegrated after bullets fired from the camp poured through it. Miraculously no one was injured or killed.

We nicknamed one gunman 'Mints', who drove us to distraction all summer with his well rehearsed one-shot sniping. Crack! And off he went handing the Armalite to his buddies, who stripped it down, shared the parts around and got the girls to hide them under skirts, jackets, prams and shopping bags. Each time Mints was arrested, he was let out, due to his age – 15. Try, reader, to imagine our sheer frustration at a cocky kid trying to take your life with as much compassion as a motorist squashing a hedgehog. So it was no small wonder then that at times we took the law into our own hands. Right or wrong.

We heard the tinny, deceptive crack of the Armalite as we pounded the pavement on Fanad Drive. Nervous voices came over the radio, someone had been hit on Central Drive. We cocked our rifles and legged it round the corner to take up firing positions. I knelt behind a low wall. Further down the road, by the shops, a group of youths was jumping up and down in celebration. They sang 'for he's a jolly good fellow' then 'Hip, Hip Hooray!' Older people stood nervously looking on. I glanced towards Ted as he writhed on the pavement; there was a bustle around him now with Jim frantically dabbing a dressing at the crimson stains on Ted's jacket. My mind flashbacked to Canada and seeing the same bloke writhing around after an accident on a live firing exercise. His legs had been peppered with shrapnel from a mortar round. Now he was lying injured on a street in Northern Ireland. Why him? An old lady came out of her bungalow and asked: 'How is he son?' She stared down at the pavement and gasped: 'Oh Jesus, Mother Mary, what's this country coming to?' Her head turned towards the shops, then back to me, I noticed a steely glint in her eye: 'We're not all like that son,' she said. I avoided her gaze and lined the sights of my rifle smack in the middle of a youth's chest as he jumped and punched the air in celebration; the image of a laughing hyena came to mind. A round was up the breech, the safety catch off and my finger on the trigger. I yearned for them to try another shot. Then a voice in my head said 'turn the other cheek son'. Ironically, Mints and Ted's paths were to cross again a few weeks later.

We didn't have to wait long before Robbo, Spick, Shakes and myself had the privilege of being shot at. As soon as we turned the corner on to Central Drive, we felt the tension – like entering a room of people knowing they were talking about you. Old women in the bus queue were shoved aside by young girls. Then came a whiplash crack! The next sound came from my own rifle. As if on autopilot, I felt the butt in my shoulder and fired. The shot went in the opposite direction; it didn't matter as long as it made the bastard think twice about shooting at us again. My tracer round carved an arc before taking a chunk of masonry out of the top of Cromore flats. The fear of military discipline helped me quickly invent a story about a gunman firing from that location. Fortunately, during the follow up operation, Nikko uncovered an Armalite in a coal shed complete with a full magazine of rounds and telescopic sight.

Back at camp, I was debriefed and asked to give a description of the gunman; I was vague. Black hair, beard, and dark clothing. Later, to my chagrin, I was driven down to Strand Road RUC station to identify a suspect who resembled my description, as I was leaving the barrack room, the lads shouted 'get the bastard'. When I arrived at the station, I was led into a room with a glass window and the suspect was paraded before me; he looked like any normal bloke who had just done a day's manual work. I tried to imagine his wife and family waiting for him. 'No, that's not him,' I said to the RUC men and returned to camp.

School holidays and hot weather conspired to bring everyone on the streets, raising tensions to boiling point. Every day, it seemed, another incident would occur resulting in injury. Most notable, though, was our Adjutant, who lost an eye as he sat in the front of a Land Rover and was hit by a rock. A few days on from my shooting incident, another section came under fire from Central Drive; the shot passed over their heads. They spotted the gunman and followed in hot pursuit all the way behind the shops and up the steps to the flats above. Lightfoot, the patrol leader, a very promising middle-distance runner, kicked a door open, leapt back behind cover and counted to 15 in case it was a booby trap. As he charged forward, he saw a flash; the next thing he remembered was lying in hospital minus a leg. Two other members of the section were injured by flying masonry.

Beck's patience was running low. He'd been one-shot snipered on numerous occasions, so when out on patrol and confronted by Mints, full of bravado, jeering and throwing stones, he snapped. He pulled his section back taking cover in a front garden and told them: 'Listen, Mints had a pistol, that's the story, OK.' 'Fucking right, let's get the bastard,' were some of the replies. Off they went again. Mints, spotting four squaddies coming back down the road, rose to the bait and taunted them. A look of surprise must have shown on his face as he watched Beck take aim and fire. The shot whizzed through his buttocks at 2,000-feet per second making him jump high in the air and run off holding his cheeks. Back at camp, when completing his report Beck wrote that he fired in self-defence as Mints raised a pistol to take aim at the patrol. Two days later it was reported in the *Derry Journal* that a woman overheard troops plotting to shoot him. Mints ended up lying face down in Altnagelvin hospital a couple of wards away from Ted, the NCO shot a few weeks earlier. Visitors popping in to catch up on Ted's recovery made a quick detour to wish Mints a swift recovery.

On patrol, we became objects of abuse, the unclean passing through a settled community, social lepers, creatures on which the inhabitants could release their life-long frustrations. All the ancient hatred built up into a head of steam. Families lived, raised children and died there. All we wanted was to get out alive, limbs intact and forget about it. Sod the Creggan. The estate became a jungle with a potential threat around every corner; it could be a bomb in a car, a sniper, a plain old brick in the head or foul abuse. The place had as many mood swings as a depressive. One moment, the streets would be clear and eerily quiet – you knew in your bones there was something, somewhere, going down. Other times it teemed with activity like a disturbed anthill, everyone and his dog were on the streets. We passed endless lines of houses with their doors open, kids kicking balls, dogs yapping, biting at your heels, endless, screaming, hate-contorted faces. At times, the hairs on your neck would stand up as you anticipated the mule-like kick of an Armalite round zipping through your flesh, a sensation you learned to put at the back of your mind, else you'd go crazy. It was the primeval feel of being a hunted animal. You have to escape the confines of this mentality else you are brutalised and lost forever to become consumed by hatred and a desire to exact revenge on your tormentors. It is then that innocents get hurt and morality flies out of the window. On my last patrol, I notice a youth acting nervously, looking furtively around and pulling up his socks even though they didn't need pulling up. My eyes scanned for the people he was signalling to, waiting for the crack of an Armalite. I move close to him and give him the evil eye, ready to smash his skull with my rifle butt if we are attacked. His young face twitches, he can't stand still, the tension is getting to him. I recognise the signs because I know the fear he feels. The street is too busy for an attack, so we leave him and move on down the street past more faces which turn in disgust as we pass by. When I get back to camp, I feel comfort in the knowledge that I will never pound the pavements of that estate again, because on my bed I find a letter confirming my release from the Army in six months time.

The peace process renewed my interest in Ireland and I felt a strong draw to go back, look around and try to understand what the conflict had been about. I was fed up with reading books and doing the odd evening course. It was time to go back and see for myself. Initially, it was my intention to explore Belfast first, but, driving off the ferry, I was drawn towards Derry like a moth to a flame. As I drove over Craigavon Bridge, the old town had a vaguely familiar feel, parts still dilapidated and world-weary mixed with modern developments. The signs led me up to the Creggan, once a strange hostile place to anyone in uniform. Gone were Cromore flats, where my shot gouged out a chunk of masonry; gone, too, were the old dreaded Central Drive shops and flats. The houses on the estate had been given a face-lift; it was a totally rejuvenated estate that looked nothing like the way I remembered it. I drove on to the City Cemetery to seek out Mints, sure he'd be lying under six foot of Irish soil, the recipient of British lead. Two hours passed, alone, up there on the hill searching for him. I didn't find his name etched on a piece of stone and was glad. Seriously. I was told later that he was working over in England sending back money to his family. The dour, grey-stoned Republican plot conveyed to me the message of eternal suffering and struggle – the culture of the victim, where history lives and no injustice is ever forgotten. Trouble is, it becomes self-perpetuating, as endless rows of stones in a graveyard bear testimony. Many of the names on the roll of honour were familiar from the books and papers I had read over the last few years. Such a waste. Again, I struggled to believe that all those years ago, in a minor way, I had been involved in this ancient conflict too, and I had been the enemy. I felt a strange affinity with the dead young men who came from parents as poor as mine, a sort of class consciousness or empathy for the underdog. Under the skin, we were not that different. If I had been born in a Republican household on the Creggan, met with inequality and the bone-headed intransigence of Ulster Unionism, maybe I too would have tried to join the IRA. With a mixture of emotions, I paid my respects to the dead of Bloody Sunday – innocents – shot by Paras, soldiers of the British Army, same as me. That made me angry and sad. Later in the week, I stood in County Donegal on Bloody Foreland, looking out over the Atlantic. I felt something akin to a spiritual affinity to the wild spirit and soft undulating beauty of dear old Mother Ireland and its tragic human history. In another of those brief moments of insight, it became clearer why the young men of the IRA had their names etched on gravestones. It felt right that I was back; now it was a time to learn and in some humble way assist in the healing process. I fought back tears and prayed, like thousands of others over the last years, that the madness was finally coming to an end. I believe it is. God bless.

FROM A 'ROOM WITH A VIEW' TO CREGGAN

If normality is defined as whatever you're used to, then normality for many youngsters in Creggan in the '70s was rioting and diving for cover during gun battles. But as Seamus Breslin explains here, this was only half the story, and life unfettered continued behind the scenes.

My family arrived in Creggan via Foyle Hill House, one of the few old buildings in the Creggan area. Obviously I wasn't there as I wouldn't come along until 1964 accompanied by the sound of The Beatles and all the other sounds associated with a house that now contained nine children. This room in Foyle Hill House was my parents' first real home – like so many other people who had to struggle through chronic housing conditions. In case you think I exaggerate the comfort, let's hear how an official describes it:

> Sanitary provision was the use of a flush toilet in the upstairs landing. Mr Breslin and family live in the front room on the right on the ground floor. It is a big, cold, damp room, windows and floor require repairs, roof is leaking. There are seven sleeping in one room. Mrs Breslin's baby was admitted to hospital a few days after birth with pneumonia. Baby has been chesty most of the time. This family urgently requires housing very soon. They are now six years on the housing list.

It would be a further year before our dream move to the luxury of Creggan and I have often thought that if ever a film was made about our time in Foyle Hill, we could call it *A Room with a View*.

Mr Thomas Breslin was allocated a four-bedroom apartment at 38 Melmore Gardens with rent, rates and cooker-hire at £1 7s 5d per week. Considering it was allocated on 3 July, I wonder who had been preparing the bigger celebrations, our family or the Americans? I couldn't even attempt to express what feelings must have gone through my mother's and father's minds on moving into the fine modern house. When Mr Herron at Rosemount Boys' developed a love among our class for the poem *An Old Woman of the Roads*, he must have known, looking at the faces of his class, that the sentiments of the verse meant so much to our parents. As in many other cases, I have often wondered how many people in Melmore know that the three-bedroom houses are actually 'four-bedroom apartments'?

My age group has very few memories of life in Creggan before the people rose off their knees in 1969. Now I wouldn't want to offend anyone, but our 'Eccles' always said that it was the Creggan people who actually fought the Battle of the Bogside. When I ask for evidence, he replies:

> How many times, if ever, did the Creggan people have to send down the Bog for reinforcements?

I'll leave the older generation to debate that one out, with each, no doubt, claiming victory over the other in the ubiquitous punch-ups after the Stardust!

As a youngster at Holy Child [school], I have a memory, real or imagined, of waiting for the RUC with Mr Tufty to instruct us in road safety. The memory sees Mr Tufty and the RUC men fleeing for their lives along Central Drive. As they say, I'm still waiting on Mr Tufty. This, though, was a defining moment from which time forward death, destruction and military occupation would become the norm. The area would be nicknamed 'the gas chamber'; so much CS had been released that the irrepressible children were making medical history by displaying immunity to the choking fumes. A newspaper report in January 1972 stated:

> . . . flesh is being torn by gas canisters used as bullets and fired head-high, by rubber bullets aimed at heads instead of feet, and sometimes tipped with metal, or, equally against the British Army's own regulations, fired with a supplementary charge of ball bearings. Troops have been discovered firing metal projectiles from catapults. Evidence for this stepping up of military violence comes from John Hume and Dr Donal MacDermott.

Further evidence for this stepping-up of military violence came some days later when 13 of the most decent civil human beings this city has produced were shot down on their own streets by the forces of law and order. Bloody Sunday had a profound effect on my family. Young Jackie Duddy's mother, who had died tragically at a young age before the *Troubles*, was my mother's sister. Their only other sister had, like so many, emigrated. The two families had shared the traditional Derry vacation for many years together, a day at the seaside. There were so many Duddys and Breslins that it was often joked we filled the one bus. It was a credit to both sets of parents that such large families had been reared so efficiently. After Bloody Sunday, the general consensus among those in our school and street was that the forces of law and order were definitely the enemy. No ambiguities or ambivalence – they were the enemy!

Like children of the Second World War, our family was evacuated down to Leenan Bay in Joe Rush's van before Operation Motorman. The older members, who had to work, stayed behind. I myself would not witness the 'invasion' of Creggan until a week after it began. Our street gang, the MDA (Melmore Defence Association), would join forces with the LFA (Leenan Fenian Army) to mount joint attacks on the enemy. Munitions and every military tactic would be used in the war. Scouts positioned at the end of each street would report the arrival of tanks and jeeps. Bottles filled with medicines, urine, paint, bleach, were thrown at the enemy. The children had become soldiers in a wider conflict. Major Manners of the Grenadier Guards became a parochial hate figure. There was a huge price on his head. The Royal Anglian 3rd Battalion took over in March 1973. Their commander described Creggan:

> It had a high ratio of young people, who had little to do other than to harass the military. The inhabitants were very aware politically, more so

than those of Belfast, and quick to complain about the Army – to the Secretary of State in person if need be.

The complaint to the Secretary of State came from the headmaster of St Joseph's who, at one stage, closed the school due to military harassment. The pupils of St Joseph's had this game they played with the Brits. Firstly, they would attack the Rosemount Barracks, letting the forces of law know they weren't wanted. The Brits would acknowledge a mutual feeling by chasing the pupils around the schoolyard, firing rubber bullets from high-speed jeeps. One of the Rosemount pupils was blinded, a teacher was nearly killed during an Army assault and still the staff managed to keep the school a relative oasis from the problems outside. I have a very real memory of our class at Rosemount lying on the ground with Mr Giles Doherty singing *Pack up your troubles in your old kit bag* as a gun battle raged outside. The IRA would leave St Joseph's with a free art class skylight, courtesy of a rocket. The Creggan camp, Piggery Ridge, and Essex would be attacked by the IRA simultaneously with rockets. A running gun battle followed right across the estate in which 200 rounds were fired by the Army. One of the Anglians would win a military medal for engaging gunmen with success. During this period the IRA fired a rocket at a Saracen on Central Drive. The hole from the rocket was until recently visible on the wall of the 'Corned Beef Tin'.

The Anglian 2nd Battalion took over from the 3rd and established 19 covert observation posts, often hidden in the roofs of houses and flats. In true gung-ho fashion, under the vigorous command of Major Drummond, violence was gradually reduced. More MBEs, MMs and BEMs would follow for these gallant soldiers.

Objective journalists would portray a more accurate image – a young man stopped 28 times being fined £25 for allegedly assaulting the soldier on the 29th occasion; of 1,000 houses in the Bogside and Creggan being searched, and 2,000 people being held for questioning; of 349 canisters of gas on one stretch of road on a night in which 800 rounds were fired on the Creggan estate. The Anglians claimed that they had rioting firmly under control and that film crews provoked it. Solution – arrest the film crews! The local Bishop, who could hardly have sympathy with Republicans, accused the Army of intimidation and terror tactics and said they greatly contributed to the escalation of violence in the city.

These British Army units had their casualties as well. Several soldiers were killed and others seriously injured in Creggan. Like the volunteers of the IRA, and the innocents who died, they were all, in a way, victims. The initial severe violence of the early '70s lulled during the late '70s and Creggan witnessed the withdrawal of the British from bases in the estate. Some may have thought that the days of Creggan being a front-line trench in a war were over. They would have been wrong, as the Hunger Strike involving a local Creggan man, Mickey Devine, would once again see Central Drive being called the 'Gaza Strip' and 'El Paso' – and that was by the local tenants' association!

Reflecting on those years, it is amazing how the spirit and resilience of the community remained strong. Local groups organised trips, parties, films and any other form of entertainment to see the people through. In our house, when the *Troubles* were serious, the neighbours would gather and play cards half-the-night. My mother helped run a women's night in the Centre and my father the men's night. The women of the street would organise bus runs to raise money for trainee priests and other causes. Also in our house, like numerous others, there were no economic passengers. All the boys worked at a variety of jobs, helping breadmen, selling Teles [copies of the *Belfast Telegraph*], sticks, brock, and cutting gardens when it took half the street with billhooks and clippers. The girls all worked in local cafés, eventually leading to jobs in the shirt factories.

My late father took all the construction work he could get, which wasn't a lot, and had many casual jobs such as papering and painting. My mother and many neighbours knitted the best of Aran jumpers and many other types. The girls would have patterns and cloth all over the floor making dresses. Despite the many social, political and economic forces that worked against the community, it was always able to hold its head high. A wide-ranging system of communal self-help was in place prior to the *Troubles*; that was cemented in the face of living under military occupation. How could anyone attempt to put a price on the voluntary work carried out within the estate by so many people?

It is with great pride that the work of those people is remembered, as are the memories of the sporting, musical and literary heroes. Once again, I wonder if Melmore Gardens could be described as the literary capital of Creggan. With writers such as myself, Kerr, Mahon, the Gallaghers and Devlin; songwriters such as our Gerald, I don't think we have much opposition! In Creggan, poverty and affluence live side by side, just like everywhere else. I have never lived anywhere else so I can't make a comparative analysis. One thing for certain is that Creggan has never looked better, and private and public housing (in the streets that have been renovated to modern standards) are much desired. Very few, if any, of the extensive Creggan diaspora ever speak of it other than with pride – this resource must be harnessed!

Most of the doors in Creggan are closed to keep out the draughts and have keys or handles that easily turn after a short knock, just like the old days in Derry. Unemployment and its subsequent side effects, such as depression, still remain a major problem. If a solution to this problem is 'out-povertying' everywhere else's poverty to secure grants, it should be handled very delicately or even the formula changed! These days, image means everything, and on behalf of my own young family, who are Creggan's past, present and future, I would like to see a positive one.

CHAPTER 8

Enduring the Most

The relentless tensions of the *Troubles* made it perhaps inevitable that strife would develop within the Creggan community itself. The '80s, in particular, would see the IRA – long a touchstone of the area – badly damaged by informers such as Creggan man Raymond Gilmour.

The Hunger Strikes were also to take their toll on the estate. The anger caused by the British Government's refusal to acknowledge the legitimacy of Republican prisoners led to some of the worst disturbances ever seen in the city. And the death of Creggan man Mickey Devine on hunger strike left his home town wounded and bereaved.

In the mid-'80s, political differences – long dormant in the estate – were to emerge as Sinn Féin began going head-to-head against the SDLP for council seats. Time and again the *Troubles* would revisit the Creggan estates in the form of bombs, shootings and paramilitary executions.

But the seemingly endless suffering expected of Creggan couldn't go on forever. Bright, brave new thinking saw the advent of political dialogue which would have been unimaginable only a decade before. By the end of the '80s, politicians from the area were becoming involved in negotiations to bring about a settlement that would provide the basis for the Good Friday Agreement.

To Hunger for Justice: The Story of Michael Devine

On the living-room wall of a house on Rathkeele Way in Creggan is a framed pen-and-ink portrait of a cheerful-looking man in his twenties wearing a slightly off-kilter pair of glasses. The glasses themselves, still stuck together with tape, are kept upstairs with other mementoes. But the face in the picture is unmistakable. It's Michael Devine, an ordinary working-class Derryman whose death was to bring the country to a standstill.

The house on Rathkeele Way is home to Devine's sister Margaret McCauley. It is also the house where Michael Devine, INLA leader, was waked after he died in the H-Blocks on hunger strike. Devine's life ended on 20 August 1981, 60 days after he began refusing food. The last of the ten Hunger Strikers to die, he continued with his fast despite immense pressure to call it off. Indeed, only weeks after his death, the strikes were over, amid considerable acrimony, with Republicans accusing the clergy of coercing the families.

Ironically, if Michael Devine had conformed and worn a prison uniform, he'd have been released from jail only seven months after he was to die. But in 1976, an IRA prisoner called Ciaran Nugent set in motion the campaign for the reintroduction of political status when he told the warders they would have to nail prison clothes to his back. This was to set in motion a train of events that would ultimately see ten prisoners – including Devine – starve themselves to death before the British Government would concede to prison reforms.

Devine's sister, Margaret McCauley, recalls that he always had a dogged streak.

> He became tough very early. He had to wear glasses as a child and was very self-conscious, so if mention was made of them he'd end up having to fight. He was very brainy as a child and loved his football, but he was a typical young fella and would get up to everything. There were only the two of us – I was seven years older – and he used to follow me around. I of course didn't want to know him!

Devine was only 12 when his father died in February 1966. It was an immense loss to him. Later that same year, Margaret married Frank McCauley and moved out, leaving her brother in the care of his mother and grandmother. But tragedy was to strike again, and in 1972 the young Creggan man returned home one day to find his mother dead in the sitting room.

> By that stage he was already involved. I'd spend my time covering up for him to my mother – and then would take him quietly by the throat later on. But he wasn't unique. All the young fellas were at it at that time. Once he was quite badly injured when a CS gas canister hit him in the groin. He couldn't go to hospital or he'd be arrested. So our doctor, who was a

> Protestant, came over to the house and worked with him. Michael still had the mark on him when he died.

After his mother died, Devine went to live with Margaret until he married his teenage sweetheart – also called Margaret. They had two children, Michael and Louise. But the difficulties posed by Devine's eventual imprisonment meant the marriage, like hundreds of others, wasn't to last. The years up to Devine's arrest were eventful as he rose through the ranks of the 'Stickies' before becoming one of the founding members of the INLA.

> We would get raided day and daily. One day they raided the house seven times. But they never got him. He was quite militant, but he was more interested in politics than in soldiering. He was socialist in his outlook and would have been involved with the IRSP.

The last time Margaret was to see her brother as a free man was 20 September 1976, the day he was lifted. There had been a robbery at a gun shop in Lifford in which a large quantity of arms and ammunition were taken. Shortly afterwards, Michael Devine and several others were stopped in a car on Central Drive, and a set of binoculars stolen in the robbery were recovered.

> Everything else was hidden away by that stage but they forgot to get rid of the binoculars, and that tied them to it. Earlier that same day, I'd got word that our granny had died and was looking for Michael to tell him. The next thing I knew he was in the barracks. I went down and, to be honest, tried to pull a bit of a move by telling the police how our granny reared us and that Michael needed to get out. But they just laughed at us. My husband Frank even offered to take Michael's place until he came back. But they told us they'd been after him for a long time and weren't for letting him go.

Devine was held in Crumlin Road prison on remand for seven months. After his conviction in 1977, he was moved to the H-Blocks where he immediately joined the 'blanket' protest. It was a rough time to be in jail. Prisoners who refused the uniform were denied furniture, exercise, visits, parcels and educational facilities. They couldn't wash and they couldn't cut their hair or beards. But the situation was to worsen when warders were accused of deliberately spilling the prisoners' slop bowls into the cells. So, as a further protest, the prisoners stopped slopping out and instead spread their waste on the floor and walls. Journalist and historian Tim Pat Coogan describes the horror in his book *The IRA*.

> The 'battle of the bowels' resulted in the prison cells, the most modern in Europe, becoming filthy, maggot-infested caves, in which young men stood naked save for their hate and a prison blanket.

The McCauley family were to give Margaret's brother their full backing for his protest despite the fact that it was very hard on both him and them.

> The conditions they had to live in were terrible. The smell from them was awful, and they had vermin walking through their beards and hair. It was very hard to look at, but you had to put your arms round them and kiss them. Many's the time I lay awake at home on a freezing night listening to the hailstones and thinking Michael wouldn't make it through to the morning. The warders would think nothing of hosing them down and turning off the heat. But he wouldn't tell you how his health was, nor would he ever complain. He would always tell you everything was great.

Because of the brevity of the visits, Devine wasted no time on small talk.

> The first thing he'd say to me would be: 'Don't tell me who's dead, I don't want to know.' I remember once our Jody, God rest him, when he was only a wee boy, asking Michael why he was in prison. I broke the 11th commandment, says Michael, I got caught!

When the first Hunger Strike began in 1980, Michael and his Derry friend Patsy O'Hara were to join it just before it ended. The protestors had five demands:

- The right to wear their own clothes
- No prison work
- Free association
- Full remission of their sentences (then 50%)
- The restoration of full visiting rights, parcels, educational and recreational facilities

The first strike was called off when the Republican leadership believed their concessions had been secured. But when the British Government attempted to introduce 'civilian-type' clothing instead of allowing the prisoners their choice of clothes, all bets were off. On the morning of 1 March 1981, Bobby Sands refused breakfast. The second Hunger Strike had begun. Sands was to die at the beginning of May, closely followed by Francis Hughes and Raymond McCreesh. Then on 21 May, Patsy O'Hara – Michael Devine's lifelong pal – became the first Derryman to die.

> Michael told me that he would be going on hunger strike about three weeks before he started. I was up on a visit with one of the children. He came out, sat down and put his hands over mine and said: 'I've something to tell you, but you can't breath a word of it to anyone. I'm starting the Hunger Strike on 22 June.' I was in shock. My eyes filled up and my stomach turned. He told me that I would have to stand by him as he needed my full support. He said he was giving me power of attorney,

> effectively telling me I would have to let him die. By the end of the visit, I said to him that I would support him. But I still thought that something would happen. I thought it would be resolved.

On the morning of 22 June, Margaret turned on her radio and was massively relieved to hear no mention of her brother. But by 11.00am, hordes of reporters had descended on her doorstep. Michael Devine had refused breakfast. For the first three weeks of his hunger strike, the Creggan man was kept in his cell, after which he was taken to the hospital wing.

> In the beginning, we only noticed a slight deterioration. Immediately he started the strike, I demanded weekly visits and then I started fighting for daily visits which I eventually got as he got weaker. Frank and myself moved bag and baggage to Belfast so we could be near the jail. Our friends and neighbours took care of our children – just as they've come to my aid throughout my whole life. It would take to my dying day to thank the people of Creggan for what they've done for me. When we got the daily visits, we did them on a shift basis. But we'd no other relatives to help us out, so we had to pretend Patsy and Theresa Moore were Michael's uncle and aunt.

Throughout the fast, the extended family would sit quietly chatting to Devine, day and night. But there was always a prison officer in the room, with a jotter, taking down every word that was said.

> Food was delivered to the room regular as clockwork every day, each meal better than the previous one. They'd just leave them there on a ledge where he could see them, until they replaced it with the next one. I think it was mental torture.

As the end approached, Devine went blind and became too weak to move his head from the pillow or his arms from the bed. His family would give him water out of a baby's feeding cup.

> Occasionally, he would be asked if he wanted to come off the strike, but he would just reply that everyone dies sometime and that it wasn't death people feared but what came after it. And he was prepared to accept whatever came next. He made me his next-of-kin and I could have taken him off. Now and again, I'd tell myself, maybe if he stopped now, he'd be okay again. And maybe I would be able to go back to normal again as well. There were times I just wanted to run away.

The former MP and prominent anti-H Blocks campaigner Bernadette McAliskey visited Devine during his fast. She was very opposed to the pressure coming from the

Catholic Church on the Hunger Strikers' families – and indeed had walked out of Martin Hurson's funeral when the priest condemned the protest. According to legend, Mickey Devine told her: 'If you walk out of mine, wheel me out along with you!'

The week before he died, Devine asked to see his two children, Michael and Louise, for the last time. He was already blind, so when they came in he asked Margaret which was which and he put his hands on their heads. He then said his goodbyes and told them he loved them.

Margaret McCauley holding a picture of her brother Mickey Devine who died in 1981 on hunger strike, 2000. (Larry Doherty)

> I was devastated. As I lifted the children down off the bed to take them out, I said to myself: 'Don't look back.' I didn't want the screw to see me crying. But being me, I couldn't help myself, so I turned round and saw Michael lying like a corpse with tears streaking down his face. It's an image that will stick with me forever.

The night before her brother died, Margaret went to a chapel in Belfast and asked God to take him that night. She couldn't stand the thought of him suffering any more. At five o'clock the following morning, Michael Devine went into a coma, and he died just under three hours later. The RUC removed his body from the prison and took it to Coleraine for reasons never explained to the family. The remains were collected and taken to Derry that evening. The coffin was met at the Bogside by an INLA colour party which accompanied the coffin to the McCauley home in Creggan. The homecoming was described in the *Derry Journal* the following day. It stated:

> The Derry Felons' Association flanked the hearse and several hundred people followed. A black beret, a pair of gloves and a belt were placed on top of the coffin along with an Irish Tricolour and the Starry Plough flag. Hundreds of people have visited the family home to pay their respects.

Unusually, Devine's cortege was not taken to St Mary's Chapel for Requiem Mass; the INLA man had expressly forbidden the flags to be removed from his coffin. The cortege went directly to the City Cemetery instead, where it was met by thousands of mourners – including one much sought-after INLA leader who jogged across the border in a pair of running shorts.

> Looking back, I have to say it was a great honour and privilege to have Mickey for a brother. There are very few people who could have done what he did. Margaret Thatcher thought she had broken the backs of the prisoners. But she was no match for their resolve. History will not ignore her cruelty in letting those ten young men die. Hell will never be full until she's in it.

'Entirely Unworthy of Belief': Creggan's Supergrass

Raymond Gilmour's story – as he tells it in his gung-ho book *Dead Ground* – is the stuff of a Jack Higgins novel. Describing himself as an 'undercover agent', he reveals how he 'infiltrated' the IRA and INLA, prevented 'countless terrorist attacks' and helped the RUC uncover 'huge quantities' of arms and explosives. Gilmour was a hero in his own mind. But in the minds of most Creggan people – and indeed of the Lord Chief Justice – he was something very different indeed: they thought he was a liar.

That Gilmour began life as a petty criminal is beyond dispute. He acknowledges himself that he was recruited by the police in the late '70s while being questioned about a botched post office robbery. The RUC had him over a barrel, but sweetened their pitch by offering him more money than his father had ever seen 'in his life'. So, Gilmour agreed to become an informer 'to save lives', though cynics might argue that the £100-a-week salary closed the deal.

It is patently unwise to go into any detail on what Gilmour alleges he saw and did over the next four years – given that no less an authority than Lord Lowry saw fit to describe him in court as a 'selfish, self-regarding man to whose lips a lie inevitably came more easily than the truth'. Suffice to say that by August 1982 Gilmour felt his role as a 'tout' was about to be uncovered, so he begged his handlers to get him out of the country. But the police insisted on him singing for his supper one more time, so he made detailed statements incriminating dozens of people he claimed were involved in IRA or INLA activities. Creggan – which had long prided itself on its tight sense of community – had produced Derry's first supergrass.

On Tuesday 24 August 1982, about a week after Gilmour disappeared, the British security services mounted the biggest arrest operation in Derry since Motorman. And on Friday, the *Derry Journal* reported that 36 people were being held on the basis of statements given by the 22-year-old Cromore Gardens man. The *Journal*, reflecting the mood of dismay in nationalist circles, published appeals by Gilmour's parents for him to rethink his position.

> Patrick and Bridget Gilmour said they had been 'stunned, shattered and shamed' by the events. In a statement, they said that they would like to say to the relatives of those arrested that 'the pain of knowing that your relatives are being held in Castlereagh or elsewhere must somehow be less than the pain of the parents whose son stands accused of putting them there'. They said that they did not intend letting their son be used by the RUC and appealed to him to think about what he was doing. They appealed to people to try and understand that Raymond is the victim of police intimidation and that they have used his personal problems to pressurise him into this dreadful action.

Within days, 31 people had been charged with offences ranging from murder, to conspiracy, to IRA or INLA membership. To a person, they denied the charges. And the police were forced to admit that the only evidence against the vast majority of the defendants was the word of Raymond Gilmour.

Attempts to get him to retract his claims were in vain. The IRA even kidnapped Gilmour's father, Paddy, in November 1982, and threatened to shoot him. But the son had cut his links with his family forever and wasn't for bending. The IRA were to release Paddy Gilmour ten months into his captivity. Gilmour himself insists he knew his family wouldn't be harmed. In his book, he claims:

> Even after the trial was over, my family would be more use to the IRA alive than dead. While they lived, there was always the chance that I would be drawn into a careless disclosure or a clandestine meeting that would give the IRA its chance for revenge.

In all, 45 people stood accused on Gilmour's word. Charges against ten were eventually dropped, while the remaining 35 were held on remand for two years until their trial at Belfast Crown Court in May 1984. At the preliminary hearing, Bridget Gilmour was bundled out of the gallery by RUC officers after calling out to her son to 'stop telling lies' about his former friends.

Opening the case, the prosecution revealed that Gilmour had received almost £5,000 during his period as a police agent, (although Gilmour himself later put the figure at almost £11,000). They said he had joined the INLA and IRA at the behest of the RUC and had been an active agent for four years. Gilmour himself was to appear in court on 16 October, and according to the *Derry Journal*, spent 12 hours giving evidence before undergoing three weeks of cross-examination.

The defence, not surprisingly, made a vigorous assault on the informer's character. He was variously described as a drug-user, a homosexual, a philanderer and a 'practised liar'. The gloves-off tactic was ultimately to prove successful and, on 18 December 1984, all 108 charges against the 35 defendants were dismissed. In his account of the case, the late Domhnall MacDermott told *Derry Journal* readers of the courtroom drama:

> There was stunned silence in the court as Lord Lowry began reading out his verdict; most of the defendants looking visibly surprised. It took some minutes before they reacted to the news. When Lord Lowry concluded his verdict, there was loud cheering and shouting from the defendants and their friends and relatives in the court. At the start of his judgement, Lord Lowry said he was not rejecting Gilmour's evidence because he was a paid informer or an accomplice, or even because of Gilmour's scandalous character. He described Gilmour as a man who was oblivious to every natural inclination and obligation, who cared nothing about bonds of kinship or friendship. The Lord Chief Justice said he considered Gilmour to be entirely unworthy of belief.

Twenty-six of the defendants were to walk free from Belfast Crown Court. Nine others, who had been convicted on the word of another supergrass, Robert Quigley, were to remain in prison for several months more until Quigley's evidence was also discredited. Quigley had broken after being arrested on Gilmour's say-so.

The Gilmour acquittals were the beginning of the end for the supergrass system. In its editorial after the case, the *Journal* reflected that the trial showed how the RUC was prepared to use any means to put away people they suspected of crimes. It stated:

> That the police, who had such an enduring relationship with Gilmour, were unable to expose him as a compulsive liar and therefore abandon him as the vehicle to use against the defendants, calls for the most stringent examination of all cases based on police estimation of the credit-worthiness of informer witnesses. The credibility that has been dealt an even greater blow than Gilmour's in this historic trial is that of the RUC. They have become Gilmour's chief victims at the end of the day.

In 1998, a decade and a half after his testimony was rejected, Gilmour was to publish his 'explosive true story' of his role as a Special Branch agent. There was some surprise that he got it to print, given his credibility problem. But there was little shock when people libelled in the book successfully sued his publishers.

To this day, there is still anger in Creggan about the divisions caused by the supergrasses. Thirty-five people were to serve the equivalent of a five-year jail sentence while on remand. But Derry people are renowned for their gallows humour in times of great adversity. And perhaps the most fitting epitaph to the whole episode was the graffiti which appeared on one Creggan wall a few days after the informer bolted.

I knew Raymond Gilmour. Thank fuck he didn't know me.

A Conscientious Objector: Eamonn Melaugh

Eamonn Melaugh has lived many lives. He's been a fitter's mate, construction worker, civil rights organiser, campaigner and politician – not to mention his perennial role as father of 11, foster father to 14, photographer and traveller. A lifelong pacifist, he was nearly jailed in England for refusing to be conscripted at the time of the Suez Crisis. And in Derry, for years his house operated as Creggan's only welfare rights centre.

Melaugh was delighted to get a house in Creggan:

> We moved to Circular Road in 1961, to a beautiful gable house with a big garden where I could grow vegetables; I thought I was in heaven. We had a big field behind us and our neighbours were excellent. Until then we'd been sharing a house with a Protestant family in Alfred Street and we'd only had a small bedroom and a dining room for the five of us, as there were then. Many people who were moved to Creggan, including my own wife, were so thankful for the housing that they broke down in tears.

A sleepy idyll perhaps, but Eamonn Melaugh's eyes had been opened during his time in England and he couldn't fail to see the problems Creggan and Derry were facing. Creggan was being developed without any coherent plan on what Melaugh terms a 'field by field' basis to relieve the overspill of Catholic families from other areas. There were no amenities whatsoever, and the only chance neighbour got to meet neighbour was outside Mass on Sunday. The estate was to become the most densely populated area in Western Europe. Meanwhile, down the hill, Derry was suffering the twin crises of poor housing and unemployment. The economic prospects for the city were bleak and the only option for young people was the boat to England. As Melaugh explains:

> I joined Sinn Féin in the early '60s in a bid to start some movement on social issues. I always argued that this should be the priority rather than constitutional matters. But I was told our task was to unite Ireland. So I went freelance. As early as 1961, I got my father to put an ad for me in the *Belfast Telegraph* looking for 'Men of Action' to do something about unemployment, poor housing and emigration. A group of about 12 or 13 of us got together, but very few were prepared to take direct action such as blocking roads or taking over Council meetings. Apathy in the town was total and complete – we called a public meeting about unemployment and only one person showed up; the group eventually fell through.

Discrimination in employment was the accepted norm and had been for generations.

> My own father, who was a first-class tailor, went for a tailor's job at the old asylum. He and seven other qualified Catholics applied, but the job went to an unqualified Protestant who had learnt to do alterations when he was in borstal.

However, when Melaugh and other early activists were to stage demonstrations calling for One Man – One Vote, One Family – One Home, and Jobs for the Unemployed, they were mocked on the streets.

> There was very little enthusiasm for civil disobedience. People believed their situation was down to the will of God and that you should suffer in silence. To a certain extent the Church damaged them by perpetuating that.

Melaugh's concerns were being shared by other radical thinkers in Tyrone, however, and the McCloskeys in Coalisland began producing pamphlets challenging discrimination and deprivation.

> In Derry, we attempted to take on bias from whatever quarter. I remember once organising a meeting with a leading Catholic and a leading Protestant businessman – both of whom employed only their own sort – and telling them both we would picket their shops unless they changed their ways.

When the campaign for civil rights got underway in earnest, it was largely based around the city centre. Likewise, a lot of the early trouble centred on the Bogside. But, as Melaugh points out, a huge number of the agitators were from Creggan. An avowed pacifist, Melaugh was alarmed with the upsurge in violence.

> I must have made hundreds of speeches, always advocating peaceful opposition but I always said that if you're attacked, you have a right and a duty to defend yourself. And I admit at times I got angry myself. On one occasion, I saw a police lorry mounting a pavement in Wellington Street and deliberately try to run over a pedestrian. And I lifted stones and threw them.

Constant raiding and searching by the British Army were to radicalise the people in Creggan.

> The brutal treatment meted out, the way civil liberties were trampled on, the obscene body searches on the streets, the smashing up of homes, all raised people's political awareness more than anything else. And the seething anger and resentment that followed Bloody Sunday left people

> queuing up to join the IRA. I believe there were so many that they couldn't take them all on. On the whole, that was understandable. The sight of 13 coffins lined up in St Mary's Church in front of weeping relatives is a sight which will haunt me forever.

Just before Bloody Sunday, Melaugh met with *Journal* employee Willie McKinney at the rally at Magilligan which was brutally broken up by the Parachute Regiment. Both men were keen cameramen. And as they exchanged yarns about the events, Melaugh commented that he hoped they never came across the Paras on Derry's streets. Only days later, Willie McKinney was shot dead in the Bogside by the same regiment. All through that period, the Melaugh household operated as an advice centre. He filled out forms, represented people at unemployment and sickness tribunals and dealt with housing problems. Dozens of people would pass through the house every day. On a political level, Melaugh was involved with the Republican Clubs for a short time 'before they became too Nationalist', and he was also an adviser to the Official IRA.

> I always argued that they should channel all their energies into passive resistance – in the manner of Gandhi. If the Indians could do it, so could the Irish. I'm still a Republican – one of the few left in Derry. And I take my Republicanism from Wolfe Tone, who said that the only way to unite Ireland was to unite the people, Protestant, Catholic and Dissenter. And if you want to unite people, you can't do it by killing them.

The values of non-violence were ones which he tried hard to instil in his children.

> Parents who reared children in Creggan in the '60s and '70s deserve medals. I've been called in by many families asking me what to do when their son becomes involved. I advised them to confront him and tell him to either leave the house or leave the organisation. It's not fair to involve the parents.

While the *Troubles* initially brought the tightly-knit community in Creggan closer together, Melaugh believes that the continuing violence eventually began to divide it.

> At first we were all in the same boat – sink or swim. But when organisations like the Provisionals, Officials and SDLP started looking for electoral support, it started to polarise the community. Animosity developed into thinly disguised hatred, as each group became a political threat to the other. And as years went on, the divisions became more apparent. The divisions in the Creggan community, both over the use of violence, and between the haves and have-nots, are now as real as cross-community ones. They're so deep that people don't even talk about it to each other. We're all to blame for this – it's facile to claim otherwise.

Melaugh's criticism of violence was to make him unpopular in certain circles.

> Events like shootings and kneecappings engender fear in families and rob them of the courage to speak out. When I would make a public statement, for about three or four days after, people would say to me 'do you not fear?' Of course I feared. But what could I do? All it takes for evil to reign is for good men to stay silent. I have been threatened many times by supporters of the Provisionals but never by members of that organisation. I think they still have a very grudging respect for my social and welfare work. Things will only move forward when the violence stops completely and Britain announces its intention to withdraw from Ireland. Our divisions can only start to heal themselves then.

Creggan's First Resident Mayor

Although he would not claim it as a defining moment, Pat Devine, the first mayor residing in Creggan, has, on occasion, recalled the class on citizenship given by the gifted teacher, Seán Breslin, who taught him at The CBS Brow o' the Hill Technical School. What stayed with him was the notion that one should be a good citizen regardless of bad government. Although not always at the forefront in his mind, he has no doubt that it coloured his attitude in his path towards public service. This journey had not the mark of inevitability about it, but was determined by events rather than by any long-term ambition to engage in politics.

Maybe something in the air around Argyle Street, where he grew up, played its part in propelling residents in the vicinity towards politics. As Pat observed:

> John Hume lived some three hundred yards away, and Joe Fagan, another SDLP mayor, was raised just around the corner.

Like most young people growing up in the 1940s and '50s, Pat was aware of political injustices and discrimination. However, it was being allocated a house in Creggan that brought him close to the reality of gerrymander. Although delighted with his new house in Creggan, where he still lives, he was unable to get a satisfactory explanation why he could not get one of the new houses being built in the Northland and Glen Road developments that were close to his home. He already knew that the preservation of Unionist control of the city depended on maintaining a religious balance in electoral wards. This meant that Creggan in the South ward was to become overwhelmingly Catholic. The Northland and Glen Road estates were in the North ward, which was expected to return a majority of Unionists, and houses there were thus more likely to be allocated to Protestants.

Like many Catholics in Derry who grew up beside good Protestant neighbours, Pat had difficulty finding a platform where opposition to Unionist injustices would not be read as opposition to Protestantism. The opportunity came along with the birth of the Civil Rights movement whose slogan was 'Civil Rights for All'.

Involvement in the Civil Rights movement and a long-term friendship with Len Green were to be initial factors in drawing Pat deeper into politics. Len, an Englishman and later an SDLP mayor, had a trade union/socialist background and had imparted his political philosophies over many informal debates between them. Membership as a steward of the Civil Rights marches and attendance at the many Civil Rights meetings were also key factors in his growing political awareness. He remembers John Hume and Ivan Cooper as stimulating presenters of arguments with Hume's contributions being particularly memorable for their clarity and logic. He also found Eamonn McCann:

> . . . an articulate and inspiring speaker who eloquently expressed the anger many felt towards Unionist misrule, but who had no positive practical proposals on how the incumbent regime should be replaced.

Mayor Pat Devine at the presentation, during his year of office, of a donation by the Ireland Fund to then Inner City Trust chairman Peter Enright. Far left, Paddy (Bogside) Doherty, 1979. (courtesy Pat Devine)

His own position, as a Nationalist, but not a Nationalist Party member, was that the idea of making one tremendous leap from Stormont to a United Ireland was simplistic and impractical. He was soon to be challenged on his own inactivity.

The occasion was a meeting in his brother Jack's house in Leenan Gardens. At a time of intense political debate, Jack had invited about 20 neighbours to his house to talk about the political uncertainties of the current situation. Eugene O'Hare, a staunch member of the Nationalist Party, was in attendance and Pat, favouring a non-violent approach to achieving a United Ireland, asked Eugene what direction was being given by the Nationalist Party. Eugene's reply was: 'Why are you not making the argument from inside the party?' Pat did not join, but for the first time considered playing a part from inside politics in effecting the changes he desired.

The Stormont election of 1969 saw good friends Len Green and Pat on opposite sides as election workers, Len working for Eamonn McCann and Pat working for John Hume, who at that stage was running as an Independent.

Pat and Len were soon to be persuaded by Hugh Doherty to join the SDLP and stand for election to Derry City Council, the body that was to replace the old Derry Corporation. He was elected with Len in 1972 and was soon to become entangled in a bizarre situation.

Len Green lived opposite Rosemount police station and, in times of violent confrontation, was asked to make representations to the police on behalf of young people accused of rioting. On one occasion he was arrested on suspicion of rioting and taken to Victoria Barracks, the RUC station in the city centre. On hearing this, Pat went to make representations on behalf of his friend, only to be 'identified' as a rioter himself. He was duly charged and sentenced to a term of nine months imprisonment, six of which he served. Pat, who holds no rancour against the magistrate, explains that he [the magistrate] had no option. The legalities were that attendance at a disturbance was enough to bring in a verdict of guilty, and that the inevitable mandatory sentence for the 'offence' was nine months in prison. He had time to reflect on the injustice of it all, although he does not complain of his treatment there. A particular regret is that imprisonment separated him from family and friends during the trauma of Bloody Sunday.

There was an interesting dilemma when he went to claim his seat on Derry City Council. The position was that, despite his prison sentence, there was a legal right to stand for election but, if challenged by another council member, he would be forced to stand down; in the event no challenges came. The decision made by political opponents not to challenge made sense, as a successful challenge would have seen him stand again. The possibility of repeated elections and challenges would only have drawn unwelcome publicity to the potential challengers. As it happened, reference was never made to the sentence, perhaps also demonstrating the widely-held belief in the injustice of it all.

He threw himself into to the work of the Council and found refreshing evidence of an enthusiasm from all parties to work for the greater good of all, despite political differences. He thought there emerged a constructive spirit released from the dead hand of the old Unionism.

Aware that executive power of local government had been reduced, Derry City Council decided it would develop 'the power of influence'. That is, intensive lobbying would become a tactic and a number of major projects would become the target. These were to include the extension of the university, a second bridge for the Foyle, the development of an airport and the construction of a shopping centre on the site that was eventually to house the Richmond Centre.

Pat was elected Mayor in 1979 and was closely involved in the lobbying strategy. After six deputations to various secretaries of state over a period of seven years, agreement to build the new Foyle Bridge finally came when Humphrey Atkins arrived with definite plans; Pat was particularly pleased that this happened in his year as Mayor of the city. He was also glad that another project was about to be launched at around the same time. An approach was made by Paddy 'Bogside', who explained his plans for the launch of the Inner City Trust, and who asked Pat to brief Marlene Jefferson, the Unionist deputy mayor, on the plans. Marlene was duly impressed and they both agreed that if anyone could make the work of the Trust a success, Paddy was the man. All-party support was to follow.

The Trust had identified derelict properties all over the inner city and proposed acquiring and refurbishing them, or building anew, but in a style sympathetic to the existing architecture. The construction of the Craft Village and the Tower Museum is evidence of the success of this strategy. Grants were made available by the Council as the work of Paddy Bogside's dream continued apace.

Pat reckoned that the idea was a winner on all fronts. As he saw it, central government, in view of the self-help element, would be embarrassed into investing in further development. He is in no doubt that the Richmond Centre was a direct result.

Another important conclusion was that the bombing campaign would be inhibited as more and more rebuilding was perceived as locally inspired. The story of the city since is one of continuing improvement.

Creggan also had its problems due to the decline in the condition of the housing stock and the attendant perceptions, from the outside, of Creggan as an undesirable area. The housing decline began to be reversed on the arrival, as area manager of the Housing Executive, of Sam McPherson; the work continues. Pat also believes that the decision to give sitting tenants an opportunity to buy their homes has had further positive consequences. The campaign to secure the future of schools on the estate was another battle won and their present high performances give him much satisfaction.

The growth of the Sinn Féin vote and tactical voting meant that he lost his seat by just three votes, which brought to an end 24 years of public service as an SDLP councillor, 18 of them as leader of the SDLP group in Council. Jimmy Clifford remains as the only SDLP councillor who is a Creggan resident. Pat enjoyed all his time in Council and pays tribute to the collective wisdom and support of fellow members Hugh Doherty, Len Green, Raymond McClean and Joe Fagan.

He is satisfied that his prediction of 17 years ago, that Creggan would become one of the best estates in Derry, is now a fact. He has no regrets about his own time in Council but is savouring the opportunity retirement has given him to renew bonds with his 12 children and 29 grandchildren.

Of his time as Mayor of Derry, he is confident that he has established three firsts:

> (1) The first mayor to have lived in a public housing estate during his year of office – he still lives in Creggan.
> (2) The first Nationalist mayor to have been elected with the aid of Unionist votes.
> (3) The first mayor to have been elected despite having served a term in prison.

FROM STREET POLITICS TO STORMONT: MARY NELIS

A fortuitous meeting a few years ago with prominent Philadelphia lawyer John Elliot has set Mary Nelis wondering if there is some genetic tendency that drives her towards politics. Mary's maiden name is Elliot so she was intrigued by the possibilities when John presented her with an Elliot genealogy. As it turned out, the genealogical research revealed that two out of four Elliot brothers left Derry for North America in the early 19th century. Mary is descended from one of the brothers who stayed. Of the emigrant brothers, one settled in Philadelphia and the other went to Canada to found a family from which is descended former Canadian Premier Pierre Elliot Trudeau, who obviously valued his Elliot line enough to include the name in his full title. Genetic possibilities apart, Mary has served quite an apprenticeship on her way to becoming a Member of the Legislative Assembly.

The Nelis family arrived in Creggan in 1960 and took up residence in Rathkeele Way. They arrived with very little and things were to get worse. Within two months of their arrival, the BSR, which manufactured record players and tape decks, closed down and her husband Billy was out of a job. Like many in similar circumstances, he took the boat for England in search of work. As Mary says of her own situation, and others like her on the estate, close observers could, by a simple calculation, link the regular pregnancies with the holiday visits of spouses.

St Mary's Church had just recently been built, the Holy Child School was offering classes for only half-a-day, and work on roads and lighting had not been completed. With young children to raise, and her husband away from home, Mary felt isolated; it took her two years to settle. She credits midwife Kay Thomas from Dunmore Gardens with breaking this isolation. Three families in the same street each had an average of 12 children, which meant that Kay was always busy in the area. This also meant she was a conduit for all the local news, as she moved between these large families in her regular ministrations. Common problems and Kay's introductions ensured a growing camaraderie with neighbours. One of Kay's stories illustrates the confusion that was common to many large families. Apparently one pregnant harassed mother sent a 'sample' to the doctor, only to be told that she had mistakenly submitted a bottle of Lourdes water; no miracles were ever claimed for Rathkeele.

Mary's energies were soon to be channelled into organising residents to demand improvements. The catalyst was the death of Patsy McChrystal's child. The tragic event was bad enough, but poor lighting, incomplete development work and unfinished roads were to make the funeral (a sad event in the best of circumstances) all the more miserable. The Foyle Hill Tenants' Association was formed to tackle the problem. Signatures were collected around the doors and letters written to the Housing Executive and local newspapers. Other members included Patsy McChrystal, Tommy McManus, John Doherty, Brendan Keenan, Mary Barr and the late John Fahy. The association initially demanded improvements in roads and lighting.

As common issues were identified, assistance was given to help other areas, such as Shantallow and the Rossville Flats, form their own associations. Sectarian divisions were ignored when help was also given to the Irish Street and Fountain estates. Fr Martin Rooney, the Administrator of St Mary's Church in Creggan, proved very helpful, making the Boys' Club's premises available for meetings and giving access to statistics, when necessary, to support a wide range of campaigns. An example of co-operative action was the purchase of a cardiac ambulance by an amalgam of associations.

One meeting was to provide a sharp lesson in Mary's political education. A group of women sought a meeting with the Housing Executive in the person of Marjorie McCullagh, only to be told that she could not negotiate with them since they were not officially tenants; all tenancies were in the names of the male heads of households only. A feminist issue, even though it may not have been identified as such, was revealed. Subsequent campaigns led to the institution of the joint tenancies of the '70s.

To support its activities, the Tenants' Association collected sixpence-a-month from every household. Bus runs to Buncrana for children were organised on Sundays during the summer, when parents prepared mountains of food for lunches and 50-seater coaches might have carried 150 children.

Tenants lobbied successfully to end dual-day schooling. Road maintenance and street lighting were improved and a campaign to prevent the building of high-rise flats on Southway was mounted. Resistance continued and protestors appeared on Southway at the same time as the mechanical diggers of the developers. So many expectant mothers turned out that one source christened them the 'pregnant petitioners'. Nevertheless, the campaign was successful and the Southway green space was preserved. The Rathlin Drive space was also developed.

Petitioners had various experiences as they engaged in the necessary lobbying. Mary was part of a deputation which met Mayor Anderson in the Guildhall. 'The first time there for an occasion other than the Derry Feis,' was the wry comment made by Mary. The petition was for play spaces for children. The reception was cool and they were ordered out. A meeting with Brian Faulkner and Bill Craig at Stormont was similarly cool, the only memorable experience being the opportunity to view the excruciating yellow socks worn by Gerry Fitt.

Mary is proud of her part in organising classes based on women's issues, or what nowadays might be called assertiveness courses. Issues raised were liable to be followed by action. Opposition to the withdrawal of midwife services led eventually to the establishment of Anderson House, a maternity unit where medical care was provided by General Practitioners. The small community centre at Kildrum Gardens, where many of the classes took place, also hosted author Siobhán McKenna who gave readings to packed and appreciative audiences.

As political activity and political debate intensified with the introduction of the Civil Rights agitation, it was no surprise that Mary, by then an experienced and knowledgeable campaigner, was recruited into the SDLP.

Increasing violence saw the role of community groups deteriorate, and people like John McChrystal and Fr Rooney spent more and more time visiting the British Army camp at Piggery Ridge to negotiate the release of numerous young people arrested by the British Army.

Mary's focus was to change with the arrest in 1976 of her son Donncha who, by then, was in the IRA. She might have read the signs earlier. When he was at St Columb's College, his prize for coming first in history was, of all things, a book written by British Army Major Anthony Farrar-Hockley. It was immediately consigned to the fire.

Her son Peter had been killed in a car accident in 1973 and Mary was still grieving his loss when Donncha was arrested in March 1976 and convicted for arms possession. From then on, his conviction, the circumstances of the period and the nature of his incarceration were to divert her from other community-based activity. Donncha's membership of the IRA was not denied when he was given a 16-year jail sentence. However, political status was withdrawn in the same month as his conviction. This was in direct conflict with the interpretation of the Republican movement. From then on, a clash was inevitable. Prison rules demanded that prisoners wear prison uniforms. IRA prisoners claiming political status refused prison clothing and prison authorities reacted by removing all personal clothing and denying prison visits.

It was four months before Mary was able to visit her son in Long Kesh, but communication of a sort was established when Fr Cahill informed her of his meeting with Donncha, who was brought out to meet him naked with unexplained marks on his back. To highlight his plight, Mary was to take street protest to a new and dramatic level.

Two friends, Theresa Deery, whose brother was in Long Kesh, and Kathleen McCann, whose husband was also imprisoned there, planned their first protest. As she tells it:

> The three of us clothed only in blankets stood outside the Bishop's door while the church bells rang out for peace.

It was the first blanket protest; a new campaign, which was to take her to many places, was born. At a Relatives' Action Committee meeting, she was put in touch with the late Danny Duffy, a Derryman resident in Philadelphia who, it was reported, had information on her Philadelphia cousin, the lawyer John Elliot who, as it turned out, shared antecedents with Mary. He sympathised with the campaign and later sent airline tickets so she could travel to Philadelphia. While there, she signed an affidavit for presentation to Amnesty International.

Anonymous donors funded a campaign tour of Europe when Mary and five other women set out 'to break down the wall of silence'. France, Holland, Belgium and Italy were among the countries visited. Demonstrations featured protestors and murals mounted on four sectioned boards. She talks ruefully of a demonstration on the Champs Elysées when some bystanders imagined they were attending some way-out fashion show.

During all the campaigning, traumatic events were impacting on the Nelis family. The house might be raided two or three times a day and everybody in the house was arrested at one time or another. The *Derry Journal* published a photograph of her daughter, taken from a security forces' dossier, which depicted her as one of the nine most-wanted women in Ireland. Two sons were arrested on the same day in 1978; John was 17 and Paddy 16. However, Paddy was to avoid the journey to Long Kesh. As exams loomed, an arrangement was made that he would have an armed escort to St Columb's College, sit his exam and then be taken away under armed guard again. By mysterious means, he vanished and Paddy was next heard of in the Republic of Ireland.

The blanket protest lasted for five years and, by the time of the Hunger Strikes, Mary had joined Sinn Féin. She worked on the Bobby Sands election campaign and has since worked locally on elections where Sinn Féin was standing.

Her previous experience as a community activist in Creggan had prepared her well for her part in developing the Dove House and Women's Co-operative projects. Considering her substantive involvement in a range of human rights issues, she believes she brings a wealth of experience to her new role in constitutional politics.

Mary Nelis was elected to Derry City Council as a Sinn Féin Councillor in 1995 and is now in her second term, and to the Northern Ireland Assembly in June 1998, where she holds the Deputy Chair of the Culture, Arts and Leisure Committee and sits on the Committee for Higher and Further Education, Training and Employment. Appropriately perhaps, she is the party spokesperson on Human Rights and Criminal Justice.

Mary Nelis MLA engages in 'debate' over security issues in the early '90s. (courtesy Mary Nelis)

LOCAL ELECTIONS IN CREGGAN

1973: THE FIRST 'FREE ELECTIONS'

The dissolution of the old Derry Corporation and the Rural Council, and the ending of the gerrymander were to bring radical changes to the city's governmental structures. In 1973, the first elections held for 50 years using Proportional Representation (PR) returned a Nationalist majority to the new Derry District Council. The momentous occasion was reported in the *Derry Journal* on 5 June under the banner headline: *Unionist Control of Derry Area Ends.*

The SDLP was to have ten members on the new 27-seat Council, the United Loyalist Group nine, the Alliance four, the Nationalist Party three and the Republican Clubs one. Area C, which encompassed Creggan, Beechwood Avenue and Marlborough, returned five Councillors: Kevin Barr (Nat), Pat Devine (SDLP), Mickey Montgomery (Rep Clubs), Hugh Doherty (SDLP) and Len Green (SDLP). Mary Nelis, who was standing for the SDLP, was runner-up.

In its analysis of the result, the *Derry Journal* commented:

> In Area C, where there were no Loyalist candidates, the SDLP had its greatest percentage, as was to be expected. But they gained what must have been a rather disappointing 49%, when they must have been aiming at 60%. The Nationalists also had their best showing in that area. They got a useful 21%. The SDLP got three of the five seats with only half the votes, but they were entitled to them because they had in fact three quotas. They got 2,480 first preferences and the quota was 839 . . . Summing up, the SDLP were aiming at 14 seats over the district. They got ten so they fell well below their highest hopes. To get their target, they would have needed in the region of 42 to 44% of the first preferences. Nevertheless, they go into the new Council as the largest party and probably feel that they can win back some votes lost to Alliance at the next attempt.

1977: THE SDLP ON THE RISE

The *Journal* prediction that the SDLP could usurp the Alliance Party was to prove very accurate indeed. So much so, that in the run up to the next elections in 1977, Fergus McAteer, the Director of Elections for the Nationalist Party complained that the SDLP was in danger of imitating the Unionists of old. He commented:

> We would ask voters to beware of one-party control of our City Council (shades of the old Derry Corporation). The SDLP seek a monopoly and this is very disturbing when we remember their Council antics on such

> issues as sharing the mayoral office. A good political balance within the Council is essential and, as Nationalists, we are seeking a presence and a voice to speak unapologetically in your name on the real issues of the day and to ensure that Derry gets her rightful share of the public purse.

McAteer's appeal was in vain and, on Tuesday 24 May, the *Journal* announced: *SDLP Triumph in Derry.*

John Hume's party took 13 of the 27 Council seats, the ULG [United Loyalist Group] eight, Nationalists four, while the Alliance dropped from four to two. In Area C, the SDLP's three sitting Councillors retained their seats and their share of the vote in the ward rose to almost 57%. Pat Devine topped the poll with 1,004 votes and Hugh Doherty also was returned on the first count. Kevin Barr of the Nationalist Party kept his seat, but Mickey Montgomery of the Republican Clubs lost his to John McChrystal (Nat).

1981: The SDLP Takes an Overall Majority

The 1981 local government elections were overshadowed by the Hunger Strikes, with reports on the counts being consigned to the middle pages of the *Journal.* The SDLP did, however, become the first party to gain an overall majority on the City Council, taking an extra seat in Area E (Shantallow) to give them a total of 14 Councillors. The combined Unionist bloc got nine seats (DUP five, OUP four), while the Irish Independence Party (IIP), formerly the Nationalist Party, took four. The Alliance Party lost both its seats. In Area C, the SDLP's Pat Devine polled extremely well, getting double the quota; he was elected along with two new SDLP Councillors, Annie Gallagher and Joe Moran. John McChrystal and Kevin Barr were returned for the IIP. The *Derry Journal* of 26 May 1981 commented:

> Although the SDLP had been hoping to get an overall majority, it had been thought a strong challenge by the Irish Independence Party would do them damage. However, that threat quickly disappeared during Thursday's counting when the IIP were fortunate to retain their second seat in the Creggan and thus their three seats for the Bogside and Creggan areas.

1985: Sinn Féin Enters, Decimating the IIP

Sinn Féin's first foray into local government elections was to have interesting repercussions for the new 30-seater City Council. They took five seats, virtually decimating the Irish Independence Party. Interestingly, the SDLP's vote also increased, though they gained no new seats. The final tally at close of play was: SDLP 14, SF five, IIP one, DUP five and OUP five.

Creggan, which was the largest constituent of the new six-seater Cityside ward, returned three Sinn Féiners: Dodie McGuinness; Hugh Brady and Mitchel McLaughlin. The IIP in the area was wiped out, however, with the former Deputy Mayor, Liam Bradley, and Councillor John McChrystal losing their seats. Pat Devine was returned for the SDLP along with new members Tony Carlin and Pat Ramsey. Sinn Féin immediately declared that they held no interest in taking the mayoralty or deputy mayoralty. The *Derry Journal* of 21 May reported:

> Councillor Mitchel McLaughlin has called on the Council to sell off the mayor's chain of office which he described as a 'hangover from the British colonial presence'. He stated that any number of local groups or worthy projects abroad, such as the Ethiopian Appeal, could benefit from the money raised from the disposal of this chain.

The Creggan Sinn Féin man was also to have a major impact at his first Council meeting the next month. Reporting from the Guildhall chamber, Domhnall MacDermott told *Journal* readers:

> Then came the moment we had all been waiting for, Sinn Féin Councillor Mitchel McLaughlin asked to be allowed to speak. As he started off speaking in Irish, there was uproar in the Loyalist camp with many of them shouting 'What's this Irish nonsense' and 'I can't understand him'. However, DUP Councillor William Hay came out with the best line, reminding Councillor McLaughlin that he was in 'Londonderry, not Letterkenny'. As the abuse continued, the Sinn Féin man kept on talking and, dare I say it, seemed to be actually enjoying the uproar he was causing.

1989: Trouble at Close of Polls

The retirement of Derry's last IIP Councillor, Fergus McAteer, saw the SDLP gain an extra seat in May 1989. The combined Unionist bloc retained 10 seats, but there were strong divisions in the Loyalist ranks. At the end of counting, the SDLP had 15 seats, Sinn Féin five, (becoming the Council's second largest party), the DUP four, the UUP three, Independent Unionists two and the UDP one. The Cityside ward, which included Creggan, returned three SDLP Councillors and three Sinn Féiners. Indeed, the only new face was the SDLP's Jim Clifford, who squeezed out his sitting party colleague, Pat Ramsey.

In Creggan, tensions over the poll gave rise to violence in the week after the election. Pat Devine's daughter, who had acted as his agent, was attacked at her home by a masked assailant who struck her in the face with a club. The SDLP leader John Hume expressed his horror the incident, commenting:

> I suppose the masked bandit who carried out the attack regards himself as a hero. He is an unmitigated coward, and I hope his actions will be condemned unreservedly by all parties in the city.

Creggan Sinn Féin Councillor Hugh Brady also condemned the attack, which he said would not be condoned by any Republican. He described the incident as 'anti-social and anti-Republican'.

1993: Record Return for SDLP

The 1993 elections in Derry were marked by allegations of cheating. Sinn Féin captured the last Unionist seat on the West Bank with Mary Nelis narrowly defeating the Independent Unionist David Davis in the Northland ward. The SDLP claimed Sinn Féin was behind a 'highly organised campaign of personation'.

> Our polling agents challenged dozens of people who then elected not to vote but to flee the polling station. Our canvass showed that invariably the persons whose votes these people attempted to take were supporters of ours.

Sinn Féin, in turn, accused the SDLP of 'begrudgery' and Mary Nelis challenged the SDLP to deny that two sitting SDLP Councillors and one former Councillor were under investigation by the Electoral Office and the RUC for alleged voting fraud.

When the dust had settled, the SDLP had taken a record number of seats, electing 17 out of the party's 18 candidates. Sinn Féin took five seats, the DUP also got five, the UUP two and Independent Unionists one. In Creggan, Jim Clifford, Pat Devine and Pat Ramsey were returned for the SDLP while poll-topper Hugh Brady and Bernie Bradley were elected for Sinn Féin.

Again there was trouble in Creggan in the aftermath of the elections. According to the *Derry Journal* of 25 May, Jim Clifford's 18-year-old daughter narrowly escaped injury when a brick was thrown through the front window of their Iniscarn Road home. Pat Devine claimed Sinn Féin supporters 'couldn't take their oil'. But Sinn Féin's Mitchel McLaughlin also condemned the attack commenting:

> It's hard to think of anything more cowardly than throwing a brick at a family home from a passing car.

1993 By-election: SDLP Stands Accused

When Hugh Brady resigned his Cityside seat only months into the new term, the DUP refused to allow Sinn Féin to co-opt a candidate in his place. There were widely differing views within the SDLP as to whether it should field a candidate or allow Sinn Féin what would effectively be a free run. Somewhat controversially, the SDLP eventually decided that while it would have supported co-option, once an election was to be held, they would have to fight it. At the elections in May, the SDLP had a majority of about 300 over Sinn Féin in the ward and so may have been expected to take an extra seat in a straight fight. It was not to be.

The SDLP approached a number of candidates before selecting Theresa Coyle to fight the by-election. Sinn Féin put up Cathal Crumley, while Labour stood Pat Muldowney. However, just three days before polling day, the SDLP's Derry chairman, Gerry Murray, resigned his office, alleging 'electoral malpractice' by his party. The *Derry Journal* front page story of 19 October stated:

> The *Journal* has learned that Mr Murray's resignation may be related to the processing of postal votes for the by-election and, in particular, to alleged irregularities concerning the SDLP handling of postal votes allegedly favouring Sinn Féin.

The SDLP vehemently denied any wrongdoing and accused Sinn Féin of an attempted smear. But the Creggan public returned Cathal Crumley with a comfortable majority, and Sinn Féin's vote in the ward increased by nine per cent. The new Councillor commented:

> People in the Cityside said that while they were not surprised at the bigotry of the DUP, which forced this by-election, they were shocked at the opportunism of the SDLP. This by-election is over now, but the signs are that Sinn Féin will capture the fifth seat in the Cityside ward in the next local government elections.

Violence at close of polls saw stone-throwing attacks on the homes of the SDLP's Jim Clifford and Sinn Féin's Dodie McGuinness.

1997: SDLP Stalwart Ousted

Cathal Crumley's prediction that Sinn Féin could take a third seat in Cityside was to prove correct. The party increased its tally of seats in Derry to eight, while the SDLP dropped to 14, losing overall control of the Council in the process. The DUP took four seats, the Ulster Unionists three, with Independent Unionist Jim Guy taking the last seat. In Cityside, the SDLP's Council leader, Pat Devine, lost his seat by four votes to party colleague Pat Ramsey, bringing to an end the Creggan man's 24-year career in local government. Jim Clifford was the other SDLP candidate elected, while poll-topper Cathal Crumley, Mitchel McLaughlin and Peter Anderson were returned for Sinn Féin. Devine's defeat was a sore one for his party; his was the scalp Sinn Féin prized most. Councillor Mark Durkan told the *Derry Journal*:

> Pat Devine was a major presence on Derry City Council and within the SDLP group and, as a result, will be a great loss. The loss of someone of his stature is a blow. Pat Devine wasn't just chairman of the group of Councillors – he had more strings to his bow.

Durkan was further to claim that electoral abuse may have played a 'major role' in the outcome of recent elections, but Sinn Féin said the SDLP was using the allegations as a 'smoke-screen' to hide its despair at Republican successes. Cathal Crumley commented:

> They are a demoralised party trying desperately to explain away our excellent performance.

Beyond 1997

Mitchel McLaughlin's commitments as Sinn Féin chairman and as a new Member of the Legislative Assembly (MLA) saw him stand down as a Councillor in 2000. This time, the DUP did not force a by-election, claiming it would be an unnecessary expense. As a result, Gerry MacLochlainn was co-opted as the new Sinn Féin member for Cityside. The next council elections are due in 2001, though local government reform and the proposed introduction of new 'supercouncils' could delay these.

Creggan Tomorrow – A Bright, Brand New Day

The tribulations of the '70s and '80s were to give way to a new dawn in the '90s. Political miracle-working – involving some from Creggan, and others from very close by – saw a new sense of confidence instil itself in the estate. This was noted by the Taoiseach, Bertie Ahern, when he visited the Ráth Mór Centre in January 1998 to close the Creggan 50th Festival. Mr Ahern told his audience:

> I'm here because I want to acknowledge the tremendous achievements of the Creggan community over the past ten years. Creggan has been pivotal in the events of the past 30 years, since the people of this city and of the North embarked on the struggle for civil rights for Nationalists and recognition of their Irish identity. The people here have shown endurance and resilience, often in the face of adversity and challenge.

Mr Ahern spoke of the success of Féile an Chreagáin, and welcomed the efforts being made by Creggan Enterprises Ltd to develop the local economy. He commented:

> I applaud all that you have already achieved by working together. You have done a huge amount to make a better Creggan. I want to see Creggan go further and I want a better life for the people of Creggan. The best way to make that happen is to ensure an end to the conflict and the promotion of full equality and justice for all here in Northern Ireland. That's precisely what I'm working to achieve. You deserve nothing less.

One man who worked tirelessly and selflessly to ensure a new beginning was John Hume MP MEP. His contribution was such that he was awarded the Nobel Peace Prize for his efforts. Throughout the *Troubles*, the SDLP leader lived at the mouth of Creggan, just off the New Road. And here, he tells how, for the first time, the people of Creggan have the chance to look to the future with real hope.

I can only pray for a bright, brand new day in the town I loved so well. For the last three decades these words from Phil Coulter's classic song, *The Town I Loved So Well,* seemed like an impossible dream. The task of solving our political problems has been daunting. The obscenity of 30 years of violence on our streets diminished and destroyed people's lives. So many of our communities were shattered. Violence prevented and distorted social and economic development and made it very difficult to resolve our political and cultural differences.

For the first time in our history we have an opportunity to look to the future with real hope. We have institutions of government which reflect and accommodate our differences. We have government ministers who care deeply about all of our communities, who understand the difficulties of our communities and who are in a position to identify solutions to those problems. We have locally accountable representatives in government who can ensure that the solutions to our problems are effectively implemented by government agencies.

John Hume MP MEP (courtesy John Hume)

Creggan suffers badly as a result of unemployment, and the last few years have seen a large number of job losses. It has always been my dream that people in Derry would have the means and opportunity to earn their living in high-quality jobs, at home, in Derry. At last, this dream is starting to develop. Traditional declining industries are being replaced by new and growing knowledge-based industries. This is why I have always placed such a high priority on education. We have a very highly trained and educated workforce. Derry is becoming known as a centre for good companies in high-quality industry. The working conditions in these knowledge-based industries tend to be very good. Many of the new jobs give a high level of training and education and so develop the workers.

It is by working very hard internationally that we have attracted these new industries, but our unemployment is still too high, particularly in areas like Creggan. We must continue our work at international level to attract more industry and to give hope to our young people that they will be able to earn a living in their home town. Continued peace on our streets will help us to achieve that goal.

Recently, there has been the development of social economy and community initiatives by Creggan Enterprises Limited and the Ráth Mór Centre to provide services to the community. The social economy is a means of generating new wealth in local communities, and keeping existing wealth within communities. In Creggan, as with other areas in Derry, the social economy has been very successful and has created over 100 jobs in the area, as well as investing considerable amounts of money into the community by way of grants and donations.

This sense of community and family is present in a very real and physical sense in Creggan's community organisations. These organisations provide a cohesive structure to the area and they meet many of the area's social needs. The community groups build people's capacity, allowing individuals to realise their potential.

Creggan is placed on a beautiful location with a spectacular view of the River Foyle. The Creggan Country Park, with its reservoirs and parklands, is a beautiful centre for recreation and a very rich environmental resource for this city. This park is undergoing a major programme of works which will enhance the natural environment. I look forward to the completion of the project.

After 30 years, our prayer is being answered. We are at the dawn of that 'bright, brand new day'. In Creggan, like many other areas of Northern Ireland, there are serious social and economic problems to be addressed. Now, for the first, we have the ability and the means to address and resolve those problems. Our people can realise their potential. For the first time in many centuries, we can begin to build a peaceful future in a country at ease with itself.